PANDORA'S BOX

ETHNOGRAPHY AND THE COMPARISON OF MEDICAL BELIEFS

T0385681

HAU
Books

www.haubooks.org

PANDORA'S BOX

ETHNOGRAPHY AND THE COMPARISON OF MEDICAL BELIEFS

The 1979 Lewis Henry Morgan Lectures

Gilbert Lewis

Hau Books
Chicago

Published as part of the Hau-Morgan Lectures Initiative in collaboration with the
Department of Anthropology at the University of Rochester.

Cover: An ill man lies on a palm-leaf mat in the porch of his wife's house, 1969.
She sits outside with their adult daughter and some children to watch over him
and shield him from harm. Photo: Gilbert Lewis.

Cover design: Daniele Meucci and Ania Zayco
Layout design: Deepak Sharma, Prepress Plus
Typesetting: Prepress Plus (www.prepressplus.in)

ISBN: 978-1-912808-32-8 [paperback]
ISBN: 978-1-912808-87-8 [electronic]
ISBN: 978-1-912808-36-6 [PDF]
LCCN: 2020950417

Hau Books
Chicago Distribution Center
11030 S. Langley
Chicago, Il 60628
www.haubooks.org

Publications of Hau Books are printed, marketed, and distributed by The
University of Chicago Press.
www.press.uchicago.edu

Printed in the United States of America on acid-free paper.

Contents

Part IV: Treatment

List of Figures

All photos are by Gilbert Lewis and Ariane Lewis. Full-size color versions of some figures, as noted, are available in the HAU Books website at www.haubooks.org/pandoras-box.

Acknowledgments

Many years ago, the invitation to present some Lewis Henry Morgan Lectures took my breath away, being such an unexpected honor. The kindness and welcome I received from Grace and Al Harris went far beyond what I had any right to expect. The occasion has left vivid memories of the warmth and friendliness that were accorded me. Fitz John Porter Poole and Stephen Kunitz memorably went out of their way to show me around Rochester, New York. I particularly wish to recall with gratitude the intellectual stimulus, advice, and friendship of Stephen Kunitz over the many years that followed.

Many others have contributed ideas or read parts of this manuscript. I would like to thank Colette Piault especially for introducing me to the work of Atcho at Bregbo and for her generous help. St John's College and the Department of Social Anthropology in Cambridge supported me while I took sabbatical leave to write and make two later visits to New Guinea. I have benefitted from the encouragement and criticism offered by Esther Goody, Jack Goody, Murray Last, Roland Littlewood, and Michael Young. The help of my family has been critical in completing this book: Ariane sharing in the fieldwork and taking many of the photographs, Jerome with comments on some of the chapters, and Nico with preparing the photographs for publication.

The people of Rauit village have made the largest contribution to this book through their kindness to me and my family, as well as their tolerance and willingness to explain things to me. I am lastingly in their debt for this.

Note: I have published extracts of some of the case material used here in the intervening years since I first wrote up the Morgan lectures. They appear in the following venues:

1986.   "The look of magic." *Man*, n.s., 21 (3): 414–37.
1987.   "A lesson from Leviticus." *Man*, n.s., 22 (4): 593–613.
1993.   "Double standards of treatment evaluation." In *Knowledge, power and practice*, edited by Shirley Lindenbaum and Margaret Lock, 189–218. Berkeley: University of California Press.
2000.   *A failure of treatment.* Oxford: Oxford University Press.
2002.   "Between public assertion and private doubts." *Social Anthropology* 10 (1): 11–21.

Preface

My Lewis Henry Morgan lectures were first given at the Department of Anthropology at the University of Rochester in 1979 and then expanded in the early 1980s with the intention of publishing them. However, they overflowed the original lectures, and I left them un-published. Now, at the kind suggestion of the Morgan Lecture Series editor, Professor Robert Foster, I have returned to the expanded type-script that grew out of the original lectures and have shortened the text. I hope it is clearer as well. I have not tried to bring it right up to date, since the gap between medical anthropology then and now is too great. However, I trust the themes I looked at then will still be of interest.

First, some background: I came into medical anthropology from ini-tial medical training and a few years' experience of hospital practice in Britain's National Health Service. Social anthropology had long attract-ed me. What was it like to be ill in a society with no access to the sort of medicine I had been trained in? The contrast lured me and seemed to be a question that medical anthropology should try to answer be-fore it was too late. I owe the quotation in my first chapter from Sir Thomas Browne to Mervyn Susser and William Watson (1962). Browne (1977) so eloquently expressed the question: Has there been progress in medicine? With Lewis Henry Morgan's *Ancient society* ([1877] 1964) in mind, this seemed perhaps a fitting theme.

In global terms of human survival, life expectancy, and demographics, progress has been made; however, in Part I, "Being ill," the first chapter raises some doubt about the specific role of medicine in that progress. In any case, medicine is concerned not just with life expectancy and demographics but also with the illnesses of individuals and providing them with care in their illness.

The other chapters of Part I describe what it was like to be ill in a Sepik village in New Guinea: first in 1968–1969 and then about fifteen years later. Rauit was the village in the West Sepik District (now called Sandaun Province) where I lived with my wife Ariane and our toddler son for two years. The people in Rauit and two other villages were identified as speakers of a distinct language called Gnau, derived from its word for *no*. I had medical supplies suitable for a village health post supplied by the public health service. I provided medical advice when the villagers asked for some, thus altering the situation, but I thought it would be wrong not to offer to help when I was able to. Care provided by nonkin or strangers raised various problems of trust and compliance; some of these problems are tackled in later chapters of this book. I aimed to observe and record as far as I could all the responses to illness that occurred in the village where we lived.

To observe and understand local experiences were the descriptive goals of my first period of fieldwork. What were the environmental and medical problems faced in that particular setting, and what did locals do about them? The collection of data came before any particular explanatory theories. At the time, few studies were devoted to medical anthropology, either ethnographically or in anthropological theory. In chapter 2, I try to describe examples from the range of illness and responses to them as seen by the outside observer, bearing in mind that it is easy to neglect common minor ailments in favor of paying attention only to illnesses that demand more serious and dramatic responses. In chapter 3, I focus on the experience of suffering a long illness and on understanding the subjective experience of isolation, dependency, and rejection, of being unable to take part in ordinary activities and social life. But do others always recognize an obligation to help? Blame for illness and the justice or injustice of suffering are issues that raise questions.

The fifteen years that elapsed between my first fieldwork and the events described in chapter 4 included the advent of national independence and changes in the organization of national and local health services. These changes involved some loss of village self-reliance. From the villagers' point of view, there were doubts about whether to trust the care provided by unrelated outsiders: What could be the possible motives for their intervening?

Part II, "Recognizing and defining illness," is about how to differentiate the particular focus of medical anthropology. It begins with a chapter on leprosy. The naming of an illness is not straightforward; the story of leprosy provides a lesson in the possible hazards of identifying the same illness in different societies. As an example of the power of labels to stigmatize, "leprosy" also has a long history. In the next three chapters, I argue for the definition of disease itself as critical in medical anthropology, both for distinguishing its distinctive scope and for conducting comparative studies. Doubts about the relevance of Western medical categories for comparative social studies of illness emerged as medical anthropology developed. Alternative modes of thought had long been a lively subject for investigation in social anthropology, especially after Lucien Lévy-Bruhl ([1910] 1923) suggested the idea of prelogical thought, but E. E. Evans-Pritchard (1937) showed the coherent logic behind a radically different view of causality. Distinctions between fact and value, particularly between medical facts and social values, were being challenged in the sociology of medicine. Discussions of truth versus belief and the verification or falsification of fact and theory in science became relevant. Thomas Kuhn's (1970) studies of changing paradigms in the history of science reinforced theoretical doubts about the objective and authoritative status of medical and scientific facts. History bore witness to the social relativity and changing nature of accepted ideas.

Illness could be seen as a form of social deviance. Strong and weak forms of relativism were proposed in medical anthropology and, more generally, in social anthropology at large. Within social anthropology, questions of translation and understanding another mode of thought were prominent. Fieldwork in the tradition of Bronisław Malinowski requires a proper grasp of the local language. How could translation and understanding be possible if there were no bridgehead of true assertions about a shared reality? Claude Lévi-Strauss held that our common humanity and our shared endowment of senses guarantee we see and speak about the same objective world ([1950] 1966: xxv, xxix). The Melanesian of this or that island is a person I might have been: anyone could be anybody. I might have spoken his or her language and used the same modes of thought.

The objective reality of disease putatively sets up a basis or independent point of reference in medical anthropology for comparing different responses, even though it is no simple matter to specify their exact scope and boundaries. Medicine is concerned with responses to many particular kinds of disease rather than with arriving at a single definition encompassing all diseases.

In other societies, traditional frameworks within which illness is explained clearly persist; the challenge for us is to understand their assumptions. We must grasp the underlying notions of what is normal and possible. Many of these had and still have meaningful connections to moral and religious beliefs. But the encounter with modern change and introduced biomedicine can upset these connections. Part III, "The experience of change," embarks on comparison by shifting to an African setting. An earlier chapter suggested that the leprosy of Biblical times changed from being a matter of priestly rules, taboos, and exclusion to a matter of atonement for sin or guilt; much more recently, the label of leprosy metamorphosed to refer to a problem for secular medicine to treat. This could be regarded as the medicalization of a religious and moral matter. The beginnings of an analogous shift in understanding and approach are the subject of the chapters on Bregbo, witchcraft, and depression. Chapter 9 describes the healing center of Bregbo in Côte d'Ivoire and its prophet healer Albert Atcho. Bregbo is a community of suffering. Atcho explained why some individuals prosper and others fail by proposing a new morality more adapted to the demands of encroaching urban life. His clients came to him with problems of infertility, childbirth, unhappy marriages, dreams of jobs and urban success, and ambitions they could not realize. Atcho called himself a healer and received official recognition as such. He preached a new understanding of the individual's own responsibility for his or her suffering; for some, he provided treatment through confession and, for others, care in a community of like sufferers.

Considerable continuities exist between the old persecutive understanding of witchcraft and Atcho's new emphasis on personal responsibility and guilt. Opinions shifted among different observers about whether or not to see what Atcho did as treating witchcraft or as practicing a form of emerging psychotherapy and community care. After reading about Bregbo, I was introduced to Margaret Field's (1960) study of an Ashanti shrine, published fifteen years before I learned about Bregbo. Many of the case histories and treatments were astonishingly similar. Field was first an anthropologist, later completing her training as a psychiatrist. She returned and studied a large sample of clients coming to the Ashanti shrine. She considered many of the women who complained of witchcraft to be clinically depressed or mentally ill. Her medical training gave her a different perspective on the problems about which the women spoke. Was this difference purely a question of psychiatric bias and different frames of understanding? Or was recognition of the prevalence of mental illness at stake? Psychiatric illness poses special problems of criteria and evidence in cross-cultural diagnosis.

Chapter 11, which focuses on the impact of events, considers whether the stress of change and adaptation to new circumstances affected the prevalence of illness and inclined priests or leaders of cults toward healing as their special activity. In practice, shifting views invite ambivalence and ambiguity. Past modes of thought are not simply repudiated.

Part IV, "Treatment," begins by examining healing actions in chapter 12. I discuss verbal techniques and moral persuasion, drawing on many insights in the literature to explain Atcho's healing work. Pierre Janet's (1919) monumental studies of suggestion and persuasion (as in both religious healing and psychotherapy) are especially relevant. He emphasized the personal qualities of the healer who provides moral direction and examined the power of the healer's personal relationship to the patient to influence or even restructure someone else's self-understanding. Not only does the healer provide the patient with support but also with an explanation and meaning for the experience of illness. The effects of repeated one-on-one interviews in molding an eventual public confession were apparent in the Bregbo community. Janet did not neglect the crucial role of the community that encouraged the patient with their support and expectations. Care, rest, and support not only cure but also make up a significant part of the healing treatment.

Returning to Gnau, it was clear that villagers demonstrated support very differently than Westerners do. Their initial approach was to provide a protective isolation of the patient; this could even go to harmful lengths in cases of protracted illness. Behind their approaches were particular ideas about the causes and dangers of illness. They also had a repertoire of substances, actions and gestures, spells, spittings, and invocations to use in healing. Most of these actions were brief and did not seem to require any intense personal rapport. But when someone important to the villagers seemed to be seriously afflicted, then a more complex and elaborate performance could be organized, sometimes involving nearly the entire village. The ritual healing took the form of symbolic enactment, almost like a theatrical performance, in which the presumed cause of the illness, taking the form of a mask or contrived image, was brought into the village, honored, presented to its victim, entreated, and finally sent away or "killed." The villagers symbolically made visible the cause, its placation, and its ending in a form of make-believe. Chapter 13 describes one such treatment, the performance of Panu'et. The appendix at the end of the book transcribes in detail exactly what participants said and how they behaved during one particular Panu'et performance.

My final chapter, "Faith and the skeptical eye," focuses on belief and questions of efficacy. Healing activities can have various functions even when causality (in our terms) is not certain. In hopes of relief, a great variety of treatments may be tried. Some people are ready to believe in miracles; for others, experience brings skepticism. Different aims and different expectations guide judgment. Questions of therapeutic efficacy—of cause and effect—are almost always difficult to answer. Compliance normally requires a willingness to believe a treatment might work. People may also question whether to trust someone else's judgment, skill, or knowledge or whether to accept what has been done in the past. The shared beliefs and opinions of people in one's own community, as well as the advice of specialist authorities, potentially carry great influence.

The sufferer's view of success or failure is not always the same as the outside observer's view. They do not necessarily judge by the same criteria or have the same hopes and expectations. The anthropologist may wish to go beyond observation to analyze people's activities and attempt to account for the outcome. Lévi-Strauss's essay on the Kuna shaman's chant for a woman in protracted labor is a famous example of this. But if an anthropologist explains success or failure in the terms of an external observer, he or she implicitly has to choose and justify the standards used. For an obstetrician (as for other medical specialists), the diagnosis and prognosis are vital for judging evidence of an effect. Follow-up, numbers, and records of failure and success would normally be expected in Western medical practice. Should anthropologists adopt different standards because the people observed do likewise? Anecdotal evidence is not enough.

Belief is not necessarily an all-or-nothing matter. Nor is allegiance to a single type of treatment a general rule. Pluralism rather than a monolithic adherence to one method and one truth better characterizes many practices in treating illnesses. The distress that can arise from demands for unswerving belief is illustrated by the predicament of a New Guinean pastor I knew who fell ill and had to choose between the local health service approach and a ritual treatment based on the non-Christian beliefs and traditions of his people. It posed a moral dilemma for him, revealing the subjective problems engendered in outlooks and beliefs that are undergoing change.

Franz Boas (1966) recorded the experience of ambivalence vividly described by Quesalid in recalling his own initiation to shamanism as his belief changed into skepticism. Likewise, in relation to Gnau treatments involving the extraction of malevolent arrows, we may ask about the sincerity of individual actors' belief in the actual or the symbolic efficacy of what they did. Issues of doubt and skepticism affected attempts to manage the treatment of leprosy in the village. People were less than ready to voice their opinions and doubts or to comply with the new treatment regimes demanded of them.

The treatment of leprosy brings out the impact of prognosis and timing on perceptions of cause and effect. According to Leviticus, the priest could decide on an uncertain diagnosis of this illness by whether the signs had changed after seven days or, in certain circumstances, after waiting another seven days. But the pace and nature of change in the signs of what is now meant by "leprosy" have none of those characteristics. Signs take far longer to change. On questions of cause and effect, knowledge of the facts about diseases may become relevant to explanations and judgments of efficacy, but for the sufferer, other criteria, such as considerations of care, familiarity, and safety, may matter more.

PART I: BEING ILL

This part describes illness and the range of local responses to it in a small New Guinean village I observed during my first period of fieldwork in 1968–69. At that time, the village was difficult to reach and had relatively little exposure to introduced Western biomedicine. The villagers had to meet a diverse range of medical problems largely reliant on their own resources.

To shed light on local illnesses and treatments, I show how villagers responded both to the small ailments of daily life and to serious sickness. Two contrasting cases are described in detail: one of acute panic and community response, the other of long suffering and gradual abandonment. They raise questions about care and their perceptions of the justice or injustice of suffering. During a later field trip fifteen years later, after national independence, access to health centers and aid posts had changed. It involved some loss of village self-reliance and raised problems for the residents in understanding the obligations and motives of the new health providers.

I begin with a brief review of the history and evolution of disease in order to ask what has been the role of human responses to illness in the rise and success of human populations.

CHAPTER ONE

Pandora's box

Hesiod's poem "Works and days" tells the story of Pandora's box, the great grave jar from which misfortune was let loose upon the world. Ills came silently while hope remained shut up inside it. Prometheus stole fire from Zeus, who in anger planned for grief to come to humans:

> Till now in peace all the days of the earth had run;
> The tribes of men had been saved from the toil that drives,
> And disease that flings the swarming Fates on our lives.
> But Pandora lifted the jar's great lid, and then
> Its plagues were scattered abroad, with mischief for men.
> Only hope remained, entrapped for evermore. (Hesiod, in Higham and Bowra 1938: 132)

It was the loss of a Golden Age when people had been free from toil, suffering, and disease. Similarly, in the story of Adam and Eve's fall, a paradise was likewise lost. Since then, have people changed or is it diseases that have changed? This was the question to which Sir Thomas Browne gave an answer in his "Letter to a friend," written around 1656:

> Some think there were few Consumptions in the Old World, when Men lived much upon Milk; and that the ancient Inhabitants of this Island were less troubled with Coughs when they went naked, and slept in Caves and Woods, than Men now in Chambers and Feather-beds. Plato will tell us that there was no such Disease as Catarrh in

Homer's time, and that it was but new in Greece in his age. . . . Some will allow no Diseases to be new, others think that many old ones are ceased; and that such which are esteemed new, will have but their time. However the Mercy of God hath scattered the great heap of Diseases, and not loaded any one Country with all: some may be new in one Country which have been old in another. New Discoveries of the Earth discover new Diseases: for besides the common swarm, there are endemial and local Infirmities proper unto certain Regions, which in the whole Earth make no small number: and if Asia, Africa, and America should bring in their List, Pandora's Box would swell, and there must be a strange Pathology. (Browne 1977: 399)

This could almost be the justification for a medical anthropology.

In *Ancient society*, Lewis Henry Morgan saw human history differently from Hesiod's grim view of a decline from a Golden Age to an Age of Iron: Morgan saw progress not decline. He worked "to bring forward additional evidence of the rudeness of the early condition of mankind, of the gradual evolution of the mental and moral powers through experience, and of their protracted struggle with opposing obstacles while winning their way to civilization" (Morgan [1877] 1964: 11). He followed two lines of investigation: first, into the "great sequence of inventions and discoveries which stretches along the entire pathway of human progress"; second, into the development of certain social institutions from a "few primary germs of thought." To have survived or not is a matter of the facts: it is the criterion of success according to the theory of natural selection. By that criterion, the human species has been successful: the species has progressed from being rare to numbering in the millions today.

We inherit our genes and with them various potentialities and susceptibilities. People can find food in very different environments, obviously an advantage for survival. "We eat all sorts of things," a New Guinean man said to me with a cheerful laugh. "You White people choose only the good things to eat, you haven't got strong teeth to eat the things we do, you can't chew up the bones." But though physiological versatility and flexible development are vital to adaptation, the evolutionary mechanism is genetic. Genes are the basis of characteristics that will potentially be shown by the organism in any environment in which it is able to develop. The genome remains the same whatever the conditions in which the individual organism grows to maturity. Acquired characteristics do not alter the genome. Indeed, it is fortunate that this is so, since most acquired characteristics in nature are the consequence of injury, starvation, disease, or senescence; only a minority are adaptive. The inheritance of naturally "acquired characters" would more likely lead to a deterioration of a species rather than to adaptive advantages (Maynard Smith 1966). The paradox of social evolution, Lamarckian though it is, is that we tend to assume the opposite and suppose that the changes we choose to make are improvements—progress rather than deterioration—because people have exercised choice, as though what people choose and like must naturally be good for them. When people can change their environment through choices and by means of skills they learn, the effects may last, significantly changing the conditions to which their children and descendants must adapt. In this sense, perhaps the effects of acquired characteristics will be inherited and may lead to genetic change in the long term.

Adaptive fitness is decided in a particular habitat here and now; nature pays no regard to a hypothetical future. However, the fate of any population will depend not only on the particular environment in which it lives now but also on whether it will be able to tolerate change. If we introduce time and speculation about the future, we alter the basis for deciding about fitness for survival. In retrospect, adaptations that were favorable in the short term may prove unfavorable in the long run. People can alter their behavior to benefit by learning from the experience of others; learned behavior leaves open a possibility for future change despite present choices. In this lies the human species' great potentiality: the diversity of cultures. In comparison with other species, human behavior is less fixed, more guided by reason, and more flexible to change and new circumstances.

Diseases in history

Evolution and biological adaptation provide some answers about disease change and human progress. History certainly supports Browne's observation that "new discoveries of the earth discover new diseases." The distribution of infectious diseases has played a significant part in the peopling of continents and historical events. In his survey of the global role of infectious diseases through the ages, William McNeill (1976) identified the major disease pools and their spread through encounters and intermingling among people through war, conquest, trade, and pilgrimage, following links between town and countryside, disseminating to different city-states and countries, and crossing mountain ranges and oceans. The ability to survive or the tragedy of succumbing to new diseases mark the history of contact, conquest, and colonization.

Diseases acted as barriers to the expansion of the Chinese beyond their southern frontiers. To the south lay fertile lands with a warm, wet climate, but to settle and thrive there, the invaders needed to accommodate to new endemic diseases and heavy parasite loads. Epidemics have provoked political instability and wreaked catastrophic effects on numerous populations. The conquest of Mexico is a notorious example of epidemic decimation. The exchange of diseases between the Old and the New World was not equal. The Old World had adapted to certain illnesses through gradual exposure over the millennia attendant upon contacts between Asia and Europe, the impact of the Mongol Empire, the Black Death, the effects of expanding communication, and trade by sea and by land. By contrast, the New World and Oceania were confronted with the sudden transoceanic introduction of diseases from the Old World, with catastrophic consequences. Few if any truly isolated societies now remain.

After an epidemic wreaked its toll, a gradual equilibrium tended to emerge, with the populations becoming less vulnerable to disastrous epidemic diseases. They entered a new era of disease proliferation when the balance changed from epidemic to endemic patterns. By the sixteenth and seventeenth centuries, populations in Europe began to grow. As McNeill (1976: 210) points out, "Europe's expansion is such a central fact of modern history that we are likely to take it almost for granted and fail to recognize the quite exceptional ecological circumstances that provided sufficient numbers of exportable (and often expendable) human beings needed to undertake such multifarious, risky, and demographically costly ventures." In the complex of factors sustaining Europe's expansion, McNeill argues that the altered pattern of infectious disease was of key significance.

The identification of causes of change

The rise of human populations is a sign of adaptive success of the species. In modern times—the last three centuries—an unprecedented sustained rise in the world's population has taken place. Assessing the contribution of medicine to this population change requires going beyond conjecture. Often facts are missing or impossible to recover. In *The modern rise of population*, Thomas McKeown (1976) summed up his research on the role of medicine. His identification of various causes for the decline of mortality in England and Wales was influential, creating something of "a conceptual revolution in the disciplines of history and medicine, overturning a long-standing general orthodoxy regarding the importance of medical science and the medical profession in bringing about the decline in mortality which accompanied industrialization in Britain" (Szreter 1988: 2). Any orthodoxy is likely to elicit critical reappraisal. McKeown argued that conjecture is not of much value without reliable evidence. He proposed instead a method of deduction based on explicit evidence by applying reasoning and current medical knowledge to a detailed series of national death records from the past. His analysis was original and persuasive.

McKeown found that, from 1838 onward, new rules of personal registration in England and Wales provided national records from which population size, birth rate, death rate, and causes of death could be calculated. These figures made it possible to discover reasons for the increase in population that occurred. From his examination of the records, McKeown concluded that the rise represented a decreasing death rate rather than an increasing birth rate. He found that the decline of mortality was due chiefly to the reduction in deaths from infectious diseases. Between the period of 1848–54 and 1971, 26 percent of the drop in mortality was due to a reduction in noninfectious mortality, but the largest proportion—74 percent—was due to fewer deaths from infectious diseases. To interpret this finding, McKeown looked for when, to what extent, and which specific infections declined. Not all infectious diseases declined uniformly, since different kinds of such illnesses existed, each with its own characteristics and particular history. We know that airborne diseases, for instance, display different potentials for exposure, risk, spread, communicability, and chances of control as compared to diseases that are waterborne or foodborne. McKeown drew graphs of the decline in death rates over the study period from each particular kind of disease, indicating exactly when an effective therapy for each was introduced. He found that, for the majority of infectious diseases, most of the decline in mortality *preceded* the introduction of an effective therapy. A few diseases, such as scarlet fever, changed in virulence over time. Rules for public hygiene and the building of sanitation infrastructure reduced the study population's exposure to infections by water- and foodborne diseases, such as typhoid, cholera, and other intestinal diseases. Changes in the prevalence of tuberculosis reflected reduced exposure after reforms in housing and working conditions were instituted, although class differences in prevalence persisted due to uneven implementation of these reforms. However, these changes did not explain enough of the decline in mortality.

McKeown concluded that the growth in population during this period could not be attributed to fortuitous changes in relationships between disease organisms and hosts. The drop in mortality was not much influenced by immunizations or medical treatments before 1935, when sulfonamide antibiotics became available. Certain medical measures were effective before 1935 in the management of smallpox, syphilis, tetanus, diphtheria, diarrheal diseases, and some surgical conditions, but these had made only a small contribution to the total decline in the death rate since 1838. By the method of exclusion, he was left with one other explanation for the reduction of mortality—namely, improvements in the human environment. Water purification, efficient sewage disposal, and improved food hygiene were introduced in the second half of the nineteenth century and reduced death from intestinal infections, but the decline in infectious diseases had actually begun before then. His main finding was therefore the negative conclusion that, contrary to common assumptions, medical science and hygiene had *not* contributed much to this era's decline in mortality. His positive finding was that improvements in nutrition explained the population increase. The most likely explanation, in McKeown's view, for the decline in mortality and the growth in population was the improvement in the population's nutrition due to greater food supplies.

Assigning credit for change

I have stepped quite far outside the limits of my competence. Why? As someone trained in medicine, I was struck by McKeown's argument that little evidence existed to support the notion that medical advances before 1935 had made much difference in the decline in mortality in England and Wales. He challenged the conventional wisdom that progress in medicine and treatments must be the chief reasons for a growing freedom from disease in modern times.

In my training as an anthropologist, however, I wondered whether medical treatments in other societies or earlier historical periods may have been more effective in reducing rates of death from infectious diseases. Is our own readiness to value what we do for the ill matched by other people's convictions in other places and in the past?

If success is judged by population numbers, medicine has recently done a great deal for people in many countries by controlling and treating the most important infectious diseases, more than occurred in the period and place that McKeown analyzed. For instance, Stephen Kunitz (1983a) analyzed records of mortality and morbidity for the largest Indigenous group of North America, the Navajo, who are a relatively poor population in an overall wealthy society. He found that medical interventions were significant in reducing mortality even in the face of minimal economic change. He traced the history of several causes of death during the past century and showed how specific medical measures brought about a decline in tuberculosis and maternal mortality among the Navajo. Such findings present a certain challenge to McKeown's analysis. Another challenge was raised by Simon Szreter (1988), who reassessed the social and political developments that succeeded in improving working conditions, housing, education, health services, and the regulation of food quality in England and Wales from 1839 to 1935. He concluded that such social interventions played a greater part in the decline of mortality than McKeown had allowed (Szreter 1988: 26). He argued that we need to examine the role of *human agency* in producing changes in health rather than just the *processes* of change. He was concerned with the political ideas and the individuals "causing" change. Political forces affected mortality by making demands for the introduction of changes—sewage disposal, better working conditions, the expansion of suffrage, and so on.

Different explanations give credit for the rise in population to different agents and forces; each of these explanations may have ideological implications (Kunitz 1987). Some turn to the role of environment, some to individual behavior, some to medical care. We can see how McKeown's conclusions might be congenial to authorities wishing to absolve the government of the need to fund costly health services. Similarly, if more weight is given to the role of individual behavior in explaining patterns of mortality, then responsibility for health may be seen as a matter for the individual. If not the individual, then the responsibility may be put on society. Kunitz refers to this contrast as one between voluntarist and determinist views of health. The voluntarists may blind themselves to the powerlessness of the poor by assuming they could change if only they decided to do so. The determinists see the problems in terms of access to care, poor living conditions, and unsafe workplaces. Kunitz's point is that explanatory theories may reflect political ideologies and deeply held assumptions about the nature of society, the existence of free will, and the requirements of justice.

My interest in these conflicting theories led me to ask what we might learn from cross-cultural comparisons of medical treatments and beliefs. But why compare?

That most distinguished medical anthropologist, W. H. R. Rivers, asked how medicine came to be differentiated from religion and magic. In his lectures published posthumously as *Medicine, magic and religion* (1924), he discussed the complex question of progress in medicine. Any study of medical practices brings constant reminders of cultural transmission, borrowing, and pluralism as factors promoting changes in human societies. Rivers argued that comparisons of different human histories demonstrate that there is no such thing as uniform progress through stages of social evolution. "It errs by giving a far too simple account of a process which has in reality been exceedingly complex" (Rivers 1924: 58). The fact of progress may be written plain and large on the page of history, but progress is not a law of nature, as H. A. L. Fisher remarked in his *History of Europe* (1935). Yet the notion of progress plays a large part in many people's intuitive ideas of both natural evolution and social development.

Neither is progress a law of nature nor have social choices always been wise and successful. Many variations must have been discarded in the struggle to survive. Hereditary variation is blind in origin, not necessarily adaptive. By contrast, purpose marks social evolution and makes it different from biological evolution. Likewise, natural selection is not a metaphor that can be applied to society. Rather, it is social choice that contributes to making change rapid in human groups, and this depends on learning and imitation. Social evolution proceeds in a sort of Lamarckian fashion through the inheritance of acquired characteristics. As Morris Ginsberg (1932: 77) pointed out, "Social change is totally different from biological change, but also far more intelligible." It does not face the mysteries of natural evolution—the chance, nondirected, tiny modifications that occurred and led over immense stretches of time from the invertebrate eye to the human eye. The process of change in nature is mindless: there is no drive toward a future goal, no teleology to give it direction. The situation is entirely different with human beings and their arts of subsistence. They try to improve these practices; they devise or borrow new solutions to practical or social problems. When they try out new practices, their bodies do not have to change or pass along new genes to the next generation. Social transmission across human groups and generations is vital both for preserving skills and knowledge and for changing them. Acknowledging this fact of transmission, however, undermines any rigid model of stages in social evolution. Contacts among societies lead to the diffusion of ideas and techniques that enable groups to jump over intervening "stages" that others may have had to pass through to reach certain skills or forms of knowledge.

It is undeniable that people alter their environments.[1] In effect, social progress has come to mean a certain kind of independence from nature, being "civilized" and not "wild." The criterion of advancement now suggests not adaptation to a particular environment but independence from one. Progress, in short, is seen as increasing human dominion over nature by artifice, going beyond a passive state of fitness, naked and defenseless, to survive. It is as though the human species turned the tables on nature regarding adaptation. Natural forces have lost the powers over people's lives they once had. Living "now in chambers and with feather beds," we are able to help some to survive who might not have if they had come into the world when our ancestors slept in caves and forests.

So far, I have been speaking of populations and diseases in history—the rest of this book, however, is really about the care and treatments given to individuals.

---

1. Since I wrote these Lewis Henry Morgan Lectures in 1979, recognition of the human impact on the environment and climate change has become the most prominent topic of serious concern around the world and throws into question the actual independence that human beings have from their natural surroundings.

CHAPTER TWO

Village illness and a panic

In ordinary practice, medicine is concerned with individuals rather than with populations. Most people are likely to think of medical practices in connection with help for particular people: someone sick in their family, children in the community, and so on. They think of medicine parochially.

The biological criteria of progress in health in general—growth in population and increase in life expectancy—refer to *mortality* (death rates) but ignore *morbidity* (disease or ill health). They take account of the numbers of people who live and die rather than the quality of their lives. Most illnesses do not kill, although they cause distress. They include a great variety of morbidity factors that pose no or little threat to life. People presumably develop good opinions about treatments largely because of what was done successfully for those who did not die from their illnesses. Medical assertions of success in treatment point to such examples. If we want to understand how people evaluate medical care, we must consider the treatments that are given.

The consequences of illness for the sick person and for those around him or her are part of the distress caused by illness. The experience of kindness and nursing care affect judgments of the value of particular treatments. Illness brings awareness of the need for help. Unlike a blind sparrow, a blind man is not likely to starve because of his condition unless no one felt any responsibility, concern, or sympathy for him. Care for others lies at the root of responses to the sick. No doubt there are links between the words and the ideas of kin, kind, and kindness; sympathy is akin to kindness. Perhaps sympathy—the feeling that allows one to recognize another's pain and needs—has also played its part in the development of medicine.

My purpose in this chapter is to give a sense of how residents of the village of Rauit, Papua New Guinea, experienced and faced illnesses in 1968–1969. In chapter 3, I shall describe a long illness and the way it exposed problems of care and responsibility for the infirm. Even though these cases come from just a single village, they show a range of the problems and the variety of responses—enough, I hope, for some wider issues to be grasped. Although my periods of fieldwork were short (1968–1969, 1975, and 1985), they spanned Papua New Guinea's change from colonial status to independence. In the interim, a village aid post was set up for the villagers of Rauit and Mandubil, supervised by the mission health service. Chapter 4 will describe how the village aid post affected village care and the work of the local health committee. The move from village morality and expectations to the aims of the National Health Plan was a huge change, requiring major shifts of assumption about care and responsibilities in treatment.

The villages where Gnau languages are spoken lie on the southern fringes of a band of settlements along the inland fall of the Torricelli Mountains. Villages to the north and west of them are slightly smaller, with land more densely filled with gardens and less room for forest to hunt in. By contrast, the village of Rauit (population c. 370 in 1969, c. 420 in 1985) has access to extensive forest, which was empty of people. The village is a cluster of six hamlets, each associated with particular patrilineal clans. Marriage is mainly within the village between different clans. Rauit men like to see themselves as hunters, but their staple food is starch, specifically sago with green leaves, supplemented by yams and taro. Their annual gardening cycle set by wet and dry seasons. They plant bananas, pandanus, pitpit, sugarcane, various greens, tobacco, and several more recently introduced food crops, as do all the people who live in these foothills.

The Gnau-speaking villages are situated behind Anguganak Bluff, which rises. steep and sheer, among the hills of the southern fall of the Torricelli range. It has represented a barrier, isolating the villages at the top or behind it from easy access. A mission settlement was started in 1958 at the foot of the bluff, but Gnau villagers had little contact with it at first since the steepness of Anguganak Cliff cut them off. In 1968, a dirt road in the river valley below was gradually extended toward the road leading to the subdistrict headquarters at Lumi.

Figure 1. The path to Rauit village along the edge of Anguganak Cliff. The Christian mission and health center are located in the valley below.

Villagers have a myth about how Anguganak Bluff was raised as a barrier to an enemy. The Opan River has to curl around its base before it can go south to the distant plain. The ridges, hills, and valleys are all forested, but near the villages, the bush is strewn with gardens. The lower-lying hills and the flatland far to the south of Rauit are almost uninhabited, containing great tracts of tall forest for hunting. The Sepik River is down there somewhere, far to the south, invisible, and elders in Rauit told me they did not know about it before White people came. They also knew nothing about the coast where the Sepik empties: they said they did not know how to swim or what a canoe was. Their environment was bush, garden, and forest. The world they knew had narrow limits, forming a rough circle around them with a radius of about ten miles. Within this circle, ten different languages were spoken in forty-two villages. Gnau speakers are likely to know one neighboring language in addition to their own and the contact language of Tok Pisin. They used to have little knowledge of most of the villages and places at or beyond the perimeter of the circle; few in the past would ever have gone to the edge of the former social horizon. The edges were known from the names of places that came into stories, genealogies, or myths.

Illness is a relatively public matter in a village. Houses are set close together, and people know each other and about each other in detail, since they spend most of every day outside and visible to others. They see illness and must cope with it at close quarters. However, to take an extreme example, the illness and death of a week-old baby passed unremarked by most villagers, unknown to some, while at another time, another illness—that of a man in his forties—disturbed the usual pattern of the whole village's life for about three months. Reactions may be very public or very private; they vary because of the sort of illness, its acuteness and severity, aspects of the person involved (who is affected, what age and status, belonging to what group), the timing of the illness and its mode of onset, and the circumstances. An accident or sudden illness can provoke concern that a gradual descent into illness usually does not.

Ordinary cases

One of the troubles with describing social responses to illness is that readers are often more curious to hear about dramatic or complicated cases than about common illnesses that people have to cope with or respond to without much fuss. As a result, anthropologists may neglect to write about care for common minor illnesses and give undue attention to complicated cases and ritual treatment. Partly this is inevitable because one hears more about them during fieldwork. In Gnau villages,

Figure 2. A Rauit hamlet at noon, 1968. Coconut palms are planted within the village but not outside it. Their distinctive leaf crowns mark the presence of a village seen from afar.

the hamlet rather than the entire village is the effective unit of daily life, of chatting, of trivial news. Unless one lives in the hamlet, many small illnesses and accidents pass unnoticed by outsiders. Home care is quiet and relatively private. The bite of a death adder understandably causes more of a commotion than an infected sore. Villagers would see the sore as something ordinary, an accident too trivial to make much fuss over, and assume it will get better soon. But a person knows if someone is ill in the same hamlet and should come without waiting to ask if there is something he or she can do to help. Whether much is done depends on how long the illness lasts.

Figure 3. A hamlet with women's individual family houses in the foreground. The thatching of the houses is made from sago-palm leaves, their walls from the large midribs of the leaves.

Matupin has just another fever. August 13, 1968, Watalu.
Matupin had gone to Namelim (the bush where he has gardens), and while working in the afternoon, he felt sick and hot and then vomited. He stayed there and slept in his garden house that night. He came back the next day feeling better. The following day, I saw him go off in the morning; however, as I was doing something in Watalu in the afternoon, his first wife called out to me to go and see him, since he was ill again. He had come back early and vomited. He was lying beside a small fire in his second wife's fenced-off cooking porch,

apparently asleep. I didn't wake him up and went to see someone else. Twenty minutes later, noisy retching came from where he was. Everyone could hear it, exaggerated looks were exchanged, someone said he's very sick and told me to go and give him an injection. I went to look. He had retched up a little water; nothing else had come up, he said, just water. He felt hot and had a headache. I offered to come back with some medicine, but he said he wanted to sleep. However, that evening, I forgot to bring him the antimalarial tablets I said I would. No one came to remind me.

The next morning, I found him on the ground in front of his first wife's house, lying in the dust. He had a headache and felt hot, but he did not feel nauseated. I gave him the tablets. He did not want to talk, just to sleep. In the afternoon, he felt better, chatted vaguely, and said he would like to smoke now. He had not smoked for two days because he had been ill. He thought the illness must be because he had cut the leaves of a big fern *nimbe'ut* that people associate with spirits and illness. He had not asked for treatment by anyone nor had he tried to treat himself, although he knows what to do for this kind of illness. He was going to wait for it to pass. He planned to sit around and wait. He was better the next day. No one did anything special about this illness.

Selpi has a swollen hand "from harvesting yams."
Selpi, a woman in her forties from the hamlet of Animbil, came to see me because of painful swelling over the knuckle of her right index finger and middle finger. She said she hadn't injured the hand and there was nothing else except the pain and swelling. She put it down to some yams. It was the time for first harvesting yams. The hand hurt so that she could not cook meals—that is, "turn" sago jelly—and her eldest daughter had to do it instead. I could not find anything to account for the swelling. I told her to rest the hand and gave her a sling. She kept it on for two days, then abandoned it when she was extremely busy with the celebration of her eldest son's puberty cere-mony and she was in high spirits. I did not see her again until six days later when the infection had come to a head and needed to be incised.

People's previous experience with illness influences how much they worry. They know fairly well what to expect with sprains, headaches, cuts, and sores; fevers are common, although they are not predictable and sometimes turn out badly. A general discussion of the effect of diseases on social life would be vain, given the great diversity of disabling effects.

Figure 4. Women boil water in a bamboo tube for cooking taro or preparing sago jelly, their staple food. The large conical mound behind them is the eroded base of a coconut palm planted long ago.

Severity, pain, inexplicability, duration, and disablement contribute in different ways to distress.

Sickness impinges on people's work and social life in particular ways. The signs and symptoms and the restrictions or embarrassment they cause affect how they are tolerated. Illness may interfere with particular tasks or roles. Mobility and strength are obvious requirements for garden work and hunting. Many Gnau rules carry a general sanction of illness if one should break them, and the penalties most often indicated give a view of what illness in general means to them: they say you will get breathless, you won't be able to manage the slippery steep paths, your joints will be stiff, your limbs will feel heavy, you will be confined to the village. Or your sight may fail; you will be confined just the same. Illness is a threat of premature decrepitude, a threat in keeping with their way of life and what they value.

The significance of illness can, however, depend more on who is affected, on his or her role and place, rather than purely on the kind of disease. If the illness is severe enough to prevent someone from doing what he or she should, that consequence may be enough to make it serious. The contingency intrinsic to illness gives it power to disrupt plans and force itself on other people's attention. Some of these points will appear later in the accounts of the illnesses of Maka and Wolai, when the flow of other events at the times they were ill affected the significance attached to their illnesses and the care they received.

Responsibility for care

The position of women

In the vast majority of societies, the stress of illness is felt immediately by the sick person's family. In an urban situation, the strains may fall on the family and not be noticed outside it, unless the sick person is critical in some way for other people's lives or for their jobs in the wider society. Illness is a mostly private matter that the family manages on its own, unless they need to hand over care of the patient to someone specially qualified because the illness is more serious. But this is not possible for people in many places. Instead, the family and the local community have to cope and rely on their own resources. It is hard to overemphasize (in fact, it is hard to imagine it properly at all) the distress of urgent need in such a community on certain occasions, as when a child screams and vomits with pain and a high fever or a man is unable to pass urine for three days and nights and lies moaning, his belly swollen. The Gnau do face such situations and have to cope on their own.

Who should help the sick person? The Gnau wife and mother is the central figure in providing basic care and nursing within her domestic group. The degree to which she is irreplaceable at the center changes with the family's stage of development. When a man feels very ill, he can move to his wife's house so she can look after him. In fact, illness is almost the only reason for a man to sleep in the same house as his wife in the village; men normally sleep apart or in the communal men's house of their hamlet. However, a woman could not turn to her husband for nursing care in the same way as he could turn to her. Upon marriage, it is the woman who moves to live at a new place, her husband's home.

It takes some time for a young woman to feel at home among her husband's kin. This shows itself in what she does when she is ill or when her child is ill. In the early phase of married life, she is likely to go back quickly to the family in which she was born, where her parents and her brothers live. Fears of the illness caused by spirits of her husband's lineage may be used to explain or justify such a move. A wife will only go back to her parents or brothers for an illness perceived as serious. Late in marriage, with daughters or a daughter-in-law to care for her and with established friendships among other women of the hamlet, her home and place are now really there; it is quite exceptional for illness to make her move from her established home. Whether a woman moves when she or her child falls ill depends on the growth of her attachment to her husband's family and place, her sense of security and support.

Bagi, a young married woman, returns home to be mothered.
I went to see Bagi, a married woman in her twenties. I had been called by her brother. She had come back from Bi'ip to her mother's house at Taki because she was feeling sick and feverish. She was lying on a sheet of palm-leaf spathe (*limbum* in Tok Pisin, *biape* in Gnau) with her head resting on the lap of her elderly mother. She was holding her mother's leg with her arm; her mother's arm was around her shoulders. She was lying about a foot and half away from the fire in the hearth of their day house. Her father, a younger half-sister and brother, and her classificatory brother and his wife were all sitting close by with her. She was lying listlessly. Beside her on the palm spathe (*limbum*) were stained nettle leaves, and she had marks of be-tel juice spat onto her lower chest and epigastrium. Her father had treated her by spitting. Her brother said she had not eaten since yesterday, she was drowsy, and had been ill for many days. She made no attempt to answer the questions I addressed to her; others answered them for her. She gave no sign that she even heard them. I examined her; she seemed floppy from lassitude or apathy, moving slowly as she walked to her mother's house so I could examine her eyes in the dark. When I finished, she walked back and sat on the *limbum*, sitting up now, looking more alert. She had a fever. I asked them about her husband, knowing he had been arrested two days before. She spoke up for the first time, saying a policeman had come to take him to jail. She spent the rest of the day sitting with her mother, who sometimes

rubbed her with nettles. I saw her throw the nettles away with the awkward gesture of someone ritually getting rid of something.

A man could not expect to get that sort of mothering. I visited Wani, a senior man. He had been treated for affliction by Panu'et, a spirit, two days before. He had a chest infection. The visitors from Animbil hamlet were gathered at the day house belonging to him and his sons, a place for guests to come and find him. But he was inside his wife's house, lying on the flat-bench bed made from the midribs of sago palm leaves. Lawusa, his married clan sister in Animbil, was sitting on the earth floor beside him. He had taken off the fur head ring and the decorative arm bands he usually wore. He said in a quavery voice that his ribs were sore still but that someone had come to spit over him to counter possible harm from a clan ancestral spirit, since he had eaten betel nut from their land. It was so dark in the hut that all I could see of him at first was his white shell phallocrypt and the gleam from his teeth when he smiled. Outside, the people who had come sat chatting; they were given a meal later that day by his family.

Self-concern: Men

Men tended to pay more attention to their own trivial or mild illnesses than women did and more readily took time off to stay at home while ill. They could afford to indulge their indisposition because they were not bound in the same way as women were by daily demands to feed and cook for their families. But both men and women sometimes acted conspicuously or histrionically when they became ill. Such behavior in men was associated with a particular explanation or some fear about the implications of what they had noticed in themselves. In women, such behavior was unattached to any elaborate explanation, so it appeared to be an end in itself. It was as though married women, having greater pressures on them not to stop work for mild illness and needing to justify abandoning their domestic duties, did so in part by making very clear to others just how ill they felt. At times of planting and harvesting, there were usually some senior men who would ostentatiously rub their aches with nettles, apparently quite ill. They claimed to be struck ill by the yam spirits during their hard work at the gardens. They would spend a day or two in the village and then go back to work. I was mystified on three or four occasions by men who appeared to be in extreme pain in one eyeball, groaning and in anguish, saying they had been struck by a yam spirit while gardening. I could find nothing wrong with their eye

Figure 5. The *warkao*, a day house where families of a localized lineage group in the hamlet can gather. They often bring their food to eat at the *warkao* in the morning and evening. It is also used to receive friends who come by for casual conversation or to provide shelter for visitors who come to the hamlet for a particular event.

except that it had become red from rubbing, which seemed to clear up by next morning. In Rauit, the men relied mostly on a nonverbal show of illness—social withdrawal, refusal of food and conversation, griming with dirt—to convey that they feel ill.

> *Silmai with a bad headache, Wimalu.*
> I came upon Silmai sitting crouched over a fire beside his house. He was in his fifties, a wily man, also sardonic, intelligent, and effective

in authority. His head was bent down on his knees, his eyes closed. Though he heard me coming, he made no movement to look at me or acknowledge my presence. Saibuten asked him if he was sick. In a gravelly voice, with no change in his bent position, he said he was, adding something about his matrilateral relatives cutting down a tree. He raised a furrowed, bleary, tired face and laid his cheek sideways on his knees. He had a headache and ached generally. Then he said he had dreamed of Balwun and Sukadel, who were matrilaterally related to him. He had sent for Sanawut to come and spit over him because he was also a matrilateral kinsperson. There were two splotches of red betel juice over his shoulder blades. We sat with him for a while. Silmai, still crouched and occasionally snapping his fingers at his forehead, occasionally gave short hard blows with the heel of his hand against his forehead (that must have hurt!). He didn't talk any more but simply growled at a dog sitting by him. He got up to urinate, came back, and lay down to sleep. Creased brow, haggard look—a bad headache.

Saibuten explained that Silmai thought his kinsmen might have been cutting down a big old tree on his mother's brother's land. The Gnau liken the relationship of a sister's son to his mother's brother's clan to that of a tree growing up from a piece of ground. This image associates the sister's son with the tree, the clan with the ground. So perhaps when a tree growing on the mother's brother's land is cut down, the sister's son will feel sympathetic pain. A mother's brother has the power, they think, to harm his sister's son by calling on his ancestors and putting a spell on such a tree and then cut it down. When the tree falls, his sister's son is also struck down. Saibuten was alluding to these ideas in his explanation. This idea had passed through Silmai's mind because of his dream. Nonetheless, he was better the next day.

Analogy in explanation

What sets the general framework in which to see sickness? An intuition of relationships between the facts (love and hate, attraction, opposition, association, unity, intention, purpose, aim, cause, the action of an agent on an object, resistance) may emerge from the perception of such forces in social life. Why should we think that causes for illness might be found inside the body rather than in visible or invisible forces in the outside world? The problem for explaining sickness maybe to find some connection between the person who is ill and his or her circumstances. The Gnau approach depended on linking patients and circumstances (which were things to be observed) with certain causes (which were not ordinarily visible). They deduced the relationships by analogies with their experience of the motivating forces in social life. They considered the events of illness in a matter-of-fact way first, trying to deduce what might be the likely cause. I sometimes found it hard to tell whether they were giving me a plain description of recent facts or a statement that implied the mystical causes of an illness. The Gnau worked out possibilities by considering the timing and circumstances surrounding the illness. Their conclusions would rest on certain components of the situation as significant for understanding how and why the illness had occurred. The cognitive process is similar to what we use in trying to decide why an accident occurred when we consider what risks attach to different components of the situation (G. Lewis 1975: 265–66). Gnau diagnoses were applied to syndromes of circumstance rather than syndromes of clinical symptoms and signs.

Ordinary experience was the source of intuitions of possible causal relationships. Villagers would speak of a spirit causing someone to be ill as "crushing," "holding," "fastening round," "tying up," "holding tight," or "pulling" on the afflicted person. The verbs express the sense of a patient crushed down, constrained, restricted by illness. The spirit could "strike" or "shoot" the patient (involving ideas of attack, hurt, disease as an enemy) or it could "stay" in her or "go down into" him (suggesting an unwanted presence, disease as an intruder). Sometimes they seemed to take this idea of entry literally—for instance, when they sucked out "arrow points" shot in by the spirit or when they tied a foul-smelling creeper around the affected part to "stink out" the spirit. They might sear the patient's skin with flaming coconut fronds to expel the spirit with heat or try to startle it with blows and bangs. For example, the son of a man with heart failure got hold of some gun powder and came by in the evening as his father slept beside a fire. He dropped the gunpowder in the fire so the noise would startle the spirit away. Both speech and behavior showed what the Gnau thought about the illness. Certain verbs described how a spirit would take notice of someone: it would "spy him out," "put its eyes" on him, "say his name," "call out" to him, "smell" him. Their guesses and deductions about the causes and processes of illness constituted attempts to find some order, to explain events, to predict and control them.

The personification of spirits based on an understanding of human behavior allowed them to guess the motives that might actuate spirits to cause illness. But despite their personification of spirits, the latter were not persons in the way people are (see also Horton 1967, 1982: 230–31). The Gnau did not know how to judge or understand spirits' purposes and motives as they would those of other people. At times, the spirits seemed capricious, as motiveless as the wind. As a result, villagers did not assign blame and responsibility to spirits with the same moral indignation as they did to people who were thought to have caused someone's illness.

Their general explanatory themes had to be observed in use to grasp their practical significance. The ideas of the localization of a spirit, its range of movement and attention, and the danger of it adding to someone's illness came alive for me when I noticed fences set up to isolate and protect someone with an illness from the influence of people passing by who might have eaten things dangerous to the patient. How many paces off would be safe? Ten paces? Twenty? If a spirit took up a local habitation so that a patient had to move from her house, how far would she have to go to avoid the risk? Such moves rarely involved distancing of more than two or three hundred yards, sometimes much less. How long would she need to stay away? How long would she have to avoid a certain food? Answers to these questions helped me observe what such ideas meant in practical terms. The ideas were based on simple analogies, but their consequences (How far to move? Could that food have been the cause even though it was eaten two weeks before the illness came on?) required people to decide what they thought in order to know what to do. They had to articulate their theories with the myriad ordinary and chance events of life. They attended to both ideas and events selectively. In theory, a particular food might cause a man or a woman to get sick. In practice, however, it was more commonly used to explain women's illnesses—not because women ate such food more than men but because they played the major role in producing it, usually working on their husband's land with plants his jealous ancestors watched over.

Sympathy gatherings: The value of support

Obligations toward kin provided the local basis and idiom of care for the sick. To watch over others, to take responsibility for those with whom one lives, was a theme they expressed in many of their actions and attitudes, such as the taboos that parents observed to protect their child and its health or in the act of the man who broke his knife or threw it away because he had lent it to someone who cut himself with it. If someone

Figure 6. A family at meal-time, showing the separation by gender and age: the mother eats with her young children while the father and an older son sit in the background, each with a separate portion.

harmed himself by misadventure or his own stupidity during a journey he took because you asked him to, then you would be held responsible for his harm. If a child fell ill when the father was away, he might blame the mother for letting harm come to the child left in her care. If a woman cut herself accidentally in the company of others, they would they say they felt "ashamed" at the sight of her blood. The most dramatic formal expression of this attitude was in the behavior expected of clan relatives belonging to other villages who would come to mourn the death of a clan member. They would come smeared in clay or mud, chanting reproaches at the waiting villagers, weeping and sobbing, "Where was

Figure 7. A family shares taro mash from a wooden bowl.

I when you needed me? They have let you die, my brother. If only I had been with you!" The weeping showed their grief; the reproach was directed at the home relatives who should have looked after the person who died. They sometimes expressed this fiercely, since they had license to shoot at the patient's house, the men's house, or surrounding trees. At times, they would even shoot toward the mourners, aiming to miss. The home mourners were expected to stay seated, grief-distracted, disregarding any arrows that flicked by them as the deceased's clan members wreaked havoc.

In any serious ailment, public gatherings would take place during the course of the illness; people hearing of it would come for the day to the hamlet where the sick person was lying. This response was meant to demonstrate concern. The Gnau referred to this as "coming to sit in company with the sick person so that he or she may get well" or sometimes as "sitting in company with the family to surround the sick person." The second phrase suggests sitting around the patient to shield him or her. The normal pattern for these sympathy visits was for the family to provide a meal for the visitors and spend the day with them. These "sit-downs" for sickness (like the ones for certain other misfortunes, as well as those during gatherings to celebrate achievements, returns from plantation labor or from jail, and the celebration of certain rites) brought people close together in a literal sense and in the figurative social sense. The ordinary run of daily life was punctuated by these sociable occasions.

Figure 8. People who remain in the village to hold a sympathy gathering for a sick man. Instead of going to their gardens, they sit next to the patient's house to support and protect him.

In sudden serious illness or catastrophe, the whole village might gather for the night, staying to surround and shield the afflicted person; they fasted in sympathy, a demonstration of communal solidarity in visible and touching terms. They "watched over the patient." When people were abruptly frightened that someone they cared for might die, they showed their anguish and grief by destroying their own possessions, breaking pots, cutting at trees. The following account I wrote about Maka's attack when people thought she might have been struck down by sorcery or a spirit illustrates the intensity and strength of these responses. Panic spread among the villagers. They went through much of their repertory of acute responses. They tried different ways of diagnosis and treatment, but Maka's problems did not end with this episode. The pace of events and the suddenness of people's reactions struck me. It is difficult to briefly portray the dense flow of activities, dramas, and distress going on in the village at this time. Some were directly or indirectly related to another man's illness, others were unconnected; however, they all contributed to a sense of the complexity—the involvement and ramifications—of village life.

Response to crisis

Panic at Watalu hamlet. Maka becomes possessed and fears she might be dying.

The background events leading up to this crisis were complicated. A large ritual "singing" for the spirit Malyi was being performed at Watalu for the long, severe illness of Dauwaras, younger brother of Maka's husband. His illness and the beginning of the Malyi singing had occupied everyone's attention recently, but *minmin* sorcery fears also lurked in the background.[1] Over the previous three months, fears about *minmin* had been spreading and intensifying. This form of sorcery was beginning to overtake the long-reviled *langasutap* sorcery as the danger most to be feared when away from the village and in strange places (G. Lewis 1977).

The panic on September 19, 1968.

It was 2:15 in the afternoon. The Malyi singing for Dauwaras continued but without verve. It was the ninth day. About fifteen men were there, mostly from Watalu. A shouted message came from outside. Purkiten, Maluna, and Mawikil got up halfway, then sat down again. The stanza of song ended. Purkiten got up, Tawo said to get water, Purkiten looked for a bamboo water tube: empty. Nearly everyone left the men's house, not hastily, but obviously something was up. It had something to do with Maka. Under her house porch, sitting on the ground near where she normally cooked her meals, Maka was

---

1. Dauwaras's illness was the subject of a book I later published (see G. Lewis 2000).

possessed. Quite close, sitting half turned toward her was Padik, her aged mother, then slightly further away were Katina and Wolusi, both young wives from Watalu; on Maka's other side, her daughters Wankyi and Kenken were sitting facing away from her and looking at the ground. Pe'alen, her stepfather, and Maluna stood in front. Purkiten was just turning away from her, having spat water sprays to either side of her. They thought the spirit possessing her was that of his dead clan brother. Purkiten called out that it should not harm her. Children had come to see what was happening and were staring with excited interest. So was I. The others just sat listening but without seeming worried or excited, not staring at her. Most looked either at the ground or in front of them, vaguely or blankly.

Maka sat on the earth, her legs extended straight in front of her, arms loose at her sides, her torso shaking rapidly (about one and a half times per second), seeming to pivot about the pit of her stomach (at the *wuna'at*, thinking center). But her general tonus looked relaxed or flaccid rather than taut and tense, the jerks of her torso were passively transmitted along her limbs, her face expressionless, lids half drooped, eyes downcast. With each shake, she made a little noise as though her breath pushed out the cry. The cries rose and fell in waves roughly in time with a deep breathing rhythm, about ten cycles per minute. The cries went *hus! hus! hus!*, changing to *he! he! he!*, then sometimes *ha! ha! ha!*, and back to *hus! hus! hus!* (*Hus!* was the most frequent cry. It sounded like someone encouraging a dog to find something, some child said, giggling a bit naughtily.) Sporadically the cries stopped and Maka spoke, her sentences starting but not all finished. Her utterances were in a higher pitch and a flatter tone than her normal speaking voice, the flow of words was partly broken or stuttered by the jerky outflow of her breathing; some of the sentences came out in one flat unbroken flow, others were interrupted by staccato *hus! hus! hus!* cries. So far as I could catch what she said, she first spoke the names of people, the father of So-and-So, as if she were questioning them; then she said something about *minmin* and Nembugil, that Maluna or his eldest son Melui would be struck at Wolwakat or Walyip: "*Melui yi-yigai wadagep Walyip*" ("Melui will d-d-dig up yams at Walyip"). She repeated this phrase a number of times. Then "*Melui wiyab . . . Melui wiyab . . . wiyab Wolwokat? . . . wiyab Walyip?*" ("Melui, it will strike you . . . strike you at Wolwakat? . . . strike you at Walyip?"; her tone implied Wolwakat rather than Walyip). Then "*Melui yai munda'an? . . . gnau . . . Walei munda'an?*" ("Where's Melui's father? . . . No . . . where is Walei?"), to which people listening answered calmly, "He's here." They did not then try to talk to her or the spirit directly. A number of times she said "*Dji bedjirabeke'in*" ("You be quiet now"), speaking gently, almost wonderingly, as if to herself or the spirit.

She became quieter, but her *hus! hus!* sounds continued. Purkiten, Mawikil, and Maluna, having sat down, occasionally commented to each other on what she was saying and soon seemed to lose interest. They went back to the men's house. Meanwhile, her husband Kantyi came over. He had been at Animbil because they were shooting a large boar there. On his arrival, Kantyi looked briefly at her and quietly sat down about ten feet away, crouching with his back to her. As the other men got up to go, they told the children to clear off. I moved slightly off to the side. I did not see Maka look anywhere except at the ground in front of her, but then she said that I was there and she felt ashamed. She paused, then I heard her get up quite rapidly and, without faltering, go inside her house. There was silence. The scene (up to this point) had lasted about twelve minutes. I went back to the men's house, where they were talking about what she said, but I heard only the tail end of this. Tawo, who had not gone to see Maka, began beating his kundu drum and the others, following his lead, began to sing.

The singing continued. In pauses, I could hear the *hus! hus! he! he!* cries again. Pe'alen slipped out. After a bit I followed. The women were sitting quietly under the porch while Kantyi and Pe'alen crouched outside. Fine rain was falling. From inside the house, Maka could be heard still sometimes calling, sometimes talking. The pauses between her cries grew longer. She became quite silent. Now it was forty minutes from the start.

In the men's house, they told me the spirit possessing her had been reproaching her for using bush that had belonged to the spirit. Singing was resumed. The singing stopped suddenly at a burst of noise, a confusion of crying and shouting, voices calling out that Maka had died. It was sixty minutes from the start. Women were crying out. People were running to Maka's house, women wailing and in tears, crying out, "She's dead!" Wosabat (the wife of Dauwaras, the sick man, Maka's husband's younger brother) was throwing her own bamboos out of her house, smashing her own cooking utensils, destroying things, desolate, grief-stricken. I called to Walei, Maluna's second son, who was rushing there, asking him what it was. His face was very tense when he said *langasutap* sorcery has struck her. Pe'alen, her stepfather, was crouching, weeping, "Maka! Maka!" Her husband was in the house with her. He led her out to me. She was dazed, pale, haggard-looking, blank-faced. I briefly examined her. People prepared to treat her and she was quiet for a short time, and then again entered possession. Wara came up with nettle leaves to do a kind of blowing, patting divination, a "smelling out" of the spirit. Maka interrupted this by walking down the slope close to her house where rubbish is thrown. She began crying for her children and announced she was going to die. She fell back, as if struck down dead. Wolei and Wara raised her and, with Kantyi supporting her too, she walked up the slope to her house. She sank down semirecumbent, Kantyi crouching behind her to support her back, weeping. Wara, who was about to treat her, kept hold of her right wrist. Padik and another elderly woman, Sawi, flung themselves wailing on Maka's chest; others grabbed at her loose arm or sobbed down over her legs.

Amid this confusion of bodies and weeping, Wara stood facing her, holding her right wrist, talking to her calmly. He called her by name, "Maka," and began to treat her by striking her with the nettle leaves. Wolei from Bi'ip was also striking her with nettles. Wara delivered sharp blows on her ears, forehead, temples, then her chest, and brushed the nettles along her arms and legs with sweeping gestures. The blows were intended to startle the spirit or sickness out of her. He did a lot of puffing and striking on the nettle leaves and puffing into or close to her ears, striking again with the nettles. Then he stood back and called, "Maka, Maka, you get up now, get up. . . . Do you mean to abandon us?" Maka—whose head was sometimes lolling back, sometimes forward—occasionally fluttered her eyelids, but they were mostly drooped nearly shut. Her right leg showed a rapid irregular tremor. Her breathing was not distressed. She did not answer. Wolei was administering the same treatment as Wara from the other side, but Wara's was a more sustained, ordered, and impressive performance. The grieving women were still sprawled on Maka's body. At one point, Wara half-knelt on Maka's jerking leg (I think in order to still or feel the jerks). Someone cried out that they must get coconut leaves. Some dry ones were brought, bunched together into a torch, and set on fire. Flame flared. Wolei moved the flames close along her arms, sides, legs, then held them briefly to her fingers and then the soles of her feet. He worked down one side of her body, then the other. Maka allowed her limbs to be held passively to the flames, giving no sign of pain, although she bent her feet down to the flames and shrank from them a little when they were held close to her side. The flames were meant to sear the spirit and frighten it off.

She mumbled something in a low voice, something about the back of her neck and three *yammami* (a type of yam, *Dioscorea esculenta*) given to her by Kalimao, Purkiten's daughter. I was told that she said it wasn't *minmin* or *langasutap* sorcery but the spirit of Tambin that had struck her because of *yammami* she had eaten. Later, Wara said he smelled out the spirit of Weikris, a deceased clan brother of Purkiten whom Maka's husband had been brought up with. Maka's own revelation about the Tambin spirit afflicting her caused people to direct their subsequent treatments to ousting Tambin from her. (I should mention that Maka was exceptional: she was one of very few women who, as a girl just before puberty, had gone through the entire Tambin performance in the men's house just as if she had been a boy; her father had only daughters, and she was the eldest one; since he had no son, he put her through the rites.)

Pe'alen had been crouching to the side of the melee around Maka. He now came up to Maka holding nettles, spat a pale juice on them, and struck her with them. He was chewing something, saying words to a spell in a low voice. Then he bent, opening Maka's mouth for her, and spat juice into her mouth. He took her hand and pulled and bent her fingers to try and make her knuckles crack. This gesture, called *lagela galbietap* ("breaking her fingers"), was done to see if they would crack, which other people also tried later. It was a kind of test: if the spirit or sickness had left her, then her knuckles would crack; if it was still inside her, they would not. Pe'alen stood up, shaking his head.

Amid the confusion of women crying, wailing, and Maka herself occasionally saying, "*Degadeyig*" ("I am dying now"), Wara and Wolei and Maluna continued striking her with nettles or brushing them along her legs, as if catching something up in them and throwing it away. All the time, more people were gathering round. Maka asked for her uncles from Bi'ip and her brother, but they were in the bush. Someone went off to call them back. Maka then said that she was dying and asked to be taken back to Bi'ip (where she was born). Supported by Wara and Wolei and followed by a long line of people, she began to walk feebly toward Bi'ip. She got about three hundred yards to the point where the path goes down muddily beside water holes, sago palms, and a fish pond. She paused, and others decided that she could not go to Bi'ip because no one was there. So they turned Maka around, who was now passive and accepting, and walked her back to Maluna's day house (*warkao*).

There they sat her on a piece of *limbum*, her legs stretched out limp, with Walei, Maluna's second son, sitting on a kerosene drum, supporting her as she rested back in his arms. Maka was quiet now, her face drained and haggard, eyes and head drooping. Padik, her white-haired mother, was at her side holding her hand. By now, no one was wailing, but some women had tears on their cheeks as they continued to gently sob. On the way back to the day house, Kantyi had stooped to the side of the path to pick some heart-shaped leaves called *langit*, which are associated with Tambin. He gave some to Wara, Wolei, Maluna, and Pe'alen. In succession, all of them first blew spells into the *langit* and then patted Maka's chest gently, chanting quietly. Then each held his leaf in the ring formed by the index finger and thumb of the semi-clenched fist of his left hand and slapped it sharply with his right palm, lifted his palm to look at the leaf, then casually threw it away. (The slap may cause a tiny tear in the leaf; they said if the tear curls upward, that indicates that the spirit of Tambin is the cause of illness. No conclusive answer came out of this.)

Others collected dry coconut leaf fronds into two piles, one on each side of Maka, about two feet away. They lit them and flames flared up. This was to make the spirit leave her because of the heat. Maka, though looking dazed and absent, obviously shrank from the flames. She sometimes showed pain when people rubbed nettles on her; she gave little cries. It was by now an hour and three quarters from the onset of her possession. She showed signs of sleepiness, her head drooped. Others told her sharply to open her eyes, to not fall asleep. She complained of the back of her neck; they repeated it, she must have been struck there, it must be treated.

After these things, Wara went and sat alone on a low seat at the back of the opened day hut. He did not talk. His self-contained air has a certain authority and impressiveness. Possibly it helps explain why he is often asked to treat others. However, there are two other reasons for him to treat Maka: first, he belongs to a collateral branch of her natal lineage, although his branch is at Animbil, not Bi'ip; second, he is Walei's father-in-law, and Walei is a "son" to Maka.

Gradually, the concentration that everyone focused on Maka began to fragment. People began talking it over, explaining things to latecomers. Maluna repeatedly described for others how he had heard noises in the bush the day before and shouted, "Who's there?" and Maka had replied. The possible tricks of *minmin* crossed their minds, I think. Pe'alen came forward again and then Wara did so. They chewed and spat nettle leaves to rub on Maka, then spat into her mouth. It was betel juice chewed with herbs, bark shavings, and ginger, hot or bitter things with strong smells, which they keep on them in their string bags. Maka was supposed to swallow the juice so it would go into her belly and oust the spirit.

Kantyi had again disappeared. After fifteen minutes he came back with a collection of leaves and herbs in a banana leaf. There were colored cordylines, the strongly perfumed leaves of *dyuelbi*, *nilape*, et cetera. He began shredding and crumpling the leaves; the scent released was strong. This done, he went outside. Wara and Maluna followed, Wolei supporting Maka. There they placed the crumpled leaves on a large *lyimungai* banana leaf, where two hibiscus flowers were stuck in the midriff. They chanted some Tambin verses in a low voice and tore the leaf down its midrib so that the scented leaves cascaded over Maka. This was also done to rid her of Tambin. The crumpled leaves contained small bits of house thatch from houses in the hamlet, and I noticed some bright feathers from the red-breasted pitta *wa'aubi*. Maka was led back and sat down in the day house, as before.

Pauwarak, a senior man from Animbil who had been a *luluai* (official village headman), now appeared. He was chewing a large wad of betel and, without saying anything, went over slowly to Maka and stood over her, looking at her. He bent and palpated the back of her neck, pinching her skin up, bent further, and seemed to nip at the fold of skin with his teeth, then straightened back up. With his forefinger and index, he delicately removed something from between his front teeth, against which his tongue was pressing; it was something tiny, which he then threw aside on the ground. He repeated this about seven times, each time palpating carefully before pinching up the fold of Maka's skin. When he had done that, he picked some leaves and blew and patted on her skin, murmuring "*pur pur pur pur*" and words. He was extracting *sigap* (arrowheads) by the Panu'et method. These were supposed to be in her neck at the back where she had complained of pain. It was not made explicit whether the spirit of Tambin or the spirit of the *yammami* or something else had shot them in her. The arrow-remover must not think or talk about the arrowheads but should keep his mind blank as he extracts them.

Next Kantyi called to Wolei to cut some bamboo. They got a fresh coconut and cut the shell away so as to leave the meat intact in a ball. They cut a small hole in it and poured the coconut water out into a basin and gave it to Maka to drink. The coconut was then cut and the inside grated into shreds. Kantyi and Wolei came back with bamboo and some green shoots that were finely cut and mixed with a little water, some salt, and the shredded coconut, then put the mixture into the bamboo to cook. The green shoots were Tambin herbs.

Another senior man, Maisu from Dagetasa, had arrived. He was Kantyi's mother's (collateral) brother. He sat down and talked quietly to Kantyi while the bamboo tube was cooking. I had forgotten about him, but then Maisu came forward holding nettles, and he repeated the patting and blowing to "smell out" the cause. He declared that he smelled the spirit of Weikris (just as Wara had). He brushed the nettles over Maka's chest as if to catch up or sweep something up from it with care and difficulty, then gathered the leaves against her skin, and threw the extracted "contents" on the ground beside him. He bent over and searched minutely in the dust and dirt for the "arrowheads" that he hoped he had pulled out, picking at tiny fragments of wood—or dirt or chipping or betel shred—discarding them as not what he had extracted. Evidently, he could not find anything right. So he repeated the whole maneuver and again searched the ground beside him. He didn't seem to find anything this time either, but he did not look dissatisfied or troubled by this. Covertly, during his search for the extracted arrowheads, Maka was looking sideways to try to see what he found, what had come out. Maka alternated sporadic interest in what was going on with drooping sleep; she rested her arm on her knee now, bent her head, and rested it on her arm.

Maisu sat down beside Kantyi. Later the cooked bamboo appeared, and Kantyi shook out its contents into a bowl, removed some coarse shreds of bark, and stirred it. When it was cool, he gave her some in a spoon, but she took the bowl to feed herself. Slowly she took about eight spoonfuls, then gave the bowl to Pe'alen (her stepfather), and he handed out a spoonful to one of her younger daughters, then to other children, her older daughters, Maluna's youngest son; they ate it without ceremony. Maluna called out that they should give some to Tuawei's puppy, but they had already finished it.

Dukini, the middle one of her uncles from Bi'ip—her father's younger "brothers," collateral line—came into the day house. He had come from a garden quite far off at Abitag. He had noticed the silenced "singsing" and wondered what had happened. Dukini went over to the kerosene drum and Walei ceded his place to him. It was now about 5 o'clock, two and three-quarter hours on from the beginning of her attack. Dukini sat down on the drum and supported Maka's sitting position. He stayed sitting there until about 8 p.m., when Maka went to Sildao's house to sleep with Sildao and Padik. Sildao is Walei's wife, Wara's daughter; Maka calls her "daughter-in-law," as she is married to Walei, Maka's husband's elder brother's son.

Half an hour after Dukini got there, her two other Bi'ip uncles also arrived along with her closest "brother," Peitu.

Many people stayed, though some people began leaving after 5:30 p.m. Chatting grew general and relaxed, Maka was allowed to doze and scratch at her nettle stings. But no one ate at Watalu that night out of concern for Maka. Dukini and Peitu stayed the night, as did Pe'alen and Padik. Kantyi did not seem anxious that evening. During the evening, Maka's two-year-old daughter came to suckle. (In fact, she had been suckling the child when Maisu went to use nettles on her chest. The child screamed.)

The next morning, Maka sat in the porch of another house with Padik beside her. She still looked exhausted but she ate some sago and leaves. She spent much of the day lying or dozing on a piece of *limbum*, her younger children sprawled with her. Later in the day, people came to sit in sympathy from the other hamlets. They had a large meal early in the day because of fasting the night before. Dukini and Peitu left that evening, judging that Maka was better. Padik stayed to help cook for Maka and her family. The next day, most people went off to garden. Maka stayed at home with her mother and the children. She looked more cheerful. On the fourth day after the attack, she went back to ordinary work, fetching food from a garden.

Moral obligation and natural duty

Such ways for people to show concern may not seem to be very comforting expressions of sympathy and support. People do not usually sit with a sick man or woman to talk to him or her or to bolster his morale. Indeed, when sick, the Gnau withdraw from social contact and conversation; they tend to refuse food. At first, what struck me about the gatherings for a sick person was the absence of the sick person him- or herself. The patient rarely showed up at them, and people did not go to see him or her unless specifically to provide a treatment.

The social withdrawal follows from their idea of the risks of normal behavior when one is ill. Men say they fear harm by contamination from the menstrual blood of women. They say spirits may strike the sick because they wish to warn them. A spirit may follow food or people it is concerned with. Therefore, it would be tactless to go to chat with someone seriously ill, for a spirit might follow, or the afflicting spirit might think the patient took the illness lightly and therefore might strike the patient harder. There are also elements of conscious deception in some people's exaggerated show of their abject state; through dirty wretchedness and feeble whimpering, they hope to make the spirit think they are not worth more bother; they are finished, wrecked.

So at the gathering, the sick person would usually be nearby but out of sight, lying half hidden in the porch of a house, on the ground to one side, or else inside a house in the dark. A visitor would not normally feel free to go inside a private house. When women are ill, companionship and physical contact are greater. A married woman needs help with young children, which other wives, sisters, or a mother-in-law will give. And women will comfort another woman openly, as shown earlier in the description of Bagi being mothered.

More often, however, it looks as if the visitors who gather to spend the day with a sick person's family scarcely pay any direct attention to the patient. As the behavior showing illness makes known the person's need largely by nonverbal signs, so the sympathy called forth in response is rarely expressed with words directed toward the sufferer. Actions can speak louder than words. The spread of concern, the variety of constraints imposed by someone's illness on many others in the community, and the way they overcast and disrupt normal village life can give a public quality to private suffering.

There are paradoxes in Gnau responses to illness. Anyone would notice pain and certain other signs of illness. Pain or weakness calls for attention. Sometimes the abnormality is obvious to others. If illness or change draws attention to a person, it can act to individuate him or her. The sufferer is singled out, as seen in the conspicuous self-neglect, the contrast with ordinary sociability, the patient's eclipse from participation in normal social life. The social gap calls the person to mind. Someone who should be there is not; a familiar voice and face are missing. The patient is there negatively, in the shadow somewhere nearby. Restrictions imposed on others by someone's illness also act as reminders. In the context of village life and community, the conventional withdrawal during illness not only makes the patient solitary but also singles out and draws attention to them.

This isolation offers a point of resemblance to their way of honoring someone for hunting achievement and in some rites of passage. Characteristically, they have a gathering and a meal at which the person being honored does not eat with the others; when he does eat, it will be separate from everyone else at the gathering. The similarity lies in the focus by exclusion (more precisely, it is noninclusion). The exclusion singles him

Figure 9. An ill man lies on a palm-leaf mat in the porch of his wife's house, 1969. She sits outside with their adult daughter and some children to watch over him and shield him from harm.

out and reinforces a sense that people have gathered to do something for him as distinct from doing it in company with him. Normally, they take it for granted that friends and relatives share food and eat in company. Food is widely used to express affection, pity, and concern, and to gain approval and prestige. In diverse situations, both when being honored and being ill, one person is marked out from the group, individuated by being different, not included when they eat together.

Those who come to sit together with the sick person show they are aware of their obligations. Selfish interests are forgotten. They speak of another's illness as "binding" them to stay at home. Hunting parties and gardening plans are disrupted. A long illness can interfere seriously with a hamlet's social and economic life. They must not dance and sing; they cannot go off for distant hunting; they may put barriers across parts of the village to protect the sick person from harmful influences, which other people might bring these if they come too near. Residents away in the bush must be called back. They must avoid using the sick person's name lest bandying it about as though he were well would attract the baleful attention of other spirits. Behind all these constraints is the feeling that if people know someone is ill, they should come take care of him or her, thinking of the patient constantly: "Your eyes should not lose him." To go off hunting as if things were normal would be to forget the sick person and show indifference. With someone lying very seriously ill, I saw people come to weep to lament his or her ruined state and impending death.

Loyalty obliged kin to come; the obligation was seldom questioned. They felt they could not leave their kin or friends to face distress alone. There was strength and security in numbers. In a number of myths, the theme of the *butabasi* (people on their own) recurs: someone is left alone to face a danger, be it from a demon witch or from human attack. It may be the woman alone in her house, the door shut, the village empty, the fateful cough outside as the demon spirit announces itself: "Eh-hei! I thought you had gone, but here you are!" Or it may be the warrior all alone in his village awaiting his enemies. The only child, the orphan, the last survivor, each is vulnerable. People should not leave them like that. "What? Is he one man all alone? Has he no friends to help him? No one to take his place?" That is the Gnau's basic view. In such small, independent communities, there was little security except through the support of kin and neighbors. In some cases of illness, the duration and severity of the constraints on others reflect the strength of social bonds as well as affection and concern for the individual who is ill. There is both a practical and an emotional side to the gathering of kin and friends. The disabled patient needs food, water, simple nursing care, and protection. The displays can perhaps be regarded as a kind of pledge that practical sympathy will be forthcoming if needed. People can also discuss what to do at the gathering and organize larger-scale treatments, which involve more elaborate rituals. In effect, the Gnau illustrate a principle of natural duty in these sit-downs. As John Rawls puts it, "A sufficient ground for adopting [the duty of mutual aid] is its pervasive effect on the quality of everyday life. The public knowledge that we are living in a society in which we can depend upon others to come to our assistance in difficult circumstances is itself of great value. . . . The primary value of the principle is not measured by the help we actually receive but rather by the sense of confidence and trust in other men's good intentions and the knowledge that they are there if we need them. Indeed, it is only necessary to imagine what a society would be like if it were publicly known that this duty was rejected" (Rawls 1973: 339). Rawls places mutual aid among the moral ideas—the natural duties—that are fundamental to society. If these duties to each other were not recognized, we might be unwilling to accept that they belong to a society, or we might say it would not be a society worth living in. The discussion of natural duties concerns duties that obtain between those regarded as equal moral persons (1973: 115). The ethnographic problem is to establish how people in another society qualify and define the range of those whom they regard as equal moral persons. Are the duties owed to all or only to particular individuals standing in specific social relationships? A marked distributive aspect comes into much of what Gnau people say about their duties to others, so they refer to family and closeness of kinship, village, and common language as the qualifying grounds they recognize. K. E. Read (1955) analyzed the distributive aspect of morality among members of one New Guinean society in his fine account of their concept of the person. Peace, government, and contact with strangers through travel made Papua New Guineans have to change and extend the distribution and range of their moral identifications. Gnau people speak about many of their obligations in terms of basic reciprocity rather than altruism or natural duty. They bind justice to reciprocity: "If I do not help my brother, who will help him? If I do not help my brother, why should he help me?" My questions about support and help provoked that sort of reply rather than reference to generosity, which was one of the first things they described to characterize a good man or good woman.

However, support in illness is not inexhaustible. In the next chapter, I will describe the bitter situation of a man who gradually felt more and more abandoned as his long and serious illness dragged on. An illness may have moral implications. Is someone to blame for it? Illness has been given moral meanings as people seek to make sense of pain and find justice or injustice in suffering.

CHAPTER THREE

Long suffering and injustice

Chronic illness can be hard to bear, especially if the sufferer is getting worse. The demands on everyone are dragged out; they exhaust resources, wear down the strength to resist, and use up the knowledge of what to do. Perhaps the patient can adapt to a disability; more often he or she has to do so aware of being overcome. Material and emotional reserves dwindle as they are drawn out over time. Kafka's *Metamorphosis* (1915) is a bitter allegory on this. In a long illness, Gnau visitors might arrive saying, "Don't bother to feed us," although of course they would be fed. There could be heavy demands on the family of the patient to provide food, tobacco, and betel nut. I remember seeing someone's face fall as another batch of visitors turned up in the unremitting succession of visits. There is also the bitter possibility of indifference. And this is what struck me in the case that follows, which contrasts starkly with the crisis over Maka described in chapter 2.

The bitterness of long illness

Wolai's end. January to August, 1969, Pakuag.
On January 1, 1969, Wolai returned from the distant hunting bush complaining of a swollen face. He said his face had been swollen for two days, but otherwise he felt the same as before—his chest had not been worse lately. He wanted liniment to rub on his face. His face

was puffy, he had his usual signs of long-standing bronchitis, and a trace of swelling at the ankles. His blood pressure was normal. I gave him the liniment he wanted and asked for a urine sample to check whether it showed signs of abnormal kidney function to account for the swelling. (Liniment is popular; the kind the public health department issues, intended for aches and sprains, is thick and dark with a fine, strong smell; people like rubbing it on and like the smell; they use it for swellings as well as aches.)

I think Wolai is in his late forties but his age is difficult to guess. He belongs to Pakuag hamlet. His daughter Kurei is about seventeen years old. In the next few days, she does not speak about her father; I asked about him. She says he still has a little swelling. The urine sample comes after six days. The trace of albumin in it does not suggest serious kidney damage. I wait to be asked to see him. Then Kurei has her puberty ceremony with two other girls on January 14. Her father keeps clear of all the celebrations, sitting out of sight by his aged mother's house. Two days later in Pakuag, a large Panu'et treatment is done in the hope of prompting the delivery of a woman who is enormously pregnant but seemingly very long overdue (in fact, because of twins). The young men are talking of running off to try and get taken on for plantation labor—it's the right time of year—and a batch do so despite the opposition from their mothers and some older men. The next day, their mothers, sisters, and brothers chase after the men who have run off to present themselves at Nuku (the next subdistrict center) for recruitment there. At one point, the very sick man at Watalu, Dauwaras, is thought to have died. There is briefly tremendous panic over him. The next day, after another puberty ceremony at Bi'ip for a girl's first menstruation, there is a second panic, this time for a woman at Bi'ip who gets possessed, thought to be struck by *minmin* sorcery. Wolai has been forgotten in the turmoil of these other events. On January 19, there is a small sympathy gathering for him that his wife's brothers from Animbil attend. The following two weeks are busy: the condition of Dauwaras (the ill man at Watalu) is desperate; Maka and another woman have further possessions and change hamlets; batches of young men run off to seek plantation labor; people chase after them; the pregnant woman has twins; fears of *minmin* burgeon, and meetings about this take place between villages; the government dentist comes to do a full village dental survey; there are sympathy gatherings to mourn the departure of the young men to the coast. Wolai is still ill but does not ask for me to treat him. On February 4, at the ceremonial breaking up of the worn Wimalu-Basilasel men's house, Wolai's elder "brother" (FeBS)[1] and his sister's husband asked me to go and see Wolai and give him medicine (fifteen days before he had a perirectal abscess that I treated—perhaps he feels that since he had to go through it at my hands, others should, too).

Wolai was sitting near the tiny house of his mother, Dabetu. His mother's and his wife's houses are set on a mudstone level hollowed out just below the main Pakuag hamlet space. He was sitting alone eating dry sago and leaves. He had taken off his shell phallocrypt and so was naked and dirty, with ashes on his skin. He complained of swelling in his face, his legs, his scrotum. He was evidently breathless. The signs were of heart failure, mild to moderate. I could not tell the cause of his heart failure. It was likely precipitated by his chronic bronchitis, damage from repeated chest infections, smoking, smoky houses, wheezy breathlessness. He was also anemic, which was adding to the problem. I gave him diuretics and digoxin to treat his heart failure and later iron for the anemia.

As soon as I had given him the immediate treatment, I went back to Wimalu where everyone was gathered. They had finished and were eating a meal to commemorate the end of the men's house. A number of Wimalu and Watalu hamlet men sat after this, chatting and laughing together. They brought up the subject of Wolai and his illness. Seilun said he was ill because he had eaten a *tambelyiti* lizard (a spiny-backed agamid lizard a bit like a small iguana; it is forbidden for most people to eat this species as food, except old men). In the following conversation (which I was recording), they first say, rhetorically and laughing, "Why should someone so young eat that? A young man like that! They must be teasing you. Or is he blind to eat something bad like that?" Then they go through the order in rules for a variety of foods, mainly for my benefit, sorting through and agreeing what the order should be. I asked who gave him the lizard to eat. A chorus of answers: "He shot it himself! His own for himself! He shot it!" I asked whether he had said that or did they see him do it. The answer came that someone saw his footprints, the remains of the head of a *tambelyiti* lizard, signs of a fire; this man had seen these signs as he was on his way coming back through some of Wolai's bush. The point of it was that no man should eat anything he has himself shot: it is like eating yourself, your own blood (G. Lewis 1980: 173–74). One man said, "He ate it, his own blood struck him." Another leaned over

---

1. FeBS stands for "father's elder brother's son."

to me, speaking in a hoarse confidential voice, "He knows the 'dog aroid' spell. . . . He knows the 'evil spell' (*nunt wola*; a kind of destructive magic), he ate it for revenge and the aroid has struck him (rebounded on him)." They went quiet at this. Selaukei explained to me, "He has swelled up." Another, remonstrating: "Hey! What are you saying?" Tawo, quietly: "K. was the one who said that." Others agree, "He said so." Grunts of assent. All right. A pause, silence. Selaukei speaks again, "That's why he's ill and lying there, and that's why we have spoken out about him."

At first, the mood is bantering. They are laughing at his alleged gross disregard for the rules of proper behavior. It brings Wolai into relief as a figure of fun to many (though not to his brothers), a bit of a failure; they show him disrespect combined with some unkindness and callousness. I wondered if Wolai's dignity and stiff reactions sometimes provoked the teasing and unkindness.

Wolai is unprepossessing in appearance. He is noticeably short, with thin arms and legs. By comparison his head looks large and heavy about the jaws and parotids, the more ill-shaped because he is bald on top. His chest is shallow and his belly domed so that when he walks with his very straight back and erect head, his belly advances first. But he is far from fat. He is covered by tinea, an unfortunately chronic fungal infection of the skin, making it flaky and grayish. His movement is generally stiff, lacking the casual grace and mobility many people show. He always seems to me to walk and sit unusually straight—I wonder whether it is because of his shortness. He does not move his head much to look around him as he walks; his erect posture and deliberate gait make him appear dignified and slightly ridiculous. He nearly always wears a very faded red *laplap* (loin wrap) cloth at his waist, going down to his knees.

He is less sociable and talkative than most men. He is often sitting by his wife's house or his elderly mother's house. As these are on a different level from the other houses in the hamlet, the physical spacing emphasizes his social distance. My mental picture of him is of him walking alone along a path or sitting erect, knees drawn up to his chest, somewhat apart from the group of others. He does not take much part in conversation, never roars to make himself heard, as the others do. He is not assertive. In the early days after my arrival, he was one of the few who did not come to look at me to find out what I was like. It was months before he would turn up, usually alone, to sit on the ground, not saying anything or asking me for anything. He does not sit around much looking after or playing with his youngest son. If he walks past Maluna's day house, he rarely calls out to pass the time of day or drop in to chat.

One afternoon, he was in the group as we were sitting in the men's house at Watalu during the Malyi ritual. Some of the others related how two evenings before, they were walking back to the village, and the man immediately behind Wolai began to tremble as if he were going into trance and about to shoot someone. Who? Wolai. Everyone went into fits of laughter and slightly belatedly, stiffly (but pleased by it, I thought), Wolai laughed with them. What strikes me in remembering that is that it is the only time I can think of seeing Wolai in the center of a laughing group, enjoying it.

His first marriage ended when his wife died in the dysentery epidemic in about 1943–44 (Allen 1983; G. Lewis 1977). It was suggested Berau might marry him after her first husband died, but she rejected him. Then a younger brother of his father and others of his powerful lineage abducted Beikalyi from Animbil for him. Beikalyi is a capable, hard-working woman with a daughter and three sons. I don't know much about her character: she seems observant, intelligent, and reserved. I notice that she frequently goes to Animbil to see her brothers and other kin there, as do her children. Her ties to her brothers are strong, and her children often go to see or stay with their mother's elder brother, for instance, if they are ill. On one such occasion, Wolai said to me that he had sent his son there because he had scabies and Wolai didn't want him at home spreading it.

As for Wolai's illnesses, apart from the chronic fungal skin infection (in the Tokpisin language, *grile*) and his general physique, he has recurrent chest infections. In my first year there, he had three that needed, I thought, some antibiotic treatment. He and Bilki, who is old and white-haired, are the two people most commonly said to be short-winded. Some say—maliciously—that Bilki must have eaten his son's or a younger brother's food. Some say that about Wolai, too—in other words, that he broke the taboo and paid the penalty, which is breathlessness, *wuna'at wola* or *dapa wola* (bad vital center, bad wind). Both have chronic loose coughs and get breathless more than they should.

Others do not treat Wolai with respect. They will joke at his expense; they can be quite good-naturedly callous. I think this may be in part because he is not good at taking teasing (he lacks "a sense of humor"); he gets cross, he is easy to bait. But I have seen him give and take teasing when he and Tuawei were peeling taro. They horseplay, cheerfully threatening each other with their knives, Tuawei holding him at arm's length, Wolai threatening to stab him. The sight was absurd, that was the joke: Tuawei, tall and strong, fending off Wolai, such a shrimp. But some of the jokes about him are cruel. On February 4, when I went by with the medicines for him, someone called out to me, "Why bother, he's an old man old wreck?" Hearers laughed. Another, mocking, rhymed, "Wolai, Wulyi, Wulyi'ai" (I'm not sure if this was just alliteration, or a play on words coming close to a Gnau obscenity *wulyi'it*).

I believe that Wolai is rather proud, sensitive about his dignity. When I first gave him an antibiotic tablet to swallow, I remember he put it in his mouth and had great difficulty swallowing it, downing large volumes of water with his head up, neck extended, but each time finding the pill still there. There were catcalls and encouragement from spectators and children watching. Wolai, absolutely miserable, grim-faced and unsmiling, eventually crunched up the tablet (which was bitter) and stalked off. Children laughed at him openly and showed disrespect in a way that I do not think they would have dared with most other senior men. When I went to see him, his first remark to me was that he did not want any medicine. Then when someone brought a dirty half-coconut shell for a cup, he immediately and angrily said, "Take that away and fetch me a good one!" The next day when I brought him his medicine, he called for water; a child came with a coconut shell, and Wolai said, "Coconut shell? Go and get me a cup!" He sounded cross. He did not like people watching when I gave him treatment. I had to inject one of the diuretics at first. He took the injection silently and with an expression of grim endurance. He hated being watched by others for this.

Three days later, as I was going to see him, the people in Maluna's day house called to me as I went past: "Don't go up to Pakuag. Selaukei has gone to do the aroid treatment for Wolai—the dangerous one. Don't go close to watch, you might be struck by the aroid." In Pakuag I found the men gathered; Wolai was inside his mother's house. His wife, Beikalyi, was inside her house with her children, except for his eldest son, who was sitting with the men. In the space in front of Wolai's two houses, as at the center of a stage, Selaukei (the same Selaukei who had shot him in the leg years before at Animbil) stood with the decorated "dog aroid" shoot he had fetched and prepared the day before at his own bush. It had a red cordyline leaf "headdress," shell and pig-tusk ornaments, yellow lily leaves, and nettles bound around its base. Parku, who is married to Wolai's only full sister, assisted Selaukei. He held the *Iyimungai* banana leaf, with three hibiscus flowers stuck in it, and the ashes. The Pakuag men remained at a distance, looking down from the open space in front of their men's house. Selaukei prepared the banana leaf by spells and spitting betel juice. They held the banana leaf over the aroid, blew smoke, and tore the leaf, then Selaukei spat betel and blew spells into the "headdress" of the aroid. The others called for Wolai to come. There was a pause as Wolai was putting on his *laplap*. Wolai came out and stood over toward the bushes by the path with his back to the spectators. Selaukei chanted very quietly beside him, then waved the aroid over him and rubbed the nettle base on his thighs and scrotum. He spat Wolai on the shoulder blades with two blotches of red betel. He put the aroid down, took a *langit* leaf (as I described in Maka's case; see chapter 2), and tried the divinatory smack on it held over his fist, then threw it away with a special throwing gesture. He repeated this two or three times. He tried to get Wolai's knuckles to crack, then made his own crack. He got water from a bamboo, and spat it out in a fine spray to either side of Wolai.

The others called out to remind Wolai about the money, and Wolai produced two shillings, which he waved in a circle around his own head and then gave to Selaukei. The people at Pakuag said they wanted Selaukei to take the aroid back to Bi'ip with him, not to throw it away at Pakuag (as it might come back and strike someone). The ceremony appeared very much to be just between Selaukei and Wolai, with Parku as assistant. The others commented afterward that this aroid spell had been specifically to rid him of the swollen scrotum. They associated the procedure with Ligawum and Libuat villages (a different isolated language group to the southeast). Hadn't I noticed how many men there had swollen scrotums?

Before the ceremony, Wolai said something to me about the possibility that he was ill because he had eaten some betel pepper catkins from the coast, which were given to him by someone just returned from plantation work. After the ceremony, he talked to me about another idea he had: the cause of his illness was destructive magic. He had stayed in December in the hunting bush. While there, two of his "daughters" (married and from a collateral line) had come from Saikel, their husbands' bush, over which there had been a furious dispute with Mandubil, a neighboring village. They brought him greens, tobacco, and bananas. Perhaps these had had spells put on them by Mandubil who were still cross about the outcome of the dispute. He thought perhaps the spells were for *belyipeg wolendem* (evil spirits).

The swelling went down quite quickly. The signs of heart failure diminished until all he had was a very little swelling of his feet. He continued to take the diuretics and digoxin. By February 14, he said he was fed up with the tablets, they stuck in his throat. I did not think it was nausea. He agreed to go on with them. All this time, he has been sleeping in his mother's house. She is tiny, and the door of her house is so small that I find it quite tricky to bend and squeeze myself through it. So far, I have hardly exchanged a word with his wife about his illness. She has not broached the subject with me. All his food and care seem to come from his mother. His daughter rarely mentions him to me; his eldest son sometimes helps with fetching water and encouraging him to take the tablets.

At Watalu, Dauwaras died at last. There was great pandemonium: grief, mourning, reproach, trance, and possession. After three days, I had to go to the coast for a meeting. I left Wolai with diuretics and discontinued the digoxin, since I was going to be away for two weeks. I left on February 20.

I saw him the day after I got back. He was now wearing his phallocrypt but he still had some leg edema. He said his illness was from his brothers-in-law, he had got it at their bush. He was sitting behind his mother's house, she was the only other person there. She, too, insisted strongly that it was his in-laws who caused the illness. I noticed that he spoke their names aloud to me (strictly forbidden for brothers-in-law). One of his brothers-in-law is his *wusai* (coinitiate). Why did he think they were the cause? He said he had no particular reason, they had had no quarrel, he just guessed, *wuna'at wosapeg* (literally, my thinking center spoke to me).

I put him back on digoxin, continued with diuretics, and gave him some iron by intramuscular injection. Over the next period, I heard people inquire after him at odd times. Some said that he still had swelling and he would die. His brother-in-law, the coinitiate, said he thought it was a ghost of a Mandubil man that had struck him. Others agreed with this view. Perhaps Mandubil people had used a vine and put bad magic on it and Wolai must have stepped over it. I did not see him every day, sometimes giving his daughter the tablets for him. On March 13, he had a bit more swelling, and he was bitter and resentful. He had had enough pills; he said he was stuffed up to the arse with pills. What he wanted was fish, bread, flour, and biscuits. Why wouldn't I sell them to his daughter? I said I wasn't running a store.

The next day, I had to give him a diuretic by injection. He jumped a bit at the prick; the needle came out, so I jabbed it back. It upset him: "Udei!" he said with pain, turned his head away, and began to snuffle. I tried to soothe him, saying, "It's all done, all over." Then I got out the tablets, which he said he did not want. His eldest son, standing just outside the hut, spoke up, "He says he doesn't want them? He's always saying that. Don't bother with him." I thought this sounded very unfeeling. For Wolai's benefit, I went on about how I knew the tablets and the injections were nasty but they were the only way for him to get better, and so on. If he didn't want them, I would not make him take them. Then without saying anything, Wolai put his hand out for them, took them, and put them in a tin to swallow later. Dabetu had been beside him throughout in the tiny dark space, telling him to put his leg in the right position, telling me to inject downward so it would course down the leg to where the swelling was. After the injection, he turned over and lay on his face on a leathery sheet (made of the base of *limbum* palm leaves), head down, snuffling. By cajoling, Dabetu got him to turn over—the mother. elf-sized, wrinkled, naked, bending over her middle-aged son who was snuffling, cantankerous, miserable in the half-dark, the door almost shut. Everything cramped, and brown: the floor, the *limbum* sheet, the walls, the firewood. Wolai turned over onto his back. He looked up at me straight faced and did a gesture as though to hit me in the face, meant as a joke; his mother smiled hopefully at me to check that I understood the gesture.

I went on to Dagetasa hamlet. There they said that Wolai's illness was going on so long because he had eaten something wrong—hornbill or the *tambelyiti* lizard—they were not sure what, but something he should not have eaten according to their rules. They said further that he knows the aroid spell, implying that they think his knowledge has turned back on him.

In the days following that, his brother-in-law (who is the most senior of them and closest to his wife) came to spit over his legs, arms, and belly against harmful spells placed on paths to protect bush or crops; he might have stepped over them. His edema improved and Wolai seemed more cheerful and cooperative. His mother was pleased and said, at least to me, she thought the pills had helped. One evening, there were bangs like gunshot from Pakuag. The people I was sitting with at Watalu immediately guessed: it was Wolai's son dropping gunpowder into the fire beside his sleeping father to startle the sickness out of him. He confirmed it next day. His father continued to feel better and had only a trace of swelling left. On March 21, I noticed unswallowed tablets from yesterday on the ground in the hut. The day after that I found him holding a hot stone in bamboo tweezers to rub against his *wuna'at*, the thinking center and vital center (at the middle of his chest, bottom of the sternum). The hot stone had been put in water in a coconut shell with herbs. He was doing this for himself because he thought that his breathlessness might come from having eaten food cooked by his wife's brother's daughter (permissible). But she was married to someone he called "son," therefore her food is cooked by a son's wife and is consequently forbidden. However, this "son" belongs to a quite separate and rather distantly connected collateral lineage, so there is not much force in the rule and the other relationship might override it. He said only one foot feels swollen, though his legs and knees are stiff. He wants to rub liniment on his hamstrings. A few days later, he put a poultice of hot sticky breadfruit bark on his legs. I found an irregularity in his pulse rate and decided to stop the digoxin. Some days later, I noticed unswallowed diuretic pills again. On April 3, since he had hardly a sign of swelling left, I stopped the diuretics.

He continued to sit around in Pakuag, seemed more cheerful. He was pleased the swelling had gone, although he said he felt his legs were too stiff for walking, the tendons pulled. Wolai and his mother continued to maintain that his leg trouble was due to his having stepped over the magic against trespass placed on their bush paths by his brothers-in-law. His eldest son denies that. Throughout May, Wolai stayed much the same, making little effort to get himself walking again, although he kept a broken old bow beside him as a stave for support.

On May 13, nearly everyone in his hamlet went off to stay at their hunting grounds. His wife and the children remained with him for the first week, then she went off with the younger ones while the two older children went to stay at Animbil. That left Wolai alone in the hamlet with his aged mother. I heard some people in another hamlet joke about his two children abandoning him. The place was empty. He was bored. Later in the month, when I walked up, I found a dog lying dead on the path in Pakuag, close to its owner's shut and barred-up house. There were flies. The dog's corpse and the flies and the silence was an image of abandonment, only a few doors from Wolai. I mentioned the dog to Wolai; he said to leave it for its owner to come back to. There was little sign of anyone taking interest in him now, no sit-downs, no people coming to chat.

Except for his inactivity, Wolai does not appear to be very ill. He is bad-tempered to Dabetu, telling her to shut up and raising his hand as though to strike her when she talks too much to me. He wants to answer me himself. His restricted life is not much relieved by interesting things. Daikun's return after being bitten by a snake on June 1 was a high point of commotion to break the dreary days.

The others returned and June drew on. There were no marked changes in Wolai, but gradually some edema returned, mainly in his scrotum because he kept sitting and made scarcely any attempt to walk. He did not ask for treatment. I asked his eldest son and daughter to find out whether he would like me to bring pills again. They doubted it but did not come back with a definite answer. Wolai said to me, after I had reminded him that the edema had gone before, that he wanted liniment to rub on his tight hamstrings, that was all, no more pills, a tin to cook in. He and his mother talk quite cheerfully to me; they say the reason he is not walking yet is because of his brothers-in-law's antitrespass magic. They complain that no one brings them game or fish. There was a sit-down gathering for him on July 5, but he and Dabetu are alone together most of the time. Beikalyi brings food and Dabetu cooks his.

Late in July, Wolai hit Dabetu. I heard the gossip about it two days before I went to take them a bit of brush turkey to eat. Dabetu came out through the door, greeting me: "Oh you've come about my eye, it's closed up. It was an argument about firewood, he hit me, my eye is closed." She had a swollen black eye with rheum gathered at the corner and a crusted scab at the lateral border. Wolai called out from inside, "He must come and do my sores." His wife, Beikalyi, from her doorway said, "Do his sores, they are on his knee and belly, his belly is bloated." Wolai had some patches of sodden raw skin leaking edematous fluid on his knees and lower abdomen, not infected. His face, legs, abdomen, and scrotum were swollen. He said, "Do something for the sores on my knees and belly; the water is in me and these have broken out; they just came up out of nothing." He looks piteous. He is crotchety with Dabetu. He agreed to take the medicine again and knew he would have to go on taking it for a long time. Over the next few days, he lost a lot of the fluid and the sore areas dried up, beginning to heal cleanly. Wolai went outside again to lie in the sun and was more talkative. He thinks it is the spirit Malyi—the same as killed Dauwaras—that has tied him down with illness for so long now; Dabetu backs him up. He says it must have been when he went to sing for Dauwaras with everyone that Malyi saw him and struck him.

Early in August, people began to leave again to hunt in the distant bush. Pakuag again emptied, except for Wolai, his mother, his wife, and their children. I left on August 7 to join the men at one camp. My wife had a supply of diuretics and digoxin for him, but two days later she set out with some people from Watalu to find me. She said Wolai looked noticeably worse; she had left diuretics with him.

Wolai died during the night on August 11. Dabetu and Beikalyi wept over him.

On my way back on August 12, we came past the Pakuag hunting camp at Lawugda along the river and the people there told us he had died. Early that morning, they had heard the distant *garamut* slit-gong beats from Rauit, announcing the death. What surprised me was that although they were his own clan, they were still there at Lawugda. Why had they not rushed back to mourn? We were walking back with a small band that included Wolai's ten-year-old son. When they told us Wolai was dead, no one showed any concern or sympathy for the son. He did not show distress; he went on as before as if nothing was different. At one point, he picked a decorative fern frond from beside the path and was about to stick it in his hair when another boy said, more or less joking, "Don't do that, your father has just died, you can't decorate yourself." Wolai's son scampered on.

We reached the village late in the afternoon. The schoolteacher (one mission placed a local "catechist schoolteacher" in the village; he was only sometimes present, but that is a different story), assisted by a strong young woman, had dug the grave to bury him. Some people from De'aiwusel, the next Gnau village, had come to mourn, and they were able to help bury him. Dabetu and Beikalyi, along with her children, went to sleep at Animbil with Beikalyi's elderly mother. They would have been in danger from Wolai's ghost if they had been alone at Pakuag. None of the Pakuag residents had come back; no one seemed to expect they would return for Wolai's death. The next day, some people wearing mud came from Bi'ip to mourn in the empty village. On the day after that, some kin from Mandubil came; they were received at Animbil because no one was at Pakuag. On August 15, his two elder children returned from a hunting camp with their mother's two brothers and mourned and wept at his grave. I asked a man from Watalu why the Pakuag people had not returned. He said, "Oh, because they are in the bush." I contrasted this with Dauwaras's death, marked by the residents' return and their wild grief. He said, "Well, Wolai was always cross and telling them off." The Pakuag and Wimalu hunting parties did not return until August 22–23. I did not hear them mourn.

On August 25, they began building a new men's house at Wimalu-Basilasel, which was the main reason why they had been hunting so long: to make ready for the ceremonies for building it. One of Wolai's lineage brothers said something to me privately on that day about not having mourned for Wolai. They had been in the bush, he said, and anyway, Wolai had not been a *wuyin* (good man or healthy one, or perhaps a well man; I failed to find out whether he actually meant his character or his state of health). On August 26, after erecting the center posts of the new men's house, Pakuag ate the ceremonial meal to send off Wolai's spirit. The same Pakuag man who had spoken to me privately before said rather cynically they had to do that quickly so that they could sing for the new men's house. Beikalyi and Dabetu and the children stayed on at Animbil until then. An elderly, forceful Pakuag woman went off to tell them they must return.

Figure 10. The clan men's house at the Rauit hamlet of Bi'ip, 1968. It shows the conspicuous size of the structure and its traditional shape, which is less noticeable in recently constructed men's houses.

The opening night ceremony for the new men's house was on August 29. Wolai's most senior brother refused to come out of sorrow or respect for the memory of Wolai, and Beikalyi wore mourning clay to it. But overall, the lack of display of grief for the death of Wolai by his family and kin was in stark contrast to what had happened when Dauwaras died.

Beikalyi went back to her house with her children. Old Dabetu decided to move to her married daughter's house in Wimalu. I saw her at odd times—little, thin, old, just as before. On October 13, she seemed well. After the evening meal, she went off to sleep, but a few hours later she was dead. Her kin from Mandubil, the village of her birth, came to mourn. She was buried at Dagetasa. Pakuag gave these Mandubil kin the payments for her own and her son's death at the same time.

*   *   *

I wrote most of that account of Wolai's illness at the time that it took place, a running record of his illness. As it went on so long, I grew concerned by his growing loneliness and bitterness. I have recorded my impressions of his character and other people's responses to him. Certainly, I was struck by his isolation, the tiny old woman looking after her crotchety son, the apparent indifference of his wife and children, the neglect, the dog dead on the path, the lack of loud grief when he died. My impulse is to comment on the way it shows how people assessed him as an individual (prickly, awkward, not much to admire) and how this evaluation of him detracted from their readiness and enthusiasm to help him. It reflects the feelings people have for someone as an individual whom they know and interact with, their obligations to him as a person with a particular social position. In this case, the long illness put heavier demands on them and in the end exposed more about how they evaluated him as an individual. The illness individuated him.

It illustrates in a more marked form the way illness can single someone out in Gnau village life. Many New Guinean societies stress competitive achievement as well as equality. This is a recipe for individualism, for giving greater recognition to the individual, which differs from societies where power and authority are fixed by ascription or depend more strictly and exclusively on group status and social position (La Fontaine 1985).

Behavior in extremity

The empty village, the dead dog, flies buzzing around it, fix in my memory an image of his abandonment: a most unfortunate, embittered man and his decrepit mother. Perhaps I read the judgment and in-difference into the picture and make too much of it. For the picture recurred to me when I read Colin Turnbull's account of the Mountain Ik (Turnbull 1974). His book raised appalling questions about indif-ference, callousness, and inhumanity. With Wolai, the question seemed to be about the judgment of an individual; with the Ik, it seemed to be about the moral degradation of a people as a whole during extreme deprivation; by extension, the book raised questions about the essential nature of human beings and society. Is this what society is like when the duty of mutual aid is rejected? Turnbull argued (1974: 239) that during starvation, the Ik were brought together by self-interest alone; they lacked any sense of moral responsibility toward each other, lacked any sense of belonging to, needing, or wanting each other (1974: 180); they were so close to death from starvation that such luxuries as fam-ily and sentiment and love could mean death (1974: 108). The Ik fit Thomas Hobbes's harsh view of the essential nature of man, not views like those of Mencius or David Hume, who put forward compassion and sympathy as essential principles of human nature and moral action and held that feeling for others is present and basic to man. So, too, is self-love.

Is egoism or altruism at the root of human social behavior? I pause on this point because of the suggestion that compassion or sympathy would prompt care for the sick in any society. People have tried to use cases of human behavior in extreme and horrifying situations as guides or clues to human nature and the roots of human action as though ex-tremity stripped humanity down to its naked essence. Turnbull's descrip-tion of the Ik has been used in this way, just as his account and inter-pretation have been questioned (Barth and Turnbull 1974; Heine 1985; Pitt-Rivers 1975). But these inquiries are both misconceived. It is surely mistaken to look for the foundations of human morality in people who are starving. Would a physiologist expect to find the essential princi-ples of growth exemplified by them? Many traps wait for someone who tries to explain the normal by examining the abnormal. Writing of his experiences at Auschwitz, Primo Levi did not conclude that man is fun-damentally brutal, egoistic, and stupid, but he did argue that in the face of driving necessity and physical disabilities, many social habits and in-stincts are reduced to silence (Levi [1960] 1987: 93). In the concentra-tion camp, the struggle to survive was without respite because everyone was desperately and ferociously alone. If someone stumbled, there was no one to extend a helping hand.

To sink is the easiest of matters: it is enough to carry out all the orders one receives, to eat only the ration, to observe the discipline of the work and the camp. Experience showed that only exceptionally could one survive more than three months in this way. All the musselmans (a word the old ones of the camp used to describe the weak, the inept, those doomed to selection) who finished in the gas chambers have the same story, or more exactly, have no story; they followed the slope down to the bottom, like streams that run down to the sea. On their entry into the camp, through basic incapacity, or by misfortune, or through some banal incident, they are overcome before they can adapt themselves. (Levi [1960] 1987: 96)

In the camp, where each person was alone and where the struggle for life was reduced to its primordial mechanism, an unjust ferocious law was openly in force: "To he that has, will be given; from he that has not, will be taken away" (Levi [1960] 1987: 80). In his chapter on "The drowned and the saved," Levi describes how the pitiless process of selection and survival worked.

Levi saw how some—a tiny few—managed to survive. Adaptation took place by cunning or by skill. Some were ruthless, some were a bit prepared for it by harsh experience. C. D. Laughlin (1978) interpreted the Ik's response to starvation as the response of people who have learned the hard way by experience, by repeated exposure to extreme deprivation. If they wish to survive in bad times, they cannot afford the same rules of morality and reciprocity as in good times. The flexibility and atomism of a hunting-and-gathering mode of life applies more stringently; nothing is spared for the old or the young; care for them may cost the survival of young adults. Lorna Marshall (1961) argued that gift-giving and reciprocity served, among other things, to control and alleviate emotional tension and aggression among the Bushmen; reciprocity and sharing were the rule and strongly sanctioned. Without any food or gifts to give, emotions normally channeled and controlled by obligatory sharing were given full expression. Perhaps this may help to explain some of the heartless and cruel behavior of starving Ik. It is hardly surprising that people's willingness to share varies with their resources, that moral behavior and rules for hard times may differ from those suited to good times. People can show generalized reciprocity, cooperation, and concern for longer-term interests when times are good, but in very bad times, negative reciprocity and short-term interests predominate and groups fragment. Marcel Mauss and Henri Beuchat's (1906) study of seasonal variation in Eskimo (Inuit) society showed that moral systems can vary under different environmental pressures. The implication is that societies will also differ in their aptitudes for coping with crises, in the kinds of acute and chronic problems they are well or ill prepared for. In this respect, people might look at social responses to epidemics or famines as a test of social strengths and weaknesses, as if in famine, plague, or crisis, the social drama would provide an epiphany or showing forth of the character and resilience of the society and its social structure (D'Souza 1988; Firth 1959: chapters 3, 4; Iliffe 1987; I. M. Lewis 1981; Lindenbaum 1979; Sen 1981; Sorokin 1946).

The frame of adaptation includes variation due to environment and to stress. It allows for altruism being part of human nature though stifled under pressure. Views on altruism have come from others besides philosophers. Anthropologists, sociologists, psychologists, and sociobiologists have analyzed varieties of reciprocity, the gift in social life. The argument of kin selection theory and of reciprocal altruism (E. O. Wilson 1975: 117, 120) is that the benefits of such behavior outweigh the losses. "While on particular occasions we are required to do things not in our own interests, we are likely to gain on balance at least over the longer run under normal circumstances. In each single instance the gain to the person who needs help far outweighs the loss of those required to assist him, and assuming that the chances of being the beneficiary are not much smaller than those of being the one who must give aid, the principle is clearly in our interest" (Rawls 1973: 333). The idea that parents have a natural impulse to care for their young, even at some sacrifice of themselves, is easy to accept as well as understandable in evolutionary terms. It is not surprising that behavior roughly possible to call "altruistic" should have evolved in animals—the thwarting of predators by communicating alarms or feigning injury to distract them, the practices of parental sacrifice, cooperation in breeding, "aunt" and "uncle" behavior in monkeys, food sharing, ritualized contests, all must have offered advantages for survival. Etymology is oddly in harmony with kin selection theory if it suggests links between kin, kind, and kindness. The evolutionary argument would reinforce the position of those who assert that mutual aid is a natural duty. Peter Kropotkin ([1902] 1939), Edvard Westermarck (1906–8), and Leonard Hobhouse (1906) were quick to compare animal and human social behavior to establish mutual aid as a factor in evolution and in the origin and development of moral ideas. Care for the ill might then have roots in the emergence and development of sympathy and mutual aid. Social life requires some recognition of others and their rights and some feeling of responsibility for their welfare. The final question we might ask about a moral attitude toward another person is whether someone cares if another lives or dies. The less we know about people, the more we can be indifferent to them; complete ignorance may amount to complete indifference.

There were elements of indifference to Wolai as his illness went on, but it may be mistaken to suppose it was simply indifference. People's abilities to respond depend on their particular circumstances at the time. There were competing calls on them, demands to participate in care for other people, the staging of ceremonies, departures for plantation work, and the flow of many events within the village. It is hard to tell exactly how different people weigh up costs and benefits in deciding on action. For in the case of Wolai, it was clear they did attempt to treat him with a number of remedies, but his illness went on and on, and as it did so, they became increasingly pessimistic about his chances of recovery. The treatment I provided probably prolonged his illness and the burdens on others of providing long-term care. In terms of their past experience with Dauwaras's suffering, they had tried to heal Wolai using many, if not nearly all, the means they knew, but without success. All they felt they could do was wait. Their traditional treatments (particular actions and rituals they performed to rid someone of illness) had failed; only caretaking was left, care that they saw not as a remedy so much as a waiting, without much hope, for the outcome.

His illness was a long one, and many people tried to help him with specific treatments. It was most difficult and demanding to sustain basic nursing care over such a long period. People's indifference seemed to be most evident in regard to such care. It is easy to judge acts and omissions by the wrong criteria—criteria appropriate to our own society but not to theirs. Their patterns of withdrawing care for an ill person are different from ours. Judgments about the primary responsibilities of a mother compared to those of a wife, as well as beliefs about the dangers or support each may bring, are not the same everywhere. In Wolai's case, the issues of acts and omissions should include my own. The varieties of omission in helping others have different moral weightings depending on how people view the probabilities of alternative outcomes and their abilities to act or do something that might make a difference. Some omissions are more blameworthy than others; it is impossible to do all good things at once, and since actions take time and omissions do not, people must make choices and weigh alternatives and priorities (Glover 1977: 92–112). Wolai's case reveals the uncertainty in the diagnoses proposed by different people; they proposed various causes that came from various sources, some based on evidence and others on speculation. Not all diagnoses were acted on nor were all proposed with the same conviction. Staging a large-scale treatment, making an invocation and spitting spell-infused substances over the patient, coming from another hamlet to spend a day at the patient's home—all of these choices demand different amounts of time and effort. However, they are relatively public gestures and receive acknowledgment from others. By contrast, the continuous daily actions of caring for a sick family member in private may be far more demanding of effort and patience than a public treatment but does not receive acclaim—indeed, people hardly refer to private caretaking at all. Men control and perform public treatments and take credit for the results; women do most of the basic daily care for sick family members, but they do it without fanfare and without reward, rarely getting much credit for it.

The visits and gatherings to sit in sympathy for the ill and the treatments organized by men were the main public responses to illness. In 1968, most people were prompt in recognizing their duty to show sympathy in the expected way, although their feelings about the individual concerned might affect what they chose to do. The response showed concern and willingness to help. However, in 1980 or thereabouts, I think Gnau people began to change their attitudes toward the ill. They now seem to feel less bound to come; the imperative to do so is gone, partly because some people now ask whether gathering to sit together has any practical value for treating the illness. They compare gathering to sit down around a sick person with getting an injection, visiting the health post, or going to a hospital (though they do little enough of that). The customary visiting has come to seem passé: occasionally they allude to this with the cliché Tokpisin phrase *westim taim tasol* (wasting time, that's all). They are more calculating about sit-downs, more likely to plan when and whether it is worth the effort, whether to come if the sick person is someone important or someone old, to come on weekends rather than as soon as they can. Twenty years earlier, the gatherings were a common feature of village life; they used to happen regardless of the week or day. However, people have become well aware of the Western calendar, the days of the week, and time patterning, even though they are largely irrelevant to village life. They rather like the notion of taking time off during weekends to rest and socialize instead of assuming responsibilities like visiting the sick. In the past, coming to sit down in sympathy for an ill person represented a recognition of duty, even if it was either spurred or curbed by feelings about the patient or the

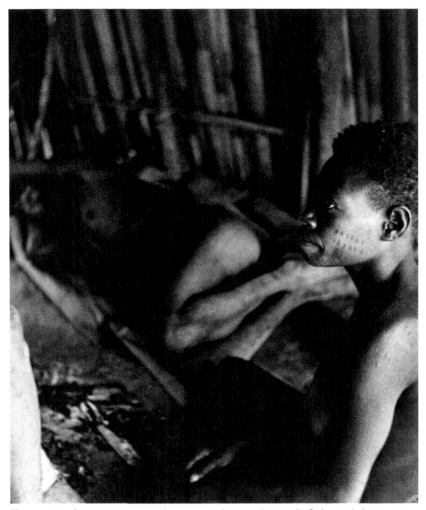

Figure 11. A young woman keeps watch over her sick father while a visitor chats.

current state of their social relationships. By 1985, sit-downs seemed to no longer be considered an adequate or worthwhile response to illness; they were viewed less as natural expressions of mutual aid than as social obligations that had to compete with other more pressing calls on people's time. Perceptions of alternative methods of treatment, the presence of a health post in the village, and various modern influences and experiences contributed to changes in attitudes about the protective and social value of the sit-downs.

Blame for illness

Care for others may be at the root of responses to the sick, but the responses are also affected by explanations given for the illness. Someone
may be thought to deserve the illness or to be ill because of personal
faults or because of the actions of other people. Consider, for example, the mother-in-law of two young wives who quarreled about a sago
palm. When she fell ill with a chest infection, she blamed her illness on
them for quarreling and suggested that a spirit of her husband's lineage
made her ill because it was cross at the lack of harmony between the
wives. Ideas like this likely increased sympathy for the sick woman. But
the question of why she should have suffered—instead of one or both
of the daughters-in-law—was ignored. There was disharmony among
the families of that part of the lineage, one member of the group had
fallen ill, and the timing fit: that was enough. It was true that one of the
daughters-in-law had earlier run off to return to her parents, perhaps
due partly to shame, partly to anger, partly to fear of being struck by a
lineage spirit if she stayed, and partly to seek comfort and sympathy. At
her parents' home, it was almost as though she were there because she
was ill (at least she was there to avoid the danger of illness). The Gnau
would leave room for ambiguity and different interpretations when they
explained illness; they often described the facts and circumstances but
drew no definite conclusion. For instance, when Daikun was bitten by
a snake, people insisted on remarking that his mother had died after a
snake bite years earlier; this was meant to draw attention to a possible
connection, perhaps a motive and an agent, whether human or spirit. But
no one spelled out who or which or what; they just raised the point, it
echoed, and they left it at that.

My aim now is to consider the effect of some explanations on attitudes toward the patient and treatment. Explanations of cause and
general theories about illness often imply advice about how to avoid
exposure to risk. You would think that people must get some blame for
their illness if they know what the risks are but do not bother to avoid it.
The suggestion that Wolai had shot the lizard himself and eaten it was
insulting and, so far as I know, no one voiced it openly to him. Explanations of illness and theories about the causes of illness often suggest
lines along which people may attribute blame. Even if they do not do so
explicitly, they may, by pointing out regularities in the process at work
in illness, provide grounds for judgments about the sufferer's foolish-
ness or thoughtlessness (or that of someone else). But it is not always

simple to do this. If we take the common Gnau case of someone complaining of aches or sudden pains after digging up yams—or especially senior men at the time of first planting, mounding, or harvesting their yams—no one implied they had been foolish; they had done their duty, the work was hard, the risk it entailed was bound to be there. The risk reflected the seriousness and worth of the work, the spirits, the magic, and the powers in it. The aches were thus a kind of testimony to them. The rather histrionic element in their behavior made me think that it was due not so much to pain but the expectation of it and the feeling they had completed a weighty task, which made them satisfied to suffer and draw attention to themselves. People can make the rights and wrongs of illness complicated by the theories they put forward to explain it. I shall argue that the complication and the possibility of complications sometimes help to meet the difficulties of reconciling illness with justice. They increase the alternatives of explanation, they meet contingencies of circumstances, and they allow people to attribute significance to events that may be deeply distressing and might otherwise be meaningless.

In many societies, people suppose that wrong action, immorality, or sin may cause illness. To an outsider who does not share their beliefs, they seem to have seized on the nastiness of illness to use it as a sanction to reinforce rules they think are right. Nature is thus portrayed as upholding morality. Taboos may identify the dangers in foods that react to breaches of certain social rules; teachings against incest warn that it causes a sort of skin disease. Such views may seem more intelligible when actual illness occurs in a context of social disruption or when the disruption is caused by illness. Diagnosis reveals some person's wrong or something wrong in the community; people make sense of the illness by discussing how it indicates past or present conflict, tension, evil, or offense. The illness may seem to be a judgment on someone or on the group that also suffers, though less directly, through his or her illness. Victor Turner's much admired analysis of the illness of Kamahasanyi (1964) is a striking account of this—the illness is taken as a social indicator by the Ndembu and as a catalyst of a social dénouement by the observer. Turner (1957: 91–92) found that such social dramas provided a limited area of transparency on the otherwise opaque surface of regular uneventful social life. Latent conflicts of interest become manifest, and kinship ties whose significance is not obvious in genealogies emerge into prominence. They show how social tendencies operate in practice and how conflict between individuals or groups, which may revolve around a common norm or contradictory norms, can be resolved in a particular set of circumstances. Partly because of Kamahasanyi's weakness when faced by his duty, relations within the village had soured into bitter but half-concealed distrust and rivalry. The village was close to the point of breaking up. Kamahasanyi's illness served to catalyze a decisive reaction in the ferment of troubles. It resolved the doubt about whether or not the members of the village were prepared to come together, for they thought Kamahasanyi had little hope of recovery unless they were prepared to reconcile their differences, to vent their hidden animosities at the ritual to heal him. The decision to use that way to treat him was an earnest token of their desire to stay together; at the least they were prepared to shelve their differences and try to get him well. The members of his village were divided in their opinions on the rights and wrongs of the situation. As in a legal case, some bargaining and dispute took place over how the rules applied to the case and over the justice and rightness of the eventual decision.

Suffering and justice

In most societies, illness has been associated in some respects with law, religion, or morals. Issues of justice and fairness come to be bound up with it. But if illness could be a punishment or the result of vengeance, it may be hard to explain why such a punishment was merited or why anyone should wish to take such revenge. The problem is to diagnose or interpret the event when people want to make sense of it in those moral terms. They do not want to leave the situation unaccounted for. Ideas about regularities in how things happen, about processes, enable people to plan their actions and interpret events. Less is left empty and unexplained. Beliefs in the ability of people and spirit agents to cause illness thrust forward issues of fairness and malevolence. Illness is then likely sometimes to catalyze or provoke conflict. Maka's case (see chapter 2) contains a collection of different diagnoses and implications: the preceding accusation of revenge on Dauwaras for an earlier death voiced indirectly through someone else's possession; Maka's own possession and the warnings to Dauwaras's brothers; the possibility she had been struck by sorcery; earlier threats from Nembugil; the switch from seeing her as merely possessed to seeing her as ill; the ambiguity about the motive of the spirit possessing her and its relationship to her husband; and the uncertainty over which among the alternative spirits addressed in the frantic succession of treatments was the one that had attacked her and why.

Diagnosis is not always sharply separate from treatment. At first, Maka was seen not as ill but as possessed, a state in which she revealed messages about danger and diagnosis. When people thought she might be dying, each possible suggestion prompted action; they tried each treatment but no one waited for an answer about which one might be right, thinking the situation was too desperate for that. There is no reason why the people involved should come to a single opinion on the merits or justice of a particular case or on the diagnosis. Over Wolai, there was more than a hint of malice in the diagnosis others gave of the lizard he supposedly had shot and eaten. I never felt I had really fathomed what he felt about his brother-in-law, whose magic against trespass was one of the explanations he gave for his illness. At times, I thought he resented him and was jealous of his influence over his wife and children—for instance, from the way he spoke his name when he should not have done so and from his remark about sending his son to him when he had scabies. There was no consensus on Wolai's diagnosis.

If we ask why illness is considered in some cases to come as a punishment or sanction of those who break social or ritual rules, the answer may be that it is because of the suffering that can accompany illness. Illness strikes the individual directly; it would be the most personal and individual form for retribution to take. Life is valued, and illness may even take it away. Legal forms of punishment have often included the infliction of pain, mutilation, or death to satisfy the spirit of revenge or to express a feeling of public outrage. They take vengeance on the person of the guilty. Sickness and punishment may have been linked because both might mean suffering pain and even death. However, even when the threat of illness occurs as a sanction for social or religious codes because of its deterrent effect, individual illnesses in practice may rarely be interpreted as retribution. In a number of cases, the Gnau suggested that the cause of an illness was antitrespass magic or the ancestors of the owners of the land attacking wives or visitors or passersby. But sometimes the sufferer had done no wrong to the owners or the ancestors; people suggested the explanation as if once the ancestor were set, like the magic planted on paths or the hidden arrowhead traps, it might easily and inadvertently strike an innocent person. A sense of justice demands that the punishment should fit the crime, but often illness will not fit. It may strike the wrong person. This cannot be reconciled with a sense of justice. If a sanction were so rigidly fixed to a particular offense that the illness automatically accused the sufferer, it would be hard to imagine how such beliefs could survive and still seem fair, given the contingencies and inconstancy of disease in everyday life. It would be difficult to reconcile the suffering in each case as rightly bound to rules that people regard as being good. These questions of responsibility and justice extend to fundamental problems of meaning, of fate, destiny, and theodicy that religions seek to answer (Fortes 1959; Obeyesekere 1968).

John M. Janzen (1978) compared decisions taken in the management of illness to legal decision-making. Both processes might involve evidence, argument, and negotiation, the transfer of rights to act or take responsibility. Societies differ in terms of the distribution of rights to make decisions, rights to control, and rights take action. In the management of the illnesses of Maka and Wolai, the lack of consensus was striking. There was no agreed-upon decision, no single specialized or authoritative source. Different diagnoses and treatments flowed on without opposition or confrontation. The moral implications raised by some of them were not publicly or squarely faced. More often it was left open or ambiguous whether the agent had struck on purpose or capriciously or by chance.

If the problem for some people is to reconcile sickness with fairness and give it a credible moral meaning, then ideas about sorcery, witchcraft, and capricious spirits offer other ways for people to do so, to explain the pain and the justice or injustice of suffering. They fix it within a framework of intention and a framework of good and evil. If they sincerely think that others can hurt, harm, or kill by sorcery, they may suppose others have used evil unjustly to get what they want or to punish those they hate by inflicting illness. For the sufferer and the circle of his friends, the sickness is certainly not deserved; it is by no means a just retribution. It is evil pain, unfairly suffered, wickedly or capriciously caused, so the right response is pity and sympathy.

Is the individual or the group at issue?

Exculpation of the sick for their deviance has been proposed as the main (or at least as one) distinguishing characteristic of the medical system (Parsons 1951; Young 1976, 1982). Ideally, the sick would be neither blamed nor stigmatized nor punished. Clearly, this is not the view in all societies, but it is surprising that the patient is not more often blamed for his or her own illness when there are so many inculpating etiologies to choose from. People may sometimes think of illness as retribution or use ideas about it to deter. But the common response in the face of actual illness is the response of sympathy, an effort to help or remedy it. If treatment resembles any part of punishment, it would be the corrective or reformative elements found in some penal systems. However, I would stress a difference between our legal and our medical systems regarding the treatment of deviance. The aims of legal and moral rules are (ideally) to preserve and protect the well-being of society; the aims of medical treatment are usually not the same, for its object is the individual, not society. Punishment may contain a number of elements: retributive, restitutive, corrective, reformative, expressive, and deterrent. The grounds given for reforming a criminal are primarily that it will benefit others. John S. Mill (1910) argues that the only purpose for which power should be exercised over a member of the community against his will is to prevent harm to others. His own good, either physical or moral, is not a sufficient rationale. The point of interest for my argument here is not the issue of coercion but the question of aim: For whose good is the treatment (or punishment) applied? The primary ground for treatment in illness is precisely not the good of others—the social good—but the individual's good. The aim is to restore to normal someone's impaired capacity to choose and act. The fundamental principle used in our legal system—that a generally accepted standard of conduct should be applicable to all alike—runs dead against the principle of our medical system that each person's needs must be assessed and their disabilities treated according to their individual state and need. If the doctor were asked to let the social cost outweigh some individual's good and decide not to provide treatment, then the way would be open for a policy that denies health services to, for example, the aged, the depraved, the chronically disabled, and so on. To make the good of others, rather than the affected individual's good, the primary consideration would be to use the social and legal principle, not the medical one, for remedial action. Part of the healer's task would then be to judge or to find out from the community whether the patient was considered to be worth treating, to merit it or not.

Medicine, in the European tradition, has focused on the individual. In many nonliterate societies, the diagnosis of illness may resemble, in the style of procedure and reasoning, the discussion of a dispute. This also prompts a question about the difference between the resolution of a dispute and the treatment of illness. How far does an approach like the one taken toward Kamahasanyi's illness, described so vividly by Turner, handle the illness as an indicator and set out to treat the social disharmony rather than the individual? If the illness is really taken to be the indicator of a social ill—disharmony—in the same sense as a certain blood sugar level or pulse rhythm is taken to indicate a particular disease, then treatment of the social disharmony should be gauged by whether or not the patient gets well. In Turner's view, the Ndembu doctor saw his task less as curing the individual patient than as remedying the ills of a corporate group; however, the interrelations between the two (the problem and its indicator) were complex. Just as medical treatment may bring a blood sugar level back to normal without the patient feeling well, so Kamahasanyi might have improved without the underlying social conflicts being settled. If the real problem was strictly perceived as the problem of social disharmony rather than the man's individual illness, then the restoration of harmony might be enough. That would alter our conventional view of the central remedial aim: to heal the individual. However, the question forces a cut-and-dried choice between ends and means that it is unrealistic; the balance between them oscillates and their interrelations are complicated. I doubt that the Ndembu would simply abandon Kamahasanyi to his sickness if the healer judged that social harmony had been restored. The method of healing may differ from those of biomedicine by portraying it as depending on the patient's ties to others. Social ties are things that people make and break; they may think they understand social ties and can manipulate or master such ties but not the internal and hidden workings of the body. In the case of the Gnau, they made few claims to understand how the body worked inside or to know herbs or drugs that would have direct effects on it. My argument here boils down to a simple point: people do what they think they can with what they have and what they think they know. People like the Gnau, who lack a belief in their ability to interfere directly with bodily processes of disease, concentrate instead on the explanation and treatment of social and spiritual aspects of illness that they feel they can understand and possibly affect. In a long illness like that of Wolai, they are more likely to reach the disheartening point of having tried most or all they know. A system of diagnosis in which the circumstances of the person who is ill play a large part in deciding what the cause of illness is and what to do about it clearly contrasts with our practice, which most often looks for the immediate signs of disease, rather than at the person who is ill and his social circumstances, as the basis on which to decide about the cause and treatment.

The differentiation of a specifically medical domain in our belief system tends to detach it from legal, moral, and religious concerns. To the extent that our scientific medicine approaches its goals of understanding the patterns and processes involved in illness in terms of impersonal, law-like regularities that pursue their course indifferent to the moral qualities of the affected person, we consider its theories of diseases and how to treat them to be universally applicable. The sounds made by the heart do not differ with the religion or the customs of the person observed, nor does the effect on him of insulin or phenobarbitone. But the doctor's dealings with a patient can never be just a matter of impersonal science; they inevitably involve social and moral interpersonal relationships. In the next chapter, I will take up some of the changes brought about in Gnau society by the introduction of a health aid post and their exposure to certain features of our medical practice.

CHAPTER FOUR

The introduction of a medical aid post

In the past, the residents of Rauit had to depend on their own resources. They did not trust unrelated outsiders to care for them when they were sick. Trust followed the outlines given by their own distributive morality. They might treat themselves by simple rest, food avoidances, or nettles as a counterirritant. For more serious illnesses, they depended on close kin. Most adults, upon deciding they were ill, left it to others in the local community to come forward and perform treatment. But on the question of confidence in foreign healers, their attitude was simple: Why should I trust strangers to help me? I see no reason for them to care about me.

In the postcontact setting, however, sick villagers have some options of treatment, whether from an orderly at the medical aid post in the village or, at a greater distance, from a nurse or a doctor. However, they may be reluctant to seek treatment. In the village, they can choose not to go to the aid post or to ignore the orderly's advice or to throw away the prescribed pills. At the hospital, among strangers, they are not so sure of being able to escape or refuse treatment. They know about common forms of treatment, such as dressings and injections, from observation and reports, but they also know of other things that might be done and seem alarming, such as intravenous drips, stomach tubes, and surgical operations, all of which violate the body. At the hospital, the doctor or nurse in charge decides what to do, and villagers feel that, once interned, they have little or no control to stop such things being done to them. For some peoples, this is reason enough to avoid the hospital. Nevertheless, they do not suppose that these ill-understood procedures are intended to harm them, something that is perhaps surprising given their suspicious regard for the mysterious things that New Guinean strangers may do. I heard nothing to suggest they supposed White people might be contriving harmful magic; it was the latter's imposition of rules and objections to local practices that appeared arbitrary or unfair to the villagers.

Figure 12. The Anguganak Mission Health Center, 1985. A line of people waits for treatment. (Color image available at www.haubooks.org/pandoras-box.)

White people's motives sometimes made no sense. They had to be accepted as things they chose to do for their own undisclosed and unknown reasons. Among the puzzles were why strangers should bother about them, and what gave them the right to interfere. Village women asked about the nurses who came to weigh their babies. The question was essentially a moral one: Why did nurses come to weigh their babies and to give them injections and tell them how to feed them? These babies were not the nurses' babies—indeed, they were nothing to them, no kin. So what concern of theirs was it if the baby was fat or thin, healthy or sick? The questions had a sharper point. Why should the nurse be able to order the child to go for supplementary feeding? In pre-Independence days, they wondered why a nurse could report the mother to a patrol officer, who might send a policeman to fetch her and her baby if she refused to come for supplementary milk. In terms of Gnau morality, one's obligations to others, one's interest in them and care for them, should depend on the kind of relationships and social closeness one has with them. The idea of having duties toward other people for the mere fact they were other human beings was not particularly intelligible. What motive would plausibly account for White strangers caring about village babies so strongly? They could see that the nurses went to a lot of trouble to come, but that still left unanswered why they should bother. Sometimes mothers did not want to follow the advice because it seemed like interference. They silently rejected it or did not come for assistance the next time.

A new medical domain

At first, village people lacked the information and experience necessary to distinguish what were the different jobs, skills, and spheres of responsibility of the White people they encountered. Both missionaries and government patrol officers (*kiaps*) in the early days of contact gave medical advice or treatment. It was no cause for surprise to local people if a priest on patrol pulled a syringe and a half-filled vial of penicillin out of his rucksack and offered to inject a sick baby. Prayer was mixed up with treatment. It was difficult to work out what was different about the patrol officer's orders for someone to allow a wound to be treated or for him to order someone else to pay a fine. It was equally hard for them distinguish the missionary's attempt to stop the practice of spitting betel juice on sores from his attempt to put an end to their masked rituals. In the period of Australian administration, patrol officers might carry out health inspections, order treatment for yaws or sores, take absconding lepers into custody, or require a mother to take her child for supplementary feeding. Missions established clinics and health centers. Patrol officers ordered people to dig latrines, bury their dead, use new sources of water, and change the position and style of houses—villages viewed these orders as part of what kiaps did. Missionaries sometimes preached against their customs, masks, dances, ritual bleeding, polygamy, sorcery, and sometimes about cleanliness, diet, clothes, water, and latrines. How was someone who had no contact with European society to recognize the different aims and motives behind all these various exhortations and reproofs?

At first, the villagers mixed them up or conflated them; they supposed they might be rewarded for compliance and punished for disobedience—and sometimes they were. They could not understand why all these changes were ordered. Some were intelligible in terms of their own ideas: flies carry "poison," germs are invisible spirits, washing cleanses female pollution. The particular setting for a practice played a part in allowing people to make sense of them. Some of the practices, particularly the equipment—bandages, lint, syringes and needles, penicillin, liniment, and pills—were clearly new and associated with the White people who brought them. The separate medical sphere to which they belonged became progressively more distinct as health care was increasingly confined to specific times, places, and people—that is, clinic schedules, the aid post, and the people whose main job seemed to be giving medical care. The activities of patrol officers and missionaries came to be differentiated. The experience of those who went to towns or centers with hospitals and surgeons, the establishment of a local health center with a missionary doctor, and the encounter with Papua New Guineans who were trained to provide medical care and use the equipment led to changes in Gnau views about how medical ideas and practices were different from other new practices and ideas that White people brought.

Figure 13. A nurse treats a child at the mission health center, 1985. (Color image available at www.haubooks.org/pandoras-box.)

Although the novelties of health care were tied up at first with the people who introduced them, the equipment and treatments were gradually put in New Guinean hands—indeed, into those of trained local people—making it clear that medical practices and knowledge were detachable from White people. The local health center gave them some exposure to the complex equipment used in Western medicine. The "real" medicine of the White people came to be seen as what went on in hospitals.

The kinds of treatment and the people who administered and controlled it were still mostly alien; even as local people took over the management of illness, they were more or less passive recipients and observers of it rather than controllers and active participants. But it would be misleading to portray them purely in a passive light as the objects or victims of administrative demands and missionary goals. People might hide or run away to avoid treatment they disliked, they might keep silent, or they might accept the pills but throw them away in private. With time, they began to recognize limits to external authority. They became more active in choosing what to accept and what to reject.

Problems of the new medical aid post

The medical aid post was built in Rauit in 1969. It was organized by the mission health center and was primarily intended to serve the needs of the village and the neighboring one of Mandubil. When health posts were set up, the mission hospital would train Indigenous men to be aid post orderlies (APO), who were expected to provide treatment for villagers' common ailments: cuts, sores, simple wounds, injuries, and common complaints such as chest infections, malaria, diarrhea, ear infections, headaches, and the like. Ideally, an APO was supposed to meet nearly all the villagers' first-aid needs for medical attention, guidance, and health education. An APO was expected to live in the village with the people he served and to be familiar with them, their language, and their way of life. He received a salary from the Public Health Department using funds allocated to the province. The village people were expected to supply him with food and to give him convenient land on which to make a garden.

None of the local men of Rauit or Mandubil had been trained as an APO and none had reached the necessary school standard. Men from other villages in the district who spoke a different language had been among the first to complete their training. The first APO sent to attend to the Rauit aid post in 1970 was one of these. He came from a nearby village. On the score of familiarity with the village and the closeness to his home, the arrangement should have been satisfactory. His wife stayed at home in their own village most of the time. But it was easy for him to return there—too easy.

The villagers were caught in a dilemma: they lacked knowledge of the skills required for the newly-introduced medicines, so they had to depend on someone who was trained. They preferred to trust those who were closest to them—those who were kin, not outsiders, especially those from neighboring places with whom they fought in the past. There may have been controls over training, examinations, and supervision, but the villagers did not know about these nor were they in any position to assess them.

Problems also arose with recognizing and meeting the reciprocity and obligations expected between the community and the health worker. After a few months, a new APO came to Rauit for a short while, but he was soon transferred to a post closer his home. A third APO replaced him who spoke the same language as the first one, although his home village was farther away, far enough to make him come with his wife. Initially, things went quite well. He settled in. He made a garden. Then a village pig raided it. He was naturally angry about this. The villagers did nothing to stop the pig continuing its depredations (a difficult thing to do anyway), so one night he shot it. This was exactly what a Gnau man in a similar situation might have done, but he would have had the support of kin in the dispute that inevitably followed. The APO instead was faced with the furious group of those who owned the pig and who seemed ready to attack him. He fled to the patrol office. The officer investigated the dispute and decided that the medical aid post should be closed for a time to teach the people a lesson: they must properly look after an APO who came to help them. The people at Rauit saw some justice in such a view and reproached the pig's owners for threatening the APO.

The medical aid post stood empty. Besides having been established to benefit the people of Rauit, it was also intended to serve Mandubil residents as well. They were the closest rivals of Rauit, their enemies in the past as well as their relatives and affines. People in Mandubil pointed out that Rauit's bad behavior had lost both villages their health post, so the right thing for Mandubil to do would be to move the post to Mandubil. In 1971, men from Mandubil went to Rauit to try to dismantle the post and take it to their village. This started a fight between the two villages. The building was not moved, but the dispute was brought before the patrol officer, who decided that the aid post, having been the cause of so much trouble, should remain closed until the two villages earned the chance to have it opened again and staffed by demonstrating good behavior for three or four years.

In 1976, the health post was reopened with a very experienced APO who came from the area. He had close ties to Rauit, although he came from a village that spoke a different language. He had married a woman from Rauit as a second wife. His first wife and family with grown children remained in his own village. At some point in 1983, he moved to work at Lumi. The missionary nurse in charge of the health center closed the post after seeing its neglected state and noting complaints about the lack of local community cooperation. She wrote, "It is a hard place for people to be stationed due to its distance, lack of available water, and the fact that the majority of people tend to be in the bush most of the time." A replacement APO was found in 1984 who came from Lumi. He soon became dissatisfied with his posting and sent complaints about how there were no people in the village, since they had all gone out to the bush and planned on being there for two or three months, so he had nothing to do. It was too long a wait for him, so he wrote a letter asking to come down to work at the health center or to be sent back to work in Lumi. He soon sent a second letter repeating his request. A hospital orderly went to investigate and confirmed that the village was empty, the APO was alone, and no one was there to bring him food. So, as he recorded in his report in April 1984, they put away all the dressings, medicine, and equipment, locked up the aid post, and left. In July, the post was found broken into, the things left in a mess. The upshot was that the health committee decided to send back the experienced APO who had married a woman of Rauit and perhaps try to find someone from the village to train as APO for the future.

This experienced man came back. But the problem was that he came from a village too close by, and he was always leaving to go home. Ideally, some of the villagers said, if they got an APO from far away, he wouldn't leave. On the other hand, if he were to go, the aid post would probably stay empty. They wouldn't get anyone else to come. When I asked others about the hours, some said they thought the APO should be there, most said they didn't know. A few thought he should be there every day, even on weekends and at night, in case they needed him. Most were vague but thought he should be there because he got "big pay from the government," and it seemed wrong that he should be paid for no work.

The village councilor and committee man did not show any particular interest in the matter. They thought that the place to lodge complaints was the patrol office and the court; no one mentioned the local health committee meetings that were intended for community participation and dealing with such matters. No one, it seemed, except the APO who attended them, knew anything about them.

I described the committee meetings in my field notebooks.

The local health committee

The local health committee meets every three months at the health center that the mission started. The local APOs all come, as well as the White nurses (women) who now run the health center. Any village councilors may come who wish to attend or bring matters up for discussion, but there are rarely more than one or two of them at any given meeting. The bunch of APOs are old friends; they meet every few months. They are all men, the oldest is probably in his late 50s, the others of various ages. There are cheerful greetings when they meet, some banter. There will be about fifteen people present at a meeting, although attendance has varied between nine and twenty-four. Minutes are kept, the meetings are chaired—of late, by the New Guinean Health Extension Officer in charge of the district hospital at Lumi (a man) but, before him, by the White Australian or New Zealand nursing sister in charge at the health center. After opening the meeting with a prayer, the nursing sister asks for items to go on the agenda: routine matters, any new instructions, suggestions, or questions raised by those present. They sit at desk benches in a classroom. At the front of the room is an anatomical chart and a plaster cast of a head and body dissected to show the arrangement of some of the internal organs. The agenda is written on the blackboard. The business is conducted in Tokpisin. Many items are about conditions of service, plans, and pay.

A meeting is held, 1985

A meeting has been called to order. After the minutes of the last meeting are read, the chairman reports that he has not had a reply to his letter about some money they should have received. He announces how much was available from the public health department grant and the Rural Improvement Programme for building aid posts. As there was enough for two, they discuss priorities. The APOs suggest where they think the new ones should go. They recall they had agreed to rebuild the dilapidated post at Rauit. The chairman then reminds them that they need to get their priorities right, that they must have the necessary staff first before they build new medical aid posts. There are places like Yilui with an aid post standing empty; they are short of men, not money. He explains the training policy, saying there is room for eight new trainees from the province per year. They can only get one applicant in from their area every so often. One of the nurses points out that some of the aid posts are staffed by two APOs at once, that there are trained people, such as P. and M. who stay at the center without jobs in the villages, and then there is N., who likes to stay at the same post as C. and is not ready to go on his own to Yilui. The chairman speaks up with strong reproach for lazy people who just think about money and not about providing a service and helping the people. He calls them *bikhet* (obstinate, arrogant, selfish), saying they have jobs when there are plenty of other men looking for work who would be very happy to take over their jobs; we can't have two men working at the same aid post unless both men are working full time. He warms to his theme: You don't get real supervision, you work when you feel like it, you can't have someone to come and assist you (*yu wok long laik bilong yu iet, nogat man iken ikam lukautim yu*). Others speak up with the example of N., who resigned and did nothing for a while, then asked to come back. At that point N., who is late, walks into the room. The other APOs greet him cheerily. The chairman goes on to say he was told at the provincial government headquarters that people who are not doing their jobs properly should have their jobs terminated.

The items followed with varying amounts of discussion and animation: the old aid post at one village was going to be demolished, so who should get the corrugated iron roof and other materials? People in the village want to use it to cover a water tank, but the nurse points out that the roof was originally paid for out of rural improvement program money (but water tanks must come out of council funds) so they cannot use it for that. They decide that the materials will go to Rauit, since they had put in their request to rebuild their aid post long before, when there was no money available. Someone asks about another village, for which they have already voted money for a medical post. Water tanks come up in the next item too because another aid post has an unsatisfactory water supply. One of them asks, "Why do they build an aid post without a clean water supply? That's not doing a job properly." The chairman reminds them that water tanks cannot be purchased out of funds for aid posts or rural improvement. One APO, who has been four years at his post, says that it is in such a mess that if a health inspector were to see it, he would close it down because there is no good water source near it. If they cannot improve it, he wants to leave and they won't be able to find anyone to replace him. He says he is not joking. He and his family have tolerated it for four years. The aid post must be rebuilt closer to the village and to water, not far away so no one comes. The chairman suggests he discuss this with the councilor of the village and the people, especially since the village is divided into two sections. Would both be ready to help?

Then there are items about the conditions of long-service leave and ordinary leave. One of them says he was asked by the pilot to pay for his airfare coming back from leave. Why should he have to pay for his fares? Why won't the government reimburse air tickets? One of the nurses replies that she has written about this matter but has not yet received a reply. There are differences that depend on whether the APO works within the mission health service framework or within the government framework. This leads to a prolonged discussion about how different individuals have had to pay for fares, how long they waited for reimbursement, whether it is fair for APOs who work for the government (*ananit long gavman*) to be treated better than those who work for the mission health service. The APO from Rauit says he thinks the provincial government at Vanimo undercuts support for the APOs in this area because they see them as part of the mission and therefore not in need of support. The chairman then has to explain about the way government and provincial allocations are fixed.

A bit later, the question of one APO's retirement comes up. He wants to retire as soon as his retirement pay and final pay come through. Then he will retire properly and another man should come to take his place. Nurse J. brings up a problem: he already works together with N. because he was forbidden to give injections until he had taken a refresher course. N. left the village where he had been posted (village X) to go help the old APO. But as N. does not have permission to do this, he is reprimanded for leaving the place where he was meant to be. The chairman slightly modifies the direct and personal reprimand by saying that it is intended as a general piece of guidance for all of them, not just N., since any of them might get involved in a serious court action if something goes wrong and he is found to have been working at a place or in a job to which he has not been appointed. In fact, village X's schoolteacher has come to lodge a complaint about the absence of the APO, since there are people with chest infections in the village and no one to give them an injection. Nurse J. reminds the old APO that she has been trying to get him to come for a one-week refresher course for seven months. He answers that it is not because he is *bikhet*, but how could he have come and left the people at his post without an APO, without treatment? What if someone died? Nurse J. reminds him that N. is there. A third APO, who happens to come from village X, volunteers to go there and help out.

A long discussion develops about some villagers' demands for a health subcenter to be started near them. This is linked to questions about the organization of maternal and infant welfare work. Under any other business, a number of APOs voice their difficulties with supplies. The amounts they are given do not last long enough; if they run out during the month, the APO has to go fetch an extra supply, and that may mean a long walk. The chairman explains about the general shortage of dressings and stresses the need for economy. The chairman also stresses that the APO must persuade people to fetch medicines and dressings that are needed for the good of the community. APOs who pay for people to fetch and carry the aid post supplies are doing wrong; they should talk this out with the village councilors and make sure people from the community do the fetching. Certainly, the APOs shouldn't have to do it themselves. But one APO declares vehemently that it is not so easy. If he fails to persuade people to go and fetch supplies, he will get the blame when the supplies run out. If they complain he does not treat them, he will have his pay cut.

Community values and the bureaucratic system

This account has not covered the whole meeting, but it conveys in immediate terms some of the clashes between individuals, community values, and those of an introduced system: the modern health care system. Problems of payment, the community, and the orderly's obligations and priorities are prominent.

The system is organized in a hierarchy of relationships and responsibilities. Local people cannot see all of it. There are more or less implicit obligations, some of which are not accepted or recognized in the same way by everyone involved. Some of the difficulty may stem from attitudes prompted by their first encounters with introduced services. The demand for them initially seemed to come more from the givers of the services than from the receivers. These matters were literally introduced by aliens. This alienated local people because the services and conditions seemed imposed on them or were unwanted, and because they were not able to understand and control it. They had been better able to do this before with their own forms of care and treatment. Foreigners brought their kind of medicine and thought local people needed it. However, there seemed to be gap between how people perceived needing versus wanting something. Since they had not asked for it, why should they now contribute to making it work? This attitude sometimes appeared in their unwillingness to work for the medical aid post or fetch supplies for it, or even to follow suggested treatments, revealing patches of blindness in what they saw as their obligations. Despite good intentions, Westerners' paternalism in the past may have contributed to the relative indifference of many of the people who, in fact, benefited from the service. Good intentions may look different to other people.

We are easily disposed to read other people's motives for them or to imagine that we can read through them. Christian missions have been greatly involved in health care in many parts of Papua New Guinea. The measures were primarily introduced for humanitarian reasons rather than as a strategy to win converts. In this area, as in other parts of the country, the local missions established the first medical services, so villagers were bound to associate the introduced health care with Christian mission action. The mission background of many APOs and the prayers that began and ended meetings of the local health committee were among the many signs of this connection. The delivery of medical services in the region was not riven by factionalism or by interdenominational rivalries. Different missions were active in the area, but local people did not say one denomination was favored or the other disadvantaged in receiving care, nor did they say nonbelievers failed to get as good treatment as Christians did. The medical services were not used overtly to evangelize, although they contributed in general to the authority and success of the missions. Rauit residents certainly appreciated the part the mission played in building and staffing a thriving local health center, which was seen as one of the main ways the mission helped them. The villagers frequently and, I think, sincerely referred to this using the Tokpisin verb *halpim mipela* (helping us). They used the same phrase in general and almost by convention to describe White people's actions and requests, sometimes in odd ways—for instance, when describing my efforts to get exhaustive genealogies from them. It began to sound ironic. The mission began providing health services and then ran the aid posts for years with some financial assistance and supplies from the public health department. Upon the independence of Papua New Guinea in 1975, health care began to shift into local hands and become integrated with services from the government.

The right to health care: National Health Plans

The epigraph to the introduction of the Papua New Guinea National Health Plan 1974–78 reads as follows: "A National Health Plan is not just a set of recommendations about what should be; rather it is the record of choices and decisions made by those who are committed to the implementation of those decisions." Among the decisions made by the government are those concerning the health of the country's population. The introduction continued: "Health planning is not just an aid to economic progress. It is concerned with providing people with a service which is theirs as a basic human right" (*Papua New Guinea National Health Plan* 1974–78: 1). It recognized the maintenance of health as one of the government's tasks and duties to society.

People have a right to health, but it is difficult to make sure that everyone in Papua New Guinea has equal access to treatment when they need it. It is challenging to provide them with the same chance to enjoy good health, as social equity would demand, given that villages are so dispersed and located in such different terrains and that the nation holds such a wide variety of societies. Who should be responsible for providing the resources needed to secure the right to health? The individual? The community? The government (Abel-Smith 1976: chap. 1)? Do the poor, rural villagers, or the ignorant have less of a right to it or need it less than others? Rhetorical as those questions may sound, people and governments indeed have to face them. The realities of limited resources push people into having to make unpleasant choices. A colonial government that provided services for its expatriate officers but did nothing for the people it governed, would be—as some have been—condemned for selfishness or inhumanity and exploitation. Government officials may argue that local village people cannot make choices for themselves because they have so little knowledge of modern medicine, so the government has an obligation to provide treatment for them whether they think they need it or not. How can local people make the right choices without sufficient information and education? Some may see this as the stuff of paternalism and dependency or interference; however, probably most would say it is the duty of a responsible government to try to provide medical services and provisions.

Cultural diversity is one of Papua New Guinea's most striking attributes. Colonial rule created a political unit from a multitude of cultures and languages. Western institutions were based on a centralized hierarchical system, and the public health service followed suit. It was meant to provide a basic standard of care for everybody regardless of their local setting. By 1974, government staff had to think afresh about the goals of their health care services and how to adapt them to meet the needs of a country on its way to becoming independent the following year. Many of the expatriate officers who had filled posts and run the services under the Australian administration were expected to leave. The National Health Plan set out the goals and principles for the future in these terms:

> Unplanned health services are those in which the allocation of resources is based on arbitrary and ill-considered criteria such as the demands of privileged groups, an influential elite or the self-interest of professionals. The government of this country is concerned with the improved health and welfare of all the people and the use of all resources in a way that best meets this aim. Planning may therefore require a deliberate choice of priorities which cuts across the demands upon which previous allocation was based . . . . Planning therefore requires involvement of the people who will benefit from it through the expression of their real needs and priorities . . . . Planning must also involve, in its decision-making process, those who are required to carry out the provisions of the plan. (*Papua New Guinea National Health Plan* 1974–78: 1–3)

The principles were that services should be integrated and participative so that people and communities are involved in making decisions about their own health. Services should be equitably distributed and available to all. The standards should be appropriate and reflect the level of community and national development. They should be efficient and allocate expensive scarce resources for maximum benefit. They should collaborate with other government departments and the communities. The officials in charge of health care planning drew up a list that ranked the health problems in the country and, on this basis, established national health objectives in order of priority. The plan listed thirteen of such objectives: among them, the first was the provision of basic health services for all through health centers and medical aid posts; second, the control of malaria; third, provision of health education; fourth, the reduction of tuberculosis and leprosy; and fifth, the decentralization of decision-making and the promotion of community participation. The second National Health Plan, published in 1986, reaffirmed the principles of the first one and put emphasis on consolidating rather than expanding services, but the principles themselves were unchanged. The strategy now was to give priority to improving the quality and efficiency of existing services; increasing the emphasis on self-reliance and community participation in health and development; and providing more effective health education and information (*Papua New Guinea National Health Plan* 1986–90: 68).

In a discussion of reasons for providing national health service that was free of charge at the time of use, Brian Abel-Smith (1976: chapter 3) proposed a number of justifications, including the efficiency of providing certain services as collective goods and the benefit to the whole community that comes from ensuring that individuals get treatment for communicable diseases, such as cholera or tuberculosis, that they might otherwise spread to others. As he further argued, it would be unfair to oblige people by law to get treated for certain conditions and also expect them to pay for it; government control and financing of certain medical services are warranted when people are unable to make informed choices about them and seldom know in advance if or when they will need a particular service; the cost of the service may be wholly disproportionate to their ability to pay and, indeed, their need for treatment may prevent them from working to earn money to pay for it. Unpredictable needs make it hard for an individual to plan how much to put aside for health care, but it is more feasible to predict the general health care needs of a community or the country as a whole. Competitive private insurance inevitably results in risk-taking and those who most need insurance coverage are the least likely to be able to purchase it. A key point that distinguishes health service provision from the provision of other things such as food and shelter—which are necessities, although no government provides them free for everyone—is that few people can make informed choices about what health problems to anticipate or for which they should insure themselves (Abel-Smith 1976: 41). Few can tell what difference treatment might make compared with doing nothing, whereas they do know their food and housing needs and can make informed choices about them.

From ideals to practice

The ideals and objectives of the Papua New Guinea health plans were channeled into specific proposals. But intentions are one thing, fulfillment is another. There are bound to be gaps between ideals and practice. Discussion at the local health committee illustrated how things may seem so different according to someone's perspective and position in a system. The local communities perhaps did not show the active involvement that the government hoped to see. Villagers were weakly aware of their obligations and what the orderlies could or should be expected to do, and health education had far to go. The orderlies gathered at the meeting sounded much like workers or professionals anywhere, with much to say about their pay and conditions. They justified themselves, they answered criticism, they did their job. But despite that, we must recall how vigorously villagers reacted when they thought Maka was dying, coming together to sit down around her house in sympathy, discussing different causes and treatments. We must then consider what the local health committee meeting represented a decade later and what changes had taken place. The village attitudes had not disappeared; place and setting still made a difference, people still moved between settings, as witnessed in the APO mobility, and their reactions still took on different colors according to place.

In the village, care and treatment were provided within a close circle of people, mostly as a matter of kinship and community obligations. Ethics of generosity and loyalty appropriate to their distributive morality lay behind them. This contrasts with health care in the national system organized in a hierarchy, with its complex division of labor, specialized jobs, and contractual obligations in which people do their work for pay. The ethics behind this system thus seem very different than the ethics of community care. If health care workers have to be paid for services, then does that mean the payment creates the obligation to act? Or do they also have a social duty? Is medical care to be put on the same level as commerce? People are loath to do that. The methods of financing medical services and rewarding those who work within them vary greatly among countries, their political systems, and their ideologies (Abel-Smith 1976: chapter 5). They imply widely divergent views about the impacts of payment on the quality of medical practices. Some argue that compensation acts as an incentive to good practices and efficiency, as a way to ration in order to prevent waste, while others argue that it distorts and undermines good practices.

Richard Titmuss's comparative study (1970) of human blood transfusion services in different countries was an attempt to address these issues by examining one particular component of the medical care system in Britain and comparing it with equivalent services in systems based on different ideologies. His study arose from wider questions about giving and taking in modern welfare systems. If medical care is a consumer good indistinguishable from other goods and services in the private economic market, all policy might become in the end economic policy. In that case, the only values that would count would be those that could be measured in terms of money. "Each individual would act egoistically for the good of all by selling his blood for what the market would pay" (Titmuss 1970: 12). What concerned him was the place allowed for altruism in modern society. The effect of the argument in favor of treating blood commercially would be to establish policies to reduce the already limited opportunities left for altruism in modern society in Britain. The National Blood Transfusion Service in Britain is based on voluntary blood donation and it represents, he argued, an extreme type of "non-economic exchange"—that is, altruistic giving to unknown people. It is a social transaction, not an economic one; the donors are giving something they value highly and without reward. Such a social gift or action is a form of what Titmuss called "creative altruism" (1970: 212). Economists arguing on the basis of theories of the "economic individual" suggest that payment would increase the efficiency of use, the safety, and the guaranteed supply of blood. However, Titmuss found that this was not so.[1] He maintained that gift relationships of the social and moral kind still have certain functions in industrialized societies. Indeed, the spread of scientific and technological developments had increased the social need for gift relationships. Modern societies require more rather than less freedom of choice for the expression of altruism in daily life.

At the beginning of this chapter, I noted that people look for sympathy and consideration in the care they receive when ill. Even if those who care for them do not know what to do or have little that they can do, the demonstration of immediate concern may still provide moral support to someone who is sick. The sympathy gatherings of the Gnau made that side of response to illness even more obvious because of the relative lack of other things they could do in most cases. The sympathy gatherings

---

1. This holds true when judged by the measurable criteria of economic efficiency (or waste); administrative efficiency (or shortages, both chronic and acute); cost per unit; purity, potency, and safety; or quality per unit.

were more than simple visiting: they provided support and opportunities for organizing more elaborate treatment. Relations with other people and with spirits played a great part in their explanations of illness. Their own treatments relied on affecting these relations rather than on materials, herbs, or instruments. Responsibility for action depended on the social and moral ties between people. Trust played a part together with the expectations and close reciprocities of kinship and community. The Gnau were expected to gather when someone was ill, partly as a duty but also as an expression of sympathy.

Care for a sick person in vital matters and decisions about treatment are rarely handed over simply and directly through mercenary exchanges. In many societies, this is demonstrated through the ambiguities about payments for treatment; they are often not considered to be payments but gifts made in gratitude according to the giver's inclination or offerings made to the spirit; in other places, the compensation is made in kind, not in cash, or the healer is rewarded with prestige or reverence. These special forms make it difficult to assess exactly how much or sometimes even how healers are paid for their work. People in many cultures seem reluctant to put a cash value on a life or on restoring health and find it hard to accept that someone deserves much confidence if money is the prime motive for healing. As Lewis Henry Morgan found, Handsome Lake told the Iroquois,

> The Great Spirit designed that some men should possess the gift of skill in medicine. But he is pained to see a medicine man making exorbitant charges for attending the sick. . . . When a sick person recovers his health, he must return thanks to the Great Spirit . . . and the medicine man must receive as his reward whatever the gratitude of the restored may tender. This is right and proper. There are many who are unfortunate and cannot pay for attendance. It is sufficient for such to return thanks to the medicine man upon recovery. The remembrance that he has saved the life of a relative will be sufficient reward. (Morgan 1851: 251)

An increase in the specialized technical knowledge required to practice medicine has brought an increasing division of labor in many societies. The choice of healer no longer rests on trusted personal ties. But the sufferer is nevertheless anxious to be fully convinced of the efficacy of care. With a choice based on professional criteria of competence and contract, trust in sympathy risks being diminished. Payment does not necessarily buy sympathy. The state or society seeks to guarantee the competence of healers by instituting special controls: examinations, shamanic tests, or ordeals. Those who pass must take a professional oath, be required to follow a special code of conduct, or adopt a certain dress to set them apart. Such standards and professional controls are intended to provide confidence in care and to replace kinship and community as the prime basis for trust.

The illness of one individual in a small village may even upset most of the community. A comparably general disturbance can only very rarely be the case in industrialized societies. If the illness of one person has effects on many, the experience of general upset may help explain why people in small societies lay stress on the social and moral causes of illness or take the illness of an individual to be a sign of something wrong in the community. The biomedical approach has tended to focus on the patient in isolation as someone with a particular kind of disease. The risk is that as we try so hard to identify the disease, we disregard the individual and his or her social context. It might seem something of a paradox that as we find out more about illnesses, we come to provide less moral support to patients. We focus on the individual, but perhaps we see the *whole person* less clearly.

Part II: recognizing and defining illness

The aim of Part II is to consider the basis for specifying the subject matter and place of medical anthropology within social anthropology in general. I begin the first chapter with the problem of identifying illnesses and of comparing like with like, for there are traps in the identification of an illness. Leprosy is a disease with a long history that provides a lesson in mistaken assumptions. The term "leprosy" had other referents in the past, and the Bible long influenced Western ideas associated with the condition. This example shows how facts and meanings linked to a particular label for a disease may change over time and differ across social settings.

CHAPTER FIVE

The meaning of "leprosy"

There is nothing in the entire range of human phenomena which illustrates so impressively the divine power of the redeemer, and the nature and extent of his work of mercy on man's behalf, as this leprosy. There are many most striking analogies between it and that more deadly leprosy of sin which has involved our whole race in one common ruin. It is feared as contagious; it is certainly and inevitably hereditary; it is loathsome and polluting; its victim is shunned by all as unclean; it is most deceitful in its action. . . . Who can fail to find in all this a most affecting type of man's moral leprosy? Like it, this too is hereditary, with an awfully infallible certainty. As surely as we have inherited it from our fathers do we transmit it to our children. (Thomson 1882: 653–54)

The moral connotations of leprosy have changed since the days of Reverand William McClure Thomson, and far more since biblical times. The significance attached to the word "leprosy" blinded people to facts. What started my interest in the terminology was an echo of those ideas and their practical consequences. When I returned to Rauit in 1983, the village where I had conducted my first fieldwork in 1968–69, I was dismayed to find that almost thirty people in the village had been told they had leprosy. Five years before, only one person, a young married man, had lepromatous leprosy, the infectious form. The government health policy in 1958 had been to segregate people with lepromatous leprosy for treatment to prevent their condition from infecting others. If they absconded from the segregated unit, a policeman might be sent to fetch them back. When I first stayed in the village, the man with leprosy had run away from the unit more than once, so he had been sent away to a hospital on the coast. His brother and father looked after things for him, while his wife, so far childless, tended their gardens.

Five years later, when I came back, he was still at the coast undergoing treatment, although the policy of segregation had changed. During his absence, however, he was betrayed by his wife and his elder brother. They were caught *in flagrante delicto* in a garden by his elder brother's wife. Not long after, with the timing of classic tragedy, the man with leprosy returned from the coast, climbing the hill with gifts, to announce that he was well again and had come home for good. In the village located before his own, someone told him what had happened. He left his gifts there on the path and went home, destroying his gardens, cutting his fruit-bearing trees and palms to "lay waste and wreck them" (*nauwom nari'in*) as he came. Then he entered the village to seek out his brother and his wife.

But the fight between the brothers that people expected was stopped, partly because the *kiap* (government patrol officer) was already aware of the incident. A solution was reached. It involved fines on both sides and a short spell of jail for the elder brother, and the betrayed husband stabbed his wife in her thigh with a bit of wood. She seemed to accept it without rancor—in fact, while I was dressing the infected wound, she talked about it, I thought, almost happily. The two of them, she and her returned husband, settled down again together.

Attitudes toward illness: Leprosy in the village

Leprosy was not just another kind of sickness for these villagers. The events I recounted above spanned more than five years. The man had slightly thickened earlobes and his eyebrows had lost some hairs at the edges, but otherwise he looked quite normal and felt strong and well. But he was fled his home on more than one occasion, was fetched by the police, and was then forced to stay in a hospital far from his village. Much trouble followed. *Sik lepro*, the Tokpisin phrase for leprosy, meant something special to the Gnau villagers.

The segregation represented by a *haus lepro* was certainly part of the meaning embodied by the disease. The *haus lepro* was a house for the treatment of lepers built down by the river at some distance from the main part of the mission and its hospital. The local people had experience with the special rules for leprosy and its segregation. The policy had changed by 1975, when I returned; people were now treated at home. Health education patrols came to find cases and educate villagers about the disease. They tried to impress on them the need for treatment, emphasizing the risk of destructive changes, the disease's horrible effects, and the dangers of contagion. But what was diagnosed as leprosy by the medical staff seemed to the villagers to be mere superficial skin blemishes. There was little that seemed to justify so much concern.

Occasionally, however, someone fell seriously ill with swellings but no injury to account for them. People thought of *sik lepro* and suggested it might be the diagnosis. With this diagnosis went the fear of spreading it to others. The way that *sik lepro* was singled out was what first struck me. Later I was to hear of other cases, including the death of a man I had known on my first visit. His belly and legs had swollen, he felt weak, he tried to walk down to the mission hospital by a path along the ridge, which passed through the nearest neighboring village. When he came to the village, the people there would not let him pass because they said his illness would infect them. They said he had *sik lepro*, so he was turned back. He died at home shortly thereafter, his belly grossly swollen. The body was buried with special haste for fear the illness might jump to someone else.

In retrospect, people in the village said he had died of *sik lepro*. To them, it was the strange swelling that was the significant marker. They had learned that there were special horrors to leprosy and, although they were not convinced by the slight skin blemishes of early leprosy, they linked them with swelling and to what they took to be a serious case of *sik lepro*.

Leviticus as a source on leprosy

The Gnau people give leprosy (in its Tokpisin form) a new meaning and range of reference. When I later looked up leprosy in the Book of Leviticus, I was struck by the amount of space given to it—a good deal more, for example, than to dietary rules. Why was so much space devoted to leprosy?

The biblical chapter on leprosy that led to so much misery is Leviticus 13. It gives detailed directions on how to identify the disease and how to deal with the leper. It says, "And the leper in whom the plague is, his clothes shall be rent, and the hair of his head shall go loose, and he shall cover his upper lip, and shall cry: 'Unclean, unclean.' All the days wherein the plague is in him he shall be unclean; he is unclean; he shall dwell alone; without the camp shall his dwelling be" (Leviticus 13:45–46).

Most of us probably think of leprosy as a disease that can be mutilating and disfiguring. We know it is contagious and slowly progressive. But behind what many of us might say in plain recall of what we know, some other images may spring to mind: a rotted, lumpy face, glazed eyeballs, a gnarled hand without fingers, the fear of contagion through touch. These are the images that lurk in Rudyard Kipling's story "The mark of the beast," with its figure of the Silver Man, and again in Sherlock Holmes's "The blanched soldier," illustrated in the fate of Ben Hur's mother and sister. With such horrors in mind, we are not surprised that leprosy has been singled out for special dread. We might accept that for the Israelites, casting out lepers was a way to protect the rest of the community.

But, if Leviticus gives such attention to leprosy, we might also ask whether leprosy plagued the ancient Hebrews more than other peoples. And what were their ideas about contagion and infection? Were they medically sound regarding other infectious kinds of sickness? Leprosy was not the only contagious disease they suffered, nor could it have been the worst or the most obvious. Was it the most disfiguring? The most deadly?

I go too fast. Leprosy is not a simple example of a contagious or infectious disease. Years may intervene between exposure to the disease and the appearance of any symptoms. People can live for years among lepers without catching it. Not all forms of leprosy are infectious; not everyone who is exposed to someone with infectious leprosy will catch it. Were the dangers of infection so much more striking or apparent to the ancient Hebrews?

And then there is something else we should notice. One of the chapters of Leviticus is about how to restore the sufferer to the community after the signs of his affliction have disappeared. So this leprosy might disappear or heal by itself. But textbooks of medicine do not write of lepromatous leprosy disappearing spontaneously or of the body becoming whole again. So what was this leprosy of the Bible?

The answer is plain. The biblical leprosy was not what we now call leprosy. The description given to the priest in Leviticus 13 make that clear. It lays out the diagnostic criteria and they are explicit. No reference is made to deformity, a loss of feeling, destructive changes, blindness, or paresis. In doubtful cases, the unclean lesions should show changes after seven days. Leprosy as we know it does not change in seven days; its advance is very slow, sometimes taking years. Various other skin conditions might fit some of the biblical criteria: vitiligo, psoriasis, or fungal infections. The instructions could cover a number of different conditions according to current medical classifications.

Doctors are familiar with the discrepancy between the biblical leprosy and the leprosy of today's medical textbook. The Bible uses the Hebrew word *zara'at* to refer to "unclean" skin lesions. This word was translated in the Septuagint as <u>*lepra*</u> (deriving from the Greek *lepros*, "rough and scaly," and *lepis*, "a scale"). *Zara'at* translated into *lepra* gave rise to derivative forms with different referents. Medical writers of the first few centuries (such as Paulus Aegineta, Aetius, Oribasus, and Polybius) used *lepra* to refer to a circular, superficial scaly eruption of the skin, a condition that was curable and not serious or contagious. Some commentators have thought that the disease they called *elephantiasis* was the leprosy of modern medical writers (Adams 1846: 1–15). It was quite distinct from *lepra* (Brody 1974; S. Browne 1975; Macalister 1902; Waldstein 1905).

But during the Dark Ages up to the Middle Ages, the word for one kind or set of skin conditions, *lepra*, came to refer to different conditions. It eventually settled as a word that applied to leprosy as we now know it.[1] What I saw happening on a tiny scale in a few villages in Papua New Guinea bore some resemblance to what had happened centuries before in Europe. The foreign name was adopted and adapted, still carrying some of the associations it had in its former reference. But the close description of observable signs given in Leviticus 13 enables us to recognize that *zara'at* did not refer to the disease we now call leprosy. It was also questionable if the symptoms called *sik lepro* in the villages were actually signs of leprosy.

The history of leprosy in the West shows the persistence of attitudes that stem from a written source and their link to a label or name. The name endures; the denotation changes. The label remains fixed in people's mind. Its moral associations have changed but not out of recognition; what it refers to almost shifts out of recognition. It shifted regardless of

---

1. The rise and fall of leprosy in Europe is a curious story. It is not clear how differences of diagnostic criteria, the spread of tuberculosis, hygienic measures, resistance, and relative immunity may have changed the prevalence of leprosy in Europe from the high number of cases in the Middle Ages (McNeill 1976: 164–68).

the instructions about making a diagnosis set out in the Bible. Instead, an inferred moral message or meaning took hold of people's imaginations. If readers are surprised to learn that the passages in Leviticus are not, after all, about the leprosy they had supposed, their surprise will cast perhaps a little light on that long story of blindness.

The Jews were not led down quite the same path as the Christians who translated the Bible. The Old Testament, the Jewish Bible, remained in Hebrew, and its adherents were expected to follow the letter of its instructions. *Zara'at* remained *zara'at*. In Talmudic tradition, leprosy was not considered contagious in a medical sense. As Danby (1933) points out, the Mishnah does not consider pagans, gentiles, or resident aliens with signs of leprosy to be unclean (Mishnah, Nega'im 3.1).[2] If a man removed the signs of uncleanness, plucked out his white hairs, or cauterized quick flesh before he came to the priest, he was considered clean. However, if he did so after he had been certified unclean, he was still unclean (Nega'im 7.4). Indeed, would we be right to suppose that the Israelites thought of *zara'at* as a kind of sickness? It is difficult to avoid assuming so when we think about it in English: we can hardly detach the words "leprosy" or "malignant skin disease" from the idea of sickness. The chapters in Leviticus are concerned with signs of "uncleanness" in the body—that is, with ritual purity and impurity. There is no discussion of measures to care for or provide remedies for people with the bodily signs that show them to be unclean. The word for "plague" (*nega*) and the one for "leprosy" (*zara'at*) both derive from roots with meanings of "smiting" (*naga*, "to smite, blast, touch, reach"; *zara'*, "to smite, strike, pierce, sting"). Leviticus 13 and 14 nowhere use the main verb *halah* (being or becoming sick) with reference to the "plague of leprosy."[3]

Something else also prompts us to question the sense in which the Israelites considered leprosy a kind of illness. The biblical chapters on leprosy describe the leprosy in a house, in garments, and in anything made of skins, which are all "unclean" because a person with leprosy is unclean. We use the idea of sickness with reference to living creatures; we do not speak of things like houses or garments falling sick.

---

2. The Mishnah was a rabbinic codification and compilation of the great body of Jewish law handed down by oral tradition. Its redaction was the work of many scholars in about the second century CE.

3. In only one phrase in the Leviticus chapters ("Behold if the plague of leprosy be healed in the leper" [Leviticus 14:3]) does another verb, *nirppa'* (to "be healed," from the root *rapa'*, "to heal, mend"), appear.

Impurity or sin

Leviticus defines the leper as one in the category of persons and things that are ritually impure. Although there is no explicit moral condemnation of the man found to be leprous, the terms for moral valuation are all there (Brody 1974: 111–12). Leviticus does not deny that leprosy is a punishment for sin; it simply ignores the idea. Rabbinical commentaries in the Mishnah connected leprosy with sin, as did the early Christian writers Justin Martyr, Origen, Chrysostom, and Tertullian. Leprosy was the external revelation of internal evil, an emblem of sin visible on the skin. For simony, avarice, and lust, a man or woman might be smitten with leprosy. By the Middle Ages, leprosy had become a disease of the soul as well as of the body (Brody 1974). A bishop, priest, or ecclesiastical jury that decided whether people had leprosy had the power to cut them off from ordinary life. The rules differed with time and place, but segregation of leprous patients was the common and persistent theme. The leper was dead to the world (in Rothar's edict, *il est mort quant au siècle*). Over the centuries following the Middle Ages, the numbers of lepers in Europe slowly declined; the moral stigma so closely bound to leprosy also slowly attenuated and changed. However, the stigma has never wholly died out (Gussow and Tracy 1970). It remains in the attitudes people still bring to the disease as well as the horror of leprosy that, for centuries, has seemed to justify segregation and the special treatment of lepers (Iliffe 1987: chap. 12; Richards [1977] 2000; Waxler 1981). Something of that stigma lingers with us still. But the question I have in mind concerns a much earlier period: biblical times.

Do the biblical rules for cleansing the leper reveal why leprosy was singled out? The cleansing of the leper required the performance of a series of rites with sacrifices. Old Testament sacrifice was a complex ritual system, and the order and forms set out for cleansing the leper were peculiar. William Robertson Smith's *Religion of the Semites* (1889) famously discussed Old Testament sacrifice, throwing light on the social context of sacrifice, ritual change, and the imagery of relationships between God and man. He took the rite of sacrifice to be the model of all complete acts of worship in Semitic religion (1889: 214), stressing its persistence despite elaborations of procedure. But its meaning has not been constant throughout its history. Robertson Smith considered sacrifice in the spirit of Julius Wellhausen's critical approach ([1883] 2013), taking account of people's changing history and political circumstances.

From sacrifice to sin

The ancient Semites were first a nomadic people, like others around them. They were born to their religion; their god was the god of their tribe, fighting with them on their side against other tribes with their allegedly false gods. The rules of the community were binding on all its members; they distinguished them from surrounding peoples and served in a period of intertribal wars to weld the people together. The rules were public, not private matters. The individual who broke them endangered the community. Equality and the solidarity of kinship, along with the authority of a father over his son, provided imagery for the relationship between the people and their god. The many holy places, a tent of the Lord, a traveling Ark of the Covenant belonged to a tribal people whose god moved with them—their shield and their strength. They conquered another people, they established a kingdom, they settled a land.

Then the imagery became that of a king, of tribute, and of homage; with this, the celebration of power and prosperity appeared. The conceptual distance widened between God and his worshippers with a monotheism suited to the idea of absolute or final justice coming from one source, a king over all, a judge whose decrees were laws. All sacrificial offerings had to be brought to a central place of worship. The priesthood grew stronger as it assumed the role of mediator between the people and God. The kingdom was a holy land.

Then the kingdom became divided and began to fall; the first to fall was Israel to the Assyrians. The power of Babylon rose, Judah was besieged, and Jerusalem taken, the Temple destroyed. The sense of celebrating prosperity was removed from worship and was increasingly replaced by a sense of guilt over offenses against God and the need to pacify his anger through expiation and propitiation. After the destruction of the kingdoms and the experience of exile, the themes of sin, punishment, and the need to atone came to dominate the entire sacrificial system, altering its character; its focus came to rest on sacrifice offered out of sinfulness. Most of Leviticus was codified and written down in the period after the exile. It bore the priestly stamp and their views of guilt and sin.

Uncleanness had to be excluded from contact with holy things. The taint of lepers required cutting them off from any contact with holy things. The rule had a religious basis, not a medical one. An underlying religious theme recurred in many details, especially in the contrast between death and life, whereby death was seen as polluting, life as the great good. Priest and Nazirite contrasted with lepers, the former two associated with holy things, the latter tainted as if by death. To forbid the mixture of holy things with uncleanness had the character of taboo.[4] The purpose was to prevent life from being contaminated and mixed with death. The means lay in obedience to God and observance of the code of holiness.

The ritual cleansing of the leper

The ritual procedure for the cleansing of the leper was a rite of passage, a readmission to the community of those who could worship together. The cleansing was not a treatment in a medical sense. The sacrificial system of Leviticus was a priestly elaboration made coherent by their conception of sin and expiation. My argument is that the leper was singled out as a human emblem of uncleanness, tainted by death, which contrasted with the image of the cleanness required for contact with holy things and epitomized in the priest and the Nazirite. But later, the priests' preoccupation over sin—an interest bound up with their mediating role and the control they exercised through sacrifice—led them to recast the cleansing of the leper as something done for the expiation of sin. Notions of sin changed from concern with actions to concern with the individual actor and his or her intentions. The earlier regard for action was closer to the attitude toward breaches of taboos.

The leper was said to be "unclean" (*tame'*). Unclean things defile. They are intrinsically unclean. So the leper had to be cast outside the camp and have no contact with holy things or defile other people. "Defile not ye yourselves in any of these things; for in all these the nations are defiled, which I cast out before you. And the land was defiled, therefore did I visit the iniquity thereof upon it, and the land vomited out her inhabitants" (Leviticus 18:24, 25).

In keeping with the character of taboo, leprosy was defined unclean, but no reason was given for why. However, one possible reason is suggested by the story of God's anger with Miriam when she, along with Aaron, spoke against their brother Moses because he had married a Cushite woman (Numbers 12:9–15). God made Miriam leprous and "as white as snow"; Aaron said, "Let her not, I pray, be as one dead, of whom the flesh is half consumed when he cometh out of his mother's womb."

---

4. A taboo is a ritual prohibition that may express either the sacredness (holiness) or the uncleanness of something that is set apart.

Miriam's leprosy is likened to the flesh of the dead, who bring uncleanness. According to the Mishnah's list of the different degrees of uncleanness, that of the leper is exceeded only by the uncleanness of bones from a corpse and by that of the corpse itself (Mishnah, tractate Kelim 1.4). The priest was forbidden to defile himself for the sake of the dead (i.e., to bury or come near the dead or to observe mourning rites) except for the death of a close kinsperson (Leviticus 21:1–4). In the case of a high priest, he could not mourn even the death of his own mother or father (Leviticus 21:10–12). The holiest place had to be kept strictly separated from any defilement by contact with the dead. The general rules about the dead, their polluting effects, and the means of being purified from such effects are given in Numbers 19. The rules for the priests were special rules of avoidance. The priests might not leave their hair disheveled or tear their clothes in mourning for the dead (Leviticus 10:6; 21:10; cf. Numbers 5:18; Ezekiel 24:17, 22). "But the leper in whom the plague is, his clothes shall be rent, and the hair of his head shall go loose, and he shall cover his upper lip" (Leviticus 13:45). In effect, he was expected to behave as one in mourning, made unclean by contact with the dead. But the uncleanness was in himself, in his own flesh, and he had to be cast out of the camp. The rules appear to liken leprosy to a living death—a notion preserved in medieval Christian thinking: *il est mort quant au siècle.*

Death and flesh "half consumed," white as though dead flesh, carried the worst taint. The taint had to be kept away from anything that was holy. Life and prosperity were good: this was the great theme that Moses, nearing the end of his life, declared for God on the day of the Blood Covenant. Correlatively, death was evil. "See I have set before thee this day life and good, and death and evil, in that I command thee this day to love the Lord thy God, to walk in His ways, and to keep His commandments and His statutes and His ordinances; then shalt thou live and multiply, and the Lord thy God shall bless thee in the land whither thou goest in to possess it" (Deuteronomy 30:15, 16).

The cleansing rites for the leper did not constitute a medical treatment. The three-phase procedure had the pattern of a staged transition: the first phase took place outside the camp and was concerned with separating the leper from the foulness that was in him so he could enter the camp; the second phase was a marginal one within the camp, where he was allowed back into civil life but was still not clean enough to enter his own house, to come in contact with family life, or to have marital intercourse; the third phase enabled him to expiate himself through sacrifice.

The third phase showed the priestly concern for sin and atonement—it was the leper's final purification that restored him clean to the community of worshippers. The priestly view of the purpose of sacrifice was that it was an expiation for a sin.

In the third phase, the offerings for sin and guilt were made. Old Testament ideas of guilt and sin differed from modern ones. "Sin" (*hatta'at*) was incurred by doing anything that was forbidden by a command of God. The root from which *hatta'at* comes is *hatta'*, which means "to fall or miss one's aim, to make a false step, to fail in one's duty." In Leviticus 4, the sins for which offerings made atonement were inadvertent ones. They involved unintended transgressions, among which were ones leading to the condition of ritual impurity. "Sin" in this sense included defilement and uncleanness. It was the action or the state that mattered, not the intention. The expiation of sin was made the central object of sacrifice and permeated the system, but its ethical sense was not spelled out. After the early, explicit statements about the rules and false steps, a growing concern emerged of awareness of sin by a people estranged from God because they strayed after false gods, foreign lovers, or luxury. The idea of sin took on a shape that is more familiar to us now.

Conclusions

The problem is this: Why were the skin conditions described in Leviticus given so much attention? "Lepers" were taken to be unclean and tainted with death. If skin conditions were seen as a mixture of the dead and the living in someone's flesh, that might explain why the person with "leprosy" was singled out—indeed, who came close to being the epitome of an unclean person, the image of someone to be outcast. The leper posed a danger to holy things and other people. The form the rules took was that of taboo. Other things were identified in Leviticus as unclean (e.g., a woman "in the days of her impurity," the hare, the stork, the bat, etc.) because of their state or inherent characteristics, not because of disease or anything they did or sin in our modern sense.

The idea that life and death must not be mixed may lie behind the command to not mix blood (which is life) with flesh (which can be eaten; Leviticus 17:14). Mary Douglas (1966) put forward a theory of taboo that made ambiguity and the mixture of kinds or the confusion of proper boundaries the heart of the matter. The leper would be taboo in this sense, being someone with a combination of dead and living flesh.

Such a view may help explain the special ruling for the man who was wholly leprous, an otherwise astounding notion: "Behold, if the leprosy have covered all his flesh, he shall pronounce him clean that hath the plague: it is all turned white: he is clean" (Leviticus 13:13).

The great theme of the code of holiness in Leviticus was, "Ye shall be holy for I the Lord your God am holy." The commands were rules for holiness, to set the people apart and make them a holy people. Those people who were most strictly separate—in the sense of dedicated to God—were the priests and the Nazirites. They could have no contact with the dead. The leper was almost the polar opposite of them, perhaps because he carried in his person a defiling taint of death that excluded him absolutely from any contact with holy things, even contact with clean people, even contact with the community. The theme in Deuteronomy 30:19 was life: "I call heaven and earth to witness against you this day, that I have set before thee life and death, the blessing and the curse; therefore choose life that thou mayest live, thou and thy seed."

I think the biblical attitude toward leprosy first arose from these religious themes. One strength in setting ritual rules—but not setting out the reasons for them or what they mean—is that they may persist even if interpretations change. The power to evoke feelings and meanings stays open for reinterpretation as times, ideas, and interests change. The rules about leprosy provide an example of this. My argument is that biblical attitudes toward leprosy had little or nothing to do with attitudes of the sort we now take toward illness. The medical sense overtook the moral meaning long after the biblical period had passed.

Henry Ernest Sigerist ([1951] 1967: 446–47), like Karl Sudhoff and some other historians of medicine, was prepared to see the Israelites as pioneers of public health because of the influence of their ideas about purity and pollution. The notion of contagion grew, they thought, from ideas of the danger of defilement through touch or closeness. The precepts of Leviticus taught people to fear contamination. These were first religious ideas, not medical ones, but they had hygienic consequences.

Another lesson in the story of leprosy concerns cultural relativity and our selective blindness. Leprosy shows how words, concepts of sin, and responses to illness may be confused and can change with time. Our impulse is to see or set a medical frame around the biblical instructions on leprosy; one might say we medicalize their leprosy. We find it difficult to think about the subject without thinking of sickness. Medical associations are so well entrenched around the word that it traps our thinking. Its meanings were different in the past; in changing, this relativity exposes our errors of interpretation. Our bias lets us listen uncritically to explanations of the biblical rules and attribute hygienic motives to them. We rationalize them in line with our own assumptions. But it perhaps comes as a shock to see that the leprosy of the Bible was not our leprosy, and to realize that, long into modern times, those passages in Leviticus were taken to refer to the same thing, even though the instructions given for diagnosing the condition clearly indicate they did not. Many people must have read them with selective blindness.

An antipositivist and strong skeptical view of Western biomedicine might say that truth and falsity depend on certain assumptions about the nature of reality. These are not constant and universal. Medicine of the kind we are familiar with is a cultural product peculiar to us, resting like any other on specific assumptions about the world we live in. Its facts are accepted to be facts only when those assumptions are accepted. To say that the reality of illness is subjective (and determined by particular cultural views) sounds like an extreme idealist position if the possibility of finding objective criteria of disease is denied. Sometimes writing about other societies in medical anthropology seems to imply that illness realities are fundamentally semantic, taking the meaning-centered approach of Byron Good and Mary-Jo Delvecchio Good (1981) but without noting their proviso that "it is not our argument that disease is not biological or that meanings of illness and symptoms are independent of physiological conditions" (Good and Good 1981: 176).

Strong versions of cultural relativity can come close to implying that all that matters is what people think. Mary Baker Eddy's ([1875] 1971) position on sickness and healing was even more idealist and subjectivist: the spirit is everything and matter nothing. From this she developed the approach of Christian Science to healing. It is clear that beliefs about the significance of illness have power to alter outcomes and experiences of illness. The history of leprosy is a vivid illustration of this point. Social attitudes to the disease have added much misery to the direct afflictions of bodily damage, as John Iliffe (1987) describes in his account of leprosy in Africa. The power of moral attitudes to blind or overcome attention to the facts of disease is an old story.

The next three chapters continue with the theme of the cultural relativity of modes of thought about illness, asking what the scope of medical anthropology should be. How critical or necessary are the facts of disease and Western medical categories in comparative social studies of illness?

CHAPTER SIX

The right diagnosis

To settle disputes it is no good appealing to a logical definition: what we need are not definitions but criteria. An elephant is a pretty clear case, but take another example—those swans which the logicians are so fond of. If the word "swan" is to describe a bird that has the characteristic, among others, of appearing white then those black birds in Australia must be called by another name, but if the criteria for being a swan are anatomical and do not mention colour, then the black and the white swans are in the same category. All the argument is about how to set up the categories, not about the creatures. They are what they are however we choose to label them. (Robinson 1964: 8)

When we make definitions or argue about them, we are primarily asking about the use of words, not about the nature of things. The question here is about the criteria of medicine to use in cross-cultural comparison. Comparison is inevitable. We name a subject "medical anthropology," so what comes into it? Medicine in other cultures. What is that? Their art of healing, says one. Their knowledge of illness, says another. Healing what or whom? Illness, the sick. But what is illness? Who are the sick? We reach the edge of a tangled argument. If we knew diagnostic facts about diseases, we could look into the variety of social responses to them, confident of comparing like with like and of distinguishing the medical facts from the social responses that a particular kind of disease happened to evoke in a particular place or situation. In infinitely varied ways, the ideas and practices of a society can affect the occurrence and outcomes of diseases.

The sting is that the categories can make a difference to what becomes of the creatures. As I discussed in the previous chapter, "lepers" were outcast. People did not notice how the reference of the word had changed; the use of a constant name deceived them. The same label was applied to different facts. Facts about things, their properties, are neutral; statements about them can be true or false. It is we who attach certain meanings and values to them. Leviticus described particular signs to look for to identify the "leper"; those ancient criteria could have provided a factual basis for comparisons, for matching like with like. People meet disease in all societies no matter how they name it or think about it. Medical categories would be helpful if they represented descriptions of identifiable facts with nonrelative truth values, not ones dependent on a particular cultural or subjective appreciation of the case.

Some decry the positivism of medical doctors, complain they are dogmatic, and doubt what they assert are facts. Biomedical criteria of diagnosis are mostly explicit and defined. They are useful for some purposes of comparison. Those who find bias in scientific medicine must usually fall back on their own derivative versions of biomedical criteria to identify the illnesses they describe so their readers know what they are writing about. They do not confront the problems of comparison and translation. But it is not possible to explain what the illness categories of other languages mean without translation or examples. It would be better to decide how to make the criteria clear.

Subjective views and the semantic approach: The aim of understanding

To understand why a feverish man calls for blankets, it helps to know he feels cold. The aim of understanding someone else's viewpoint is crucial in medical anthropology and medical sociology. "If there is anything unique about sociology, it is its preoccupation with the social reality of human life which, while never wholly independent of other levels of reality, can be treated usefully as a reality in itself. . . . While the physician can use biophysical science to explain the signs he labels as illness, he himself cannot explain the behavior of the sufferer by reference to that science. For the task of explaining the 'illness behavior' of the sufferer, and for the task of explaining the 'diagnosis behavior' of the man who treats him, 'scientific medicine' is simply irrelevant" (Freidson 1970: 211).

Eliot Freidson provides a reason to see this as the proper preoccupation of medical sociology and medical anthropology. But the social reality he speaks of would have to be relative to particular people. One person's views are not more or less real than another's, for the reality in question depends on what they think and feel. Each is an authority for his own case. Subjective reality is the sort of reality that prompts, "Well, that may be how it seems to you, but it's different for me." It makes reality not independent of but always relative to culture and, ultimately, relative to individuals.

Shall we hypnotize the starving man to think that he has feasted? If truth were all subjective, we could, and the starving man would grow fat, as in the story recounted in Pierre Henri Cami's short play, "Un radeau de la 'Méduse', ou naufrage et gastronomie" ("A raft from the 'Medusa'; or, Shipwreck and gastronomy") (Cami 1972: 92–99). The captain of the good ship L'Entre-côtes sees a raft at sea, on it twelve people shipwrecked and seemingly dead. But, no! They are stretched out snoring. It is the first time he has heard of shipwrecked snorers on a raft floating lost at sea. And what is more, they are all grossly fat. Woken up, the shipwrecked people beg the captain to let them digest in peace, but one of them hands him the logbook as they resume their snoring. From the logbook, he learns of the hypnotist (fortunately, their companion in shipwreck), who for the past three months on the raft has kept them from starving by stuffing them each day through hypnosis with dream feasts of rich food.

Is thought so magically omnipotent? We do not grow fat on dreams of food. A burned child fears fire, and we will not be able to persuade him or her otherwise. Ernest Gellner (1970) scoffs at the excesses of charity in those anthropologists who consider the truth of concepts wholly relative to the culture which maintains them. We cannot say to each his own truth, because some propositions, if believed and acted on, will eliminate those who hold them to be true. With time and ingenuity, many errors are eliminated, so we may make progress in the accumulation of objective knowledge. The more extravagant, the more dangerous, and the wilder hypotheses will strike against reality.

The fundamental question at issue here is an ancient one about realism or idealism. The commonsense view is that the world will not come to an end when my existence ends: this is a central tenet of realism. Most would accept it as the only sensible hypothesis, even though the opposed theory of idealism is not refutable. In its simplest form, idealism asserts, "The world (which includes my present audience) is just my dream"

(Popper 1972: 38). Karl Popper puts forth the case for realism as the only sensible hypothesis (1972: 32–47).

Yet it seems clear that some anthropologists know, as Bertrand Russell teased (1945: 684), that idealists are virtuous and materialists are wicked. The idealist position may appeal to the anthropologist because much fine work in the field has required an imaginative effort to gain entry to the worlds in other people's minds. The anthropologist needs to learn how they classify experience and the assumptions by which they interpret their experience and give value to it.

But I doubt that any anthropologist seriously adopts the extreme idealist position. The view that the diseases of biomedicine are just cultural constructs may come to look like an idealist position if we deny the possibility of finding objective criteria. Some people have, indeed, been convinced that disease has no objective status. It was, of course, the view affirmed by Mary Baker Eddy in *Science and health*: her third principle was that "God, Spirit being all, matter is nothing"; her fourth was that "life, God, omnipotent good deny death, evil, sin, disease." On the basis of her belief that the spirit is everything and matter nothing, she developed the Christian Science approach to healing (Eddy [1875] 1971). An extreme position on the cultural relativity of disease (that scientific views about diseases are *just* one other case of a culturally specific view of illness, having no special status) would be, like Eddy's, an idealist position, opposed to the realist view that we can acquire knowledge of things as they are, existing in the way they do independently of anyone's thoughts or feelings about them.

The construction of social reality

It is one thing to say that a person who does not have a thermometer or never heard of one has no way of knowing his or her body temperature in degrees centigrade or Fahrenheit. It is quite another to say that someone has a fever if he or she feels hot. And we have no reason to accept what the thermometer measures as what somebody's temperature really is, since our belief in the thermometer is a matter of where and how we were brought up. Something rather like that can be considered a criticism of medicine.

> For health scientists and clinicians the most fundamental reality is biological. Everything else is somehow less "real." This ideological

bias is an artifact of socialization into biomedical science and the modern medical profession. It is a very powerful ideology, however; one in which behavioural and social science teaching in medical schools has had little impact. If there is a single concept in social science which challenges this ideology, it is the idea of the social construction of reality. (Kleinman et al. 1978: 329)

But what does this phrase "social construction of reality" imply? That the truth of any assertion about reality, including physical reality, must depend on particular cultural conventions? It is a wording that would seem to put all knowledge in the same boat. Émile Durkheim's theory made culturally determined knowledge the model of all knowledge, and it has sometimes been taken to authorize a view that reality, including physical reality, is a social construct dependent on particular cultural conventions (Durkheim and Mauss [1903] 2017). The remark that biological reality is most fundamental to health scientists and clinicians because of their ideological bias tallies with that relativist view. The psychiatrist and anthropologist Arthur Kleinman, however, does not consider biological facts to be purely conventional (1980: 41).

To explain why someone holds a particular belief does not necessarily mean explaining it away or showing that it is somehow dubious or ill founded. Indeed, the idea of a social construction of reality implies that we should try to investigate how people came to hold their views, the social influences that have shaped them, as well as the content of those ideas. The circumstances that have led one person to know about thermometers and another not to are contingent, historical, or accidental; they are not relevant to the epistemological question of whether it is possible to know what somebody's temperature is. Whether a person has measured his or her temperature is also a matter of historical fact, but it is not a contingent matter that what the thermometer measures is the body temperature of that person in degrees.

I am conscious of belaboring a point. Nearly everyone assumes that a commonsense, objective reality exists. There would be no reason to harp on this point if there were no skeptics. But the influence of skeptical philosophies of knowledge lies behind some of the critiques of medicine in medical anthropology. Our knowledge of the world depends, of course, on our faculties for perceiving it. Bats flying in the dark hear things we cannot, bees finding flowers in the sun see things we cannot; their abilities must seem mysterious or magical until we learn that bats perceive echoes above a pitch audible to humans or that sunlight gets polarized and determines how bees dance. All our experience and knowledge reflect a particular endowment of senses, capacities adapted for solving some kinds of problem but not all, weaving a certain mental fabric (Popper 1972: 71–72, 257–61). Our unaided perception of the world has evident limits and particularities. Things will stay hidden from us and thus cannot become data or facts for us until we invent some means to identify them. This means that our knowledge of the world depends also on the historical events and discoveries that have provided us with the means to know it.

There is also variation in what people pay attention to. We perceive the world selectively. We give it meaning by relating what we perceive to our understanding and past experience. The intensity of the sensation of pain does not follow automatically from the extent or nature of an injury. Fear of implications for the future may intensify pain felt by the surgical patient or, by contrast, the hope and chance to escape the risk of death may diminish an injured soldier's awareness of pain. Henry Beecher's studies on pain and its relief (1959) have shown the power of ideas about the meaning of a situation to modify the experience of it. Mark Zborowski (1952) described differences in the response to pain of people of Jewish, Italian, Irish, or "Old American" extraction. He attributed these differences to cultural attitudes—concern with immediately relieving pain versus a desire to know its cause and the implications it might hold for future illness; a desire for sympathy and company; values set on silent fortitude, self-reliance, and so on. Pain, like fear and anxiety, is open to many influences. Its subjective reality cannot be denied by reference to facts. The experience of illness is what the assumptions and constructions held by a particular person in a particular cultural milieu help to make it, that is, its subjective reality. However, the disease, as distinct from the experience of it, is not a subjective matter.

Observation is theory-impregnated in the sense that it is selective and influenced by ideas about what is relevant. In a larger sense, we are bound to observe selectively. Theories, whether they are explicit or not, will guide what we take to be relevant in deciding for or against something. We use a thermometer to measure the fever of sickness but not to measure how cold hatred is or how hot passion is.

Other views of illness illustrate the variety of cultural views. Whether or not some condition should be called illness is more a matter of interpretation rather than stark disagreement. There are some things we would not regard as illness that other societies do, and vice versa. For instance, Gananath Obeyesekere (1976: 207–15) describes "the way that

Ayurvedic conceptions create diseases that could hardly exist in a different belief system," an example being a class of illnesses that affect men and women through *dhatu* loss, as in the loss of semen through nocturnal emission. Then again, Marjorie Topley (1970: 421–37) reports that some women from Kowloon, Hong Kong, regard measles as an inevitable, natural, and necessary part of growing up. The child must cleanse its system of a hot poison passed from the mother's womb into the child. The poison erupts in "pustules" and thus corrects the imbalance of hot and cold. Measles may be a dangerous transitory process, a crisis, just as childbirth may be, but Kowloon women do not consider it to be an illness. Rather, they treat it more as a rite of passage, although it may involve medical treatment and complications just as childbirth may (Kleinman 1980: 87, 93). People's judgment about whether they are ill or not may also differ because they have never experienced what it is like to have better health, so they may accept a condition—say, lassitude from anemia—as something normal, knowing no alternative.

However, the striking cultural variation lies in how people explain the causes of illness and how they treat it rather than in basic disagreements about whether some condition is an illness. They direct attention to different aspects of the illness and the circumstances surrounding it. In almost any account of illness, some of the underlying assumptions are apparent. For instance, Rauit villagers gave scant notice to bodily signs and symptoms—the clinical features by which we usually diagnose an illness. They put cases of all the following diseases or conditions in a single category: acute renal failure, arthritis, congestive heart failure, pneumonia, perirectal abscess, diarrhea, common cold, aches in hip and thigh. This was a category that distinguished the type of illness by making an inference about its spiritual cause rather than deducing it from the signs or symptoms manifested or reported by the sufferer. Such a classification limits the possibilities of discovering regularities of nature in producing diseases. If the Gnai were to try to predict the outcome on the basis of past experience, they would have to find features common to congestive heart failure, acute renal failure, and the common cold.

With any classification of illness, we can inquire into the principles on which it is based, the assumptions it makes, and the information it conveys. The Gnau do not assume that examining bodily signs and symptoms will reveal the cause of illness; they are simply not concerned with classifying illnesses by clinical features. What matters to them in serious illness is finding out the cause so they will know what to do to treat it. Therefore, they distinguish between kinds of illness in terms of their causes—this, to them, is diagnosis, as it often is for us, too, although in different terms and on the basis of different kinds of evidence. A diagnosis in Gnau terms will convey almost no information about the bodily condition of the person who is ill. While I lived among them, I had to find out what features they paid attention to in order to discern the cause. Understanding these features helped answer the question of what information was conveyed in their diagnoses.

Yet the Gnau, like all other people, start to speak of illness only after recognizing some change in a person. There is nothing to explain, no reason to classify by cause or sign, or to treat illness except when something has been recognized as requiring a response, whether explanation or treatment. The values we all set on life, self, our capacities to move, see, taste, think, and so on provide an intelligible reason why people everywhere tend to create various classifications and explanations around a common core of experience in illness. "Of all the objects in the world, the human body has a peculiar status: it is not only possessed by the person who has it, it also possesses and constitutes him" (Miller [1978] 2011: 14). A person is conscious of the body as him- or herself: it is the self. For this reason, I have argued that "illness is a distinctive form of misfortune sensed by the sick person in ways which other misfortunes, like his house burning down, are not. And since some diseases destroy or maim the individual, having the power to alter or abolish a living identified member of that society, it seems to me unlikely that any society would fail to distinguish at least part of the whole field of disease from other misfortunes" (G. Lewis 1975: 356). There may be uncertainties about the boundaries between illness and nonillness, difficulties of recognition and calculation, but a common core remains. The significance attached to it is another matter. As Karl Jaspers put it,

> Whether illness is understood in religious or moral terms as guilt or atonement, or assessed as some derailment of nature ("had God so foreseen he would not have created the world") or whether it is interpreted as a testing challenge to the self or a constant sign of human powerlessness, a memento of human insignificance—these are all mere expressions of the general concern and are not in any sense insight. By interpretations such as these man reassures himself about this really unbearable fact; they may help some individual patients to a self-evaluation, console them or emphasise their misfortune. (Jaspers [1913] 1963: 778)

The attitude someone adopts will reflect cultural assumptions about what sort of state illness is. They are not necessarily single or exclusive. Jaspers ([1913] 1963: 414–27, 773–90) traced how people give existential significance to illness, how they confront their condition and have to interpret it. He wanted to know its content, portent, to bring out the meaning of the facts. Is it meaningful or meaningless? Is the illness seen as part of the self ("This is just how I am"), something one is tied to as inextricably as one's age, sex, race, body? What has nature added, what comes from within? What has been sent or added by something else or someone else? Does sickness come by one's own fault, on purpose, by design, or by accident?

This aim of understanding the personal significance of an illness is clearly different from the aim of classifying it. The metaphysical questions asked above are certainly not obtrusive in every illness. But in general, they create attitudes toward illness and make a frame for interpreting it. The sufficiency of an explanation depends on what questions are asked. It is only by confining the questions about poor health to those concerning the body that we may think we know enough when, for instance, we find that someone has tuberculosis and we know what kinds of processes may follow from it. If we alter our approach to ask why that person fell ill then and there, much more must be answered: poverty, poor food, inadequate housing, and pollution may all have played a part in bringing about the illness, making any search for a full explanation endless. In illness, a desire for simplicity, to find a single or ultimate cause for it, has often misled people to rest content with explanations that are far from complete; many factors extrinsic and intrinsic to the body, not single causes, contribute to the occurrence of illness. Individuals faced with ill health must circumscribe what specifically they want to find out about it. The value to them of answers will often turn on the relevance of the factors to treating or controlling the situation. Ordinarily, it is the particular, not the general, that matters in an illness.

The traditional biomedical view depends on three kinds of criteria: (1) the patient's subjective feelings; (2) the manifest signs and symptoms that the doctor observes and examines; (3) occult signs that have to be detected by special means, such as radiography or clinical laboratory tests. But there are many other ways to classify a sick person. We may view the person as an organism coping with its environment; as a member of society filling certain roles; or as an individual personality responding to his or her culture. We may classify patients according to the diseases that makes them ill; the extent to which their personal functioning is limited by their illness; the symptoms they are experiencing; the length of time they have had the disease and are likely to have in the future; or the course of their illness, that is, whether it is chronic and of disabling intensity, progressive, remitting, or recovering (Shepherd et al. 1966: 18, quoting Gruenberg 1963). The variety of criteria is useful for different purposes. The attention given to the meaning of illness by many recent medical anthropological writers takes the enterprise in one direction, the semantic one. Horacio Fabrega (1974) reviewed the implications of biomedical notions of disease, pointing out that diseases, as defined by orthodox medical indicators, are imperfectly correlated with social behaviors. He proposes viewing disease as the independent variable and looking at whether and in what respects behavior varies directly in response to it. We have a relatively precise framework for describing biomedical structures and functions and how they break down. However, as he notes, our judgments on biomedical standards, norms, and cut-off points between health and disease have been derived mainly from studies of people living in urban industrialized settings. We should be cautious about attributing timeless, universal validity to them. To extend them to people in different settings or other periods may entail the questionable supposition that what are normal standards in urban populations must also be so for them.

The subjectivity of illness

Michel de Montaigne, who clearly stressed the power of ideas about illness to affect one's experience of it, stated:

> How many people have not been made ill by the mere force of imagination. . . . But even though knowledge could really do what they say, blunt the point and lessen the bitterness of the misfortunes that attend us, what more does it do than what ignorance does, much more simply and manifestly? The philosopher Pyrrho, in peril of a great storm at sea, could offer his companions no better example to follow than the serenity of a pig, their fellow-traveller, which was looking at the tempest with perfect equanimity. . . . In my opinion, that faculty [imagination] is all-important, at least more so than any other. The most grievous and the most common ills are those that fancy puts upon me. I like this Spanish saying from several points of view, *God defend me from myself.* (Montaigne [1588] 1927: 585, 566)

People do not make up all ideas of illness by themselves; most knowledge of illness is learned from others. We tend to take whatever is taught or prevails in our society for our own beliefs. The Gnau have their own ideas about human development, growth, and susceptibility to illness or harm at different stages of life (G. Lewis 1980: 134–85). Food taboos are one facet of this. To them, few types of food are neutral: food is not just food or always food to all persons. Nearly all types have valences that make their use right or wrong for certain kinds of people, for people in particular relationships, or for people in particular situations. Their notions about the presence of spirits, their attachments to places, their movements, their temper, and their interests animate the landscape through which people move, facing varied hazards to health. Spirits are part of the Gnau world, although they are neither directly visible nor quite predictable. When people work in their gardens, for instance, they are cautious and observe proper behavior because the spirits are present, watchful—and indeed, after certain events like planting—activated and aware.

> In cutting things down they see themselves as cutting down things which belong to certain spirits, or in which these spirits have a protective jealous interest. The same sense of a possessive jealous interest, of things that belong to certain spirits, goes with crops ready for picking or harvesting, and prepared sago. When cutting is involved the imputation is that spirits are annoyed or angered at the injury or destruction of their things; when things are taken, the imputation is of their anger or spite at the loss of what they hold dear, protect or benefit and hoard. . . . But these ideas are part of the complex ambivalent views they have about the power of spirits which also has its other face—that of benefit, securing crop growth and abundance, aiding people's efforts to produce their food. . . . The benefits must be sought and so the risks must be run. They are not wholly predictable and avoidable risks, even though people carefully observe proper prescribed forms of behaviour in gardening. (G. Lewis 1975: 314)

The Gnau move in an environment that is, as it were, variously magnetized by the concentration of spirit powers. Place is one of the coordinates of presence and danger and so is time. For how long does an action or event carry risk? The interval between an event and choosing it to explain someone's illness reveals something of how they think about the risks involved in certain actions and how they remember people and events. Trivial actions may become significant only by coincidence; however, certain deaths, certain quarrels, or certain rituals in the past may be recalled to explain an illness long afterward, thus showing how they stayed in the mind. In this perspective, illness comes to resemble accidents, natural misfortunes, bad luck, mischance. The risks in external things are simply there, intrinsic, and hard to predict. The danger may be recognizable only later because it has been revealed by the illness. People can hardly be blamed for it. The external field (places, powers, activities) interacts with an internal field (the person, his or her particular strengths and vulnerabilities).

These ideas are bound to make a discussion of illness between Gnau villagers sound highly circumstantial to alien ears. The conversation seems wayward, attention to detail appears desultory. They can pick out the possible relevance of certain actions and do not need to make explicit the assumptions behind their deductions. On the surface, the discussion sounds like a description of recent events with a jumble of items of observation, but it can also be taken as more than a statement of plain facts. A convalescent woman visited her married daughter the week before she had a relapse: they may recall the visit but leave unsaid that the point of recalling it is that the lineage spirits of her daughter's husband in his hamlet would have noticed her weak condition and may have struck her. A newborn baby dies: people may mention that the baby's grandmother had come to see the mother and baby straight from cutting some bamboo at a clump located in a particular place. On the surface, this is simple narrative about recent events; it is also the evidence from which the Gnau deduce the cause. Talk about recent events is shot through with potential implications to listeners who are alerted by illness. Such conversations form the content of Gnau case histories, answering their typical questions: What has someone done to become ill? What did she eat to make her ill? What struck him that he doesn't know about? Do you think it might be a spirit, or what, or is he just sick? The form of a case history stems from their assumptions.

If there are general grounds for doubt about how to justify beliefs, medical knowledge is not spared them. The relativist position applied to biomedicine has had some support in medical anthropology.

A recent article of mine (Young 1981) . . . argues that all knowledge of society and sickness is socially determined, and that anthropologists cannot legitimately claim access to demystified facts. What they can claim, and what would set their accounts of sickness off from those of others, is a critical understanding of how medical facts are *predetermined* by the process through which they are conventionally produced in clinics, research settings, etc. Thus, the task at hand is not simply to demystify knowledge, but to critically examine the social conditions of knowledge production. (Young 1982: 277)

The relativist argument is not particularly directed at medicine. But if the discussion should conclude with a clear decision, then that judgment would presumably also apply to medicine. Observation shows that people may be sincerely convinced of a truth not believed in a different society. Durkheim ([1912] 1968) argued that rules and categories belong to a society and reflect its social structure. People accept the essential beliefs of their society because nearly everyone in their community do so. We are prone to believe what we are told when it comes to us from a respected authority. Society and culture, due to our upbringing and dependence on them, have the power to establish our beliefs and what we take to be true. At one extreme, it might be argued that belief results from social pressures.

To argue that belief is wholly relative to culture, however, would deny a place for objective knowledge; it would grant no privilege to certain systems of knowledge (e.g., physics or medicine) as forms of knowledge that approach objective facts. Anyone wedded to this view in its extreme form (i.e., that truth is relative to the society) must face a question: Why does he or she believe that? It is like the problem of the Cretan who says all men are liars. If I believe it, I cannot argue a special case for my assertion being true in the nonrelative sense unless I exempt my own belief from my theory about all other beliefs. As Ernest Geller stated:

Relativism is interesting at least in that it takes what others consider to be a problem, and uses it as a solution. The problem: truth is different on the other side of Pyrenees—so how can it be truth? The relativist turns this upside down: for him it is not so much a problem, but rather a solution. Truth *is* that which is locally believed: it is tied to locality, time, space or culture, as are dress, manners, or cookery. (Gellner 1979: 47)

Nothing can be universally true by the normative view of relativism: there are no universal independent criteria. Gellner scorns that view: it is no guide for anyone. It is like an unhinged road sign that we could push in any and every direction. "No sane man would follow such an unhinged signpost and no sane man should suppose that he can derive guidance from relativism" (Gellner 1979: 49).

Why then should anyone hold on to the relativist view? Ideas accepted in another society might seem to an outside observer transparently false, but the ideas were not foolish or easy to falsify in the contexts in which they were used. The observer wrongly presumed to know what question or problem was relevant, what the criteria or the rules of evidence were. Language was critical. For Edward Sapir,

> Human beings do not live in the objective world alone, nor alone in the world of social activity as ordinarily understood, but are very much at the mercy of the particular language which has become the medium of expression for their society. . . . The fact of the matter is that the "real world" is to a large extent unconsciously built up on the language habits of the group. No two languages are ever sufficiently similar to be considered as representing the same social reality. The worlds in which different societies live are distinct worlds, not merely the same world with different labels attached. (Sapir 1929: 209)

If Sapir were right, each culture must have its own vision of reality, created and expressed in its particular language. This would mean, in effect, that people are bewitched by language, living on a Prospero's isle of shared meanings, where the spell of language cannot be broken (Hollis 1977: 163; Gellner 1979: 53). But anthropologists in the field face the problem in reverse: they cannot enter the isle or discover the fabric of the inhabitants' vision until they take on the local language as their own.

For Peter Winch, too, ideas of reality depend on language; each language belongs to a mode or form of social life with its own view of reality, its own rules on criteria for judgments about truth and reality.[1] He objects that E. E. Evans-Pritchard was "wrong, and crucially wrong, in his attempt to characterise the scientific in terms of that which is in accord with objective reality" (Winch 1970: 80). If Evans-Pritchard wished to go beyond merely registering that a Zande believer in magic has a different conception of reality from a member of a scientific culture and to argue that the scientific conception agrees with what reality actually is while the magical conception does not, Winch (1970: 80–82) opposes

---

1. Winch seems to take an extreme relativist position (see Gellner 1979: 144–45), although he does not endorse that reading of his views (Winch 1970: 249–59).

him on the grounds that the data needed to experimentally test a scientific hypothesis must use criteria that only makes sense to someone who is already conversant with scientific activity and accepts its methods.

This is one path to a skeptical position toward biomedicine. It is based on the view that conceptions of reality are rooted in and depend on language and society. But many reject it (e.g., Hacker 1972: 176; Hollis 1970, 1977: 143–64, 1982; Lukes 1970, 1982). They point out that we cannot begin to try to understand the meaning of utterances in an unknown language without assuming, first, that the other speakers perceive the world more or less as we do (then we can try to relate their utterances to some equivalent of ours and to the world) and second, that the speakers are rational beings (whose beliefs are, on the whole, rationally connected and whose utterances express those beliefs). "Some overlap in concepts and percepts is a necessary condition of successful translation. The sine qua non is a bridgehead of true assertions about a shared reality" (Hollis 1970: 216).

These assumptions about an independent objective reality and their basic rational conceptual commitments provide the only basis from which we can begin to understand the language and beliefs of people from another culture. How can translation occur without there being the same facts of the world described in the two languages? We must assume that people in the other culture are trying to make themselves understood, just as we must impute rationality to them. Indeed, we should impute rationality wherever possible, allowing irrationality when it is necessary to do so but with the proviso that irrational beliefs need further special explanation.

The relativity of scientific knowledge: Kuhn's argument

Another influential critical analysis of science deserves attention: Thomas Kuhn's (1970) analysis of change in scientific methods and theories. Kuhn argues that the effect of a scientific education is to initiate young scientists into a particular community. The community has a tradition, a shared culture. Learners are shown typical examples of the problems and solutions that characterize that particular branch of science. These establish a model of proper methods for them to emulate. The process of learning which methods are normal in that branch resembles entry into any new community, where newcomers must assimilate its traditions and rules. But from time to time in the course of normal work in some established branch of science, abnormalities occur that are hard to explain. The gathering force of obtrusive doubts and questions may impel members to face a crisis of confidence in what they thought they knew. They rethink their assumptions and accepted arguments, and out of this they conceive a major shift in theory.

Kuhn called this a shift of paradigm. It alters the problems addressed as well as the methods needed for solving them. "And as the problems change, so, often, does the standard that distinguishes a real scientific solution from a mere metaphysical speculation, word game, or mathematical play. The normal scientific tradition that emerges from a scientific revolution is not only incompatible but often actually incommensurable with that which has gone before" (Kuhn 1970: 103). When he writes that competing viewpoints are incommensurable, Kuhn means they have failed to make complete contact because they disagree about the list of problems to be resolved. When competing paradigms become incommensurable, "Proponents of competing paradigms practice their trades in different worlds" (Kuhn 1970: 150; see also 111–35). Shifts of opinion are clear in the history of medicine. Are they comparable? Leprosy is a problem for medicine now. In the Bible and in the Middle Ages, it was treated as a theological problem or a ritual matter for the priests. The shift from one view to the other involved medicalizing the issue, which took a long time. It serves as an example of differences of opinion or outright disagreements about the nature of a problem to be solved. In many parts of the world, there have been periods of competition between medical and religious views of the problems of witchcraft and sorcery.

Kuhn's analysis of scientific revolutions is bound to appeal to the relativist: consensus identifies what the scientific problems are. Teachers and prevailing authorities establish the consensus among incommensurable paradigms; when the paradigm changes, so, too, do views of the world, what is real, what the problem is. But in a postscript (1970: 198–207), Kuhn states that those who accuse him of arguing that science and the choice of paradigm are subjective—that there is no recourse to reasons for supporting one over another—or who claim he holds a relativistic standpoint are seriously misconstruing his position. He does not doubt that scientific development like biological development, is a unidirectional and irreversible process. "Later scientific theories are better than earlier ones for solving puzzles in the often quite different environments to which they are applied. That is not a relativist's position and it displays the sense in which I am a convinced believer in scientific progress" (Kuhn 1970: 205).

Why bother here with such grand issues?

By now I owe the reader an explanation for this excursion into fields that are not mine. Work in medical anthropology confronts anyone who undertakes it with striking evidence of the relativity of views on illness. An anthropologist cannot fail to be aware of the possibility of ethnocentric bias. But acknowledging this is not the same as adopting the relativist stance that "truth can be no other thing than that which satisfies some local criteria and that there are no universal independent criteria by which a confrontation between local ones could be judged" (Gellner 1979: 48). To take the position of the normative relativist and assert that truth is always relative means endorsing any and cultural views. But the issue of the relativist position and the status of medical knowledge is not solely theoretical: people's health and lives are on the line. If we regard truth as whatever happens to be believed locally, then we have no good reason for judging between alternative cultural theories of illness—and thus no good reason for choosing to intervene or provide treatment.

Relativity applied to illness has three strands: the first is descriptive and empirical—we describe the differences of view we find; the second is analytic and philosophical—we may question the nature of this knowledge, the epistemological status of what we or others believe; the third is normative—we judge the justification for different views, say what we think is true or what we think ought to be done. A concern for forms of social life and different worlds of socially constructed meanings is understandable. But in the study of sickness and treatment, we cannot evade questions of how theory relates to fact. We must admit the possibility that some theories about illness are false or lead to responses that produce worse outcomes than others; we must reckon with the awful knowledge that the deaths of some people were escapable yet were not escaped. In a brief picture of the conditions and quality of life in sixteenth- and seventeenth-century England, Keith Thomas (1972) describes the experience of ordinary people, particularly the poor, with chronic poor health, frequent diseases, the early deaths of many of their children, and so on. He points out that they had no other standards by which to expect less misery or to see their lot as piteous; they simply had to accept what they experienced. Something like that situation still prevails in many parts of the world. It is the situation of, for instance, a woman who has been anemic nearly all her life. She accepts her lassitude as something that is normal for her. Only after her anemia is remedied can she realize that it was not a given.

Relativists are spared possible moral pressures that might provoke them to judge or act in relation to what people think or do in another culture. They can try to understand and analyze what others think and abstain from judgment. This would justify inaction or indifference. But if sometimes they see other people doing things that make a sickness worse, it is not so easy to say nothing and do nothing. Someone who would adopt the subjectivist or the normative relativist arguments to justify passivity or noninterference is challenged by Bernard Williams, who states, "I am only saying that it cannot be a consequence of the nature of morality itself that no society ought ever to interfere with another, or that individuals from one society confronted with the practices of another ought, if rational, react with acceptance. To draw these consequences is the characteristic (and inconsistent) step of vulgar relativism" (Williams 1975: 39).

The Fore people of New Guinea (Lindenbaum 1979) suffered from a highly distinctive and inevitably fatal disease that they called *kuru*. They maintained it was caused by sorcery and tried all sorts of ways to treat it and to control the sorcery. They kept failing. After much investigation, an atypical virus that spread in a certain way was discovered to cause the disease. No action against sorcerers or against magical bundles could have stopped it. The facts *do* have implications for the fate of theories. A concern with concepts and the problem of translating them from one language into those of another may disguise what is really been at issue here: the relationship between theories and facts. Individuals, people, cultures, languages, cities, and villages do not live such wholly self-contained lives that they never face the challenge of alternative ideas or theories or the problems of choice between them. For Gellner (1979: 48–50), this is the most devastating objection to relativism. People all meet challenges of translation, of new concepts, of judgment and choice. They manage to surmount problems of translation because communication itself involves sharing some perceptions and some basic logic. Otherwise, we could not even tell we were in conflict.

CHAPTER SEVEN

Normality and values

To designate something to be a disease is at bottom a moral un-
dertaking, with moral consequences. It involves declaring that some
things are undesirable and influencing the life of the person said to
possess them by singling him out as bearing an undesirable attribute.
Because it is a fundamentally moral task, I suggest, the designation
of disease does not rest on a scientific foundation. . . . Technically,
medicine is equipped to demonstrate that some signs, symptoms and
complaints run a given course or lead to certain consequences. That
the consequence is bad or undesirable is for all men to judge, not
merely for the physician. (Freidson 1970: 342)

Scientific medicine emerges from a background of folk ideas about
illness. During most of our historical past, as for most people in the
world now, scientific views of disease played little or no part. Biomedicine achieves its peculiar autonomy by maintaining the objective character of its scientific knowledge: the facts of sickness are as they are whether someone knows about them or not, whether anybody likes them or
not. But a critic might argue that talk of scientific medicine camouflages
a practice that is subjective and evaluative. The critical questions concern
standards of normality and actual practice. The medical scientist cannot suppose his or her current theories constitute some privileged final
state of knowledge to be the lasting arbiter and authority for our standards. Current knowledge is continually being changed, corrected, and
improved. The aim of scientific medicine may be objective knowledge

free from cultural bias. But this task is incomplete, full of difficulty and complexity. In his innovative chapter on medicine as a social institution, Talcott Parsons (1951: chap. 10) proposed a sociological approach to illness. This approach holds that members of a society may look at sickness as forms of deviance that were potentially disruptive to the functioning of society; they may also consider medicine to be the means to control such deviance. Indeed, medical authorities may assume their own standards and experience represent what is normal.

Stephen Kunitz (1983b) suggested a subtle version of this line of argument in his analysis of the historical roots and ideological function of disease concepts in three primary-care specialties. His main point was that patterns of disease prevalence and techniques of investigation can influence the ways doctors think about disease. As infectious diseases waned or came under control, degenerative diseases were left more exposed and became more obtrusive as problems. Infectious diseases were easier than degenerative diseases to view as specific disease entities. The degenerative ones were more suited to physiological explanation, since they revealed the effects of wear and tear, modes of life, maladaptation, and stress. It was more difficult to restrict their investigation to the laboratory. To understand and treat them, researchers had to take account of the habits, work, and family situations of the patients. This required a broader view of disease. Social and psychological aspects of illness crept back into concepts of disease, at least in some fields. Those attracted to some medical specialties would be more likely to share an "expansionist" view of what is relevant to understand the illnesses they deal with. That is, they would be more likely to include social and psychological factors of deteriorating health as part of the medical field because they must take them into account, for example, in pediatrics, general practice, and community medicine. Practitioners in these fields also claim that they have expertise in family, social, or developmental problems and that this may properly be called a medical expertise. In short, they are likely to hold expansionist views of the province of their medical specialty.

Illness as deviance

Eliot Freidson (1970: 205–358) considered the actual circumstances of practice and explained why so often in medicine the desire to be scientific outstrips performance. Someone in a consulting profession is subject to pressures and temptations from which a researcher, pursuing "pure science," may be spared. From the sociologist's perspective, illness is a form of social deviance which people in our society *think* has a biophysical cause and requires biophysical treatment. The sociologist is concerned with social reality. If someone is thought to be sick, various social reactions may follow from that belief, whether or not the differences perceived in the patient's state or behavior in fact have the biophysical basis attributed to them. As Freidson put it, "In the sense that medicine has the authority to label one person's complaint as an illness and another's complaint not, medicine may be said to be engaged *in the creation of illness as a social state which a human being may assume*" (1970: 205).

One strand of his study involved identifying the social facts that follow from the recognition of an illness; another entailed investigating the role of medicine in making or defining an illness. If a certain disease has been identified, then certain social consequences follow. What matters about this recognition is not the factual truth of the assertion that certain changes result from this disease but the fact that people believe they do and respond accordingly.

It is no surprise that people everywhere pay attention to sickness and relate it to values. Behavior or attributes that people disapprove of according to their prevailing cultural standards have indeed sometimes been considered signs of disease or medical abnormality. Attitudes past and present reveal shifts between confident moral and medical views— for example, with regard to alcoholism, suicide, and homosexuality. The possibility of conflating medical with moral issues has allowed for a variety of abuses. In the USSR, for example, political dissidents were judged (with certification by psychiatrists there) to be mentally ill (Wynn 1983). Jaroslav Hašek satirized such political misuse of medicine in *The good soldier Svejk*. The job of the army doctors in the hospital where soldier Svejk was sent was to find out and declare men fit for military service because their country needed them.

> In those great times the army doctors took unusual pains to drive the devil of sabotage out of the malingerers and restore them to the bosom of the army. Various degrees of torture had been introduced for malingerers and suspected malingerers, such as consumptives, rheumatics, people with hernia, kidney disease, typhus, diabetes, pneumonia and other illnesses . . . There were stalwart men who endured all five degrees of torture and let themselves by carried off to the military cemetery in a simple coffin. But there were also pusillanimous souls who, when they reached the stage of the enema, declared that they

were now well and desired nothing better than to march off to the trenches with the next march battalion. (Hašek 1974: 62)

Evaluation is inherent in the notion of illness

Freidson's (1970: 205–52) point was that medicine uses normative criteria to pick out what it will pay attention to, and this involves an evaluation of what is normal, proper, and desirable. Evaluation is as inherent in the notion of illness as it is in notions of morality. He argued that "medicine is a moral enterprise like law and religion seeking to uncover and control things that it considers undesirable" (1970: 208). The characteristic social meaning ascribed to illness is that the changes—the deviance—noted in the sick person—the deviant—are not thought to arise through any deliberate choice by the actor. Rather, they are thought of as essentially beyond his immediate control. In principle, the sick person is not held to be responsible for his deviance. The illness is condemned rather than the person who suffers it.

The thrust of Freidson's argument goes from the first observation "that illness can be analyzed as both biological and social deviance" (1970: 211) toward the position that

disapproved behavior is more and more coming to be given the meaning of illness requiring treatment, rather than of crime requiring punishment, victimization requiring compensation, or sin requiring patience and grace . . . With the growth of medical science, more and more human behavior began to seem to stem from specific "causes" over which prayer, human choice, and will had little control. And medical discoveries allowed the successful treatment of such problems. From this core of scientific discovery grew a vague halo of authority that encouraged the wholesale extension of medical definitions of deviance into areas of behavior previously managed by religion and law. (Freidson 1970: 248)

He directed the force of his critique at the spurious "medicalization" of certain behaviors, situating the tendency in a historical context in the interpretation of mental illness, alcoholism, and, more vaguely, of attributes associated with poverty and crime.

The profession of medicine has extended the sweep of the label of illness. Physicians act as moral entrepreneurs. There is good reason for the sociologist to examine what they do rather than take on trust the label

"illness" wherever it is applied through consensus by medical professionals. This would be unwise in the light of history, which testifies to the
past errors of misguided "science," suggesting that "today's unwitting,
unstated assumptions will not all survive" (Freidson 1970: 210). The diseases of modern medicine are an extremely heterogeneous collection in
which not all have "the unambiguously scientific status of a compound
fracture" (1970: 211).

A consulting profession and the practice of pure science

As a consulting profession, medicine is committed to treating rather
than merely defining and studying people's ills. In the everyday practice
of professional medicine, questions of reward or the urgency of making
a diagnosis or demands for treatment expose practitioners to pressures
and temptations that may compromise a critical objective stance. Doctors sometimes have to make decisions without enough evidence; furthermore, when some matter is urgent, they may be justified in acting on
incomplete evidence.

Do medical criteria of normality involve value judgments? Some argue that such judgments are ultimately subjective or emotive. According
to this view, in disputes about morals, we move from sorting out questions of fact or logic to resolving them and then to a last phase when "all
that is at stake is a clash of feelings or commands or intuitions or arbitrary postulates" (Bambrough 1979: 135). In matters of right and wrong,
we may still disagree even though we speak the same language and agree
about the facts of the case.

Such a sharp separation between fact and value, however, cannot
always be made; the borders are not always clear-cut. For instance, if
I describe a clock and say it often breaks down, my true description
of it comes close to supplying you with my evaluation of it (see Williams 1976: 52–61). When standards are clear or when they are subject
to strict social conventions, factual description may amount to evaluation. Words that seem to be value terms turn effectively into descriptive terms: a "good" clock keeps time and does not break down. Similarly, when the physiological functions of an organ or system are clearly
known, a factual description of how it is working veers close to passing a
verdict on whether it is in "good" condition or not.

The next difficulty is the role of emotions in moral judgments and
in medicine. Moral judgments express something about the person who

makes the judgment as well as about the thing judged or evaluated. Two aspects of this obviously affect the recognition of illness: emotions are almost inevitably bound up in responses to sickness; they may even pose obstacles to the objective assessment of the sickness. There are strong evolutionary and adaptive reasons for linking malfunction and the sensations that accompany it (like pain, nausea, weakness) with responses that lie within the range of emotions like dislike, hatred, fear, and desire to escape. It is no surprise that diseases should provoke strong feelings of suffering, such as pain, misery, disgust, anxiety, or abhorrence. Nor is it surprising that these strong negative feelings and the impulses of sympathy and concern for others should have contributed to the elaboration of complex moral attitudes to sickness.

However, social deviance cannot be identified with disease. Samuel Butler satirized the folly of mixing them up for the readers of his imagined *Erewhon* ([1872] 1945), where disorders and bodily failures were punished but misbehavior and criminal acts were considered as more or less severe fits of immorality to be treated with solicitude. No doubt some criminal acts may result from mental disorders, but it would be rash to equate criminality with these disorders and the cure with inculcating a willingness to keep the law (Wootton 1959). Conformity to social rules is not always a sign of health or mental health. Not all ways of life nor all social institutions are equally desirable and salutary. Consider the following example of unemployment masquerading as sickness. The rate of growth in the population of Mauritius was becoming a serious problem by 1952. This was partly the result of bringing malaria under control, which allowed Mauritius to halve its infant mortality rate in less than five years. As children grew up, mass unemployment among them became one of many unintended consequences of the demographic changes brought about by medical science. There was no public scheme of financial assistance or relief for the unemployed or their families, but those who were sick or certified to be sick were eligible for public assistance. In practice, the system worked to encourage both large families and official illnesses: the larger the family, the larger the cash relief if the worker was certified to be sick or only "fit for light work." This incentive inevitably encouraged people to resort to medical services of all kinds. Richard Titmuss found that

> the heavy consumption of drugs is in part attributable to the public assistance system. A structure of values has been created which (1) increasingly makes it important to be regarded as sick, (2) gives relief

in cash or in kind, but generally refuses to provide modern drugs and injections, and (3) this leads the individual to the moneylender, the private doctor, and the chemists' shop to buy drugs privately. These practices reinforce each other and, during the last ten years of falling mortality, have been accompanied by a tenfold rise in the cost of public assistance. This increasingly heavy burden on the island's budget is, however, due to unemployment rather than to a genuine rise in morbidity. A rapidly growing problem of unemployment is masquerading as sickness which is being partially relieved under public and charitable poor-law systems. (Titmuss 1962: 210)

Thus, if the ability to hold a job is to be taken as a sign of social competence and therefore of health, then judgments about the health or disability of individuals may depend on the state and saturation of the employment market. Someone could be called "healthy" one moment and "sick" the next because the employment market changes. Thus, the definition of illness as a failure of social competence becomes circular.

Fine phrases cannot, however, obscure the fact that adjustment means adjustment to a particular culture or to a particular set of institutions; and that to conceive adjustment and maladjustment in medical terms is in effect to identify health with the ability to come to terms with that culture or with those institutions—be they totalitarian methods of government, the dingy culture of an urban slum, the contemporary English law of marriage, or what I have elsewhere called the standards of an "acquisitive, competitive, hierarchical, envious" society. (Wootton 1959: 218; see also 265)

Adjustment in this sense is, as Roger Bastide noted (1972: 58) a version of the ancient adage: *vox populi, vox Dei*. People tend to consider their own ways to be the standard for normality. They want to call those who differ "abnormal"; they find strange customs unhealthy or repugnant. This is, of course, the vulgar tendency of prejudice, but it also appears in mental health professions. The social side of psychiatry is obtrusive at every point and has always been so.

Subjective reasons and the meaning-centered approach

Irving Hallowell ([1955] 1967: 253) was doing fieldwork among the Ojibwe when, one night, an elderly man became panic-stricken after he found a toad hopping inside his tent. He was unable to kill it at first because of his panic, but after much effort, he managed to do so. Then he spent part of the night with a flashlight searching for toads outside the tent, weighting down its edges with stones so none could get in, and stayed awake the rest of the night waiting for morning. The Ojibwa people that Hallowell knew in the 1920s and 1930s were still living as forest trappers. They were frightened of snakes, toads, and frogs, yet they did not fear wolves or bears. The snakes were not poisonous; the toads and frogs were harmless. But the Ojibwe feared them as creatures that might be associated with evil, used in magic, or have spirit owners who would use the creatures to creep up and do them harm. Even though the elderly man was a Christian, he told Hallowell about the malevolent attributes of toads, stories of monster toads, the taboos that, if broken, led to affliction by toads.

The contents of the elder's fears were molded by his culture, but it turned out there was more to them than that. Hallowell noticed that other Ojibwe teased the man about his fears, considering them to be excessive; he even saw another man pick up a toad and deliberately put it near the elder. The latter said that, as a boy, he had crushed a toad that shocked him by crawling up his leg inside his pants. A toad crawling over someone was considered to be retribution for breaking rules about telling myths. Outside observers, like Hallowell, face the problem of evaluating unfamiliar behaviors and attitudes. They may not be able at first to tell whether these represent abnormal reactions or a pattern considered normal in the culture. This example also reminds us that people within a society can discriminate the normal from exaggerated or abnormal responses.

We can grasp an actor's point of view, but that does not suffice. A cultural belief may provide a reason for why people act a certain way, but the cause of their beliefs is still unknown. If they give good reasons for expecting rain (black clouds are gathering), they explain both why they expect it and why they act as they do (such as carrying an umbrella). But the weaker and weaker their reasons for expecting rain (perhaps someone has thrown something in a sacred pool, portending death), the more we are reduced to explaining only why they act as they do but not why they expect rain or death. A rational person can reason rightly from false premises. We might say that he or she acts rationally, given their beliefs. A certain man may think he is a poached egg, so he goes to find a piece of buttered toast to sit on. Although we have found a reason for his *action*, as Martin Hollis points out (1977: chap. 6), we have not found one for his *belief*.

Purely subjective criteria may make all actions seem equally rational; purely subjective criteria may make us think we are sick. But we can have delusions about ourselves; physicians may make mistakes in diagnosis. And the assertions of people in other cultures about diseases can also be wrong. Hollis tells us not to be distracted by our habit of accepting objectively bad reasons as good-from-the-agent's-point-of-view to the point where we confuse the distance between the ideally rational and the ideally irrational.

At each level—the individual, the local community, the human species as a whole—we confront problems of normal standards. Western knowledge of biology and physiology is incomplete. Much is known about some physiological functions, which has depended partly on discovering suitable techniques of investigation. Suffering has been a spur to discovery. Changed patterns of disease, as Kunitz pointed out, have also changed how people think about disease and normal standards. This history of changes also shows that Western medicine has made some advances. Part of the confusion between social or moral judgments and biomedical criteria has been disentangled and made clear—but not all. The doubts of medicine are by no means all dispelled, especially in regard to psychiatric illnesses.

Diseases are not natural entities in the way that individual people or organisms are. The classification of disease represents an ordering of selected data about the ways in which people may be sick. Behind the classifications lie more specific theories about how the facts are interconnected. Biomedical criteria for classifying disease can provide a means to compare things seen as similar in relevant medical respects. Some facts about human diseases depend on circumstances; however, this does not necessarily mean they are arbitrary. "Normal" human standards are not easy to specify in global terms. Nevertheless, humans cannot change their biological constitutions as they change their clothes, their politics, or the environments in which they choose to live.

CHAPTER EIGHT

No simple definition

It is easy to think of disease with the model of infectious disease in mind, as an illness is caused by a specific entity: the germ. We name the disease and its cause by the same name. The false step comes next: the disease *is* its cause. But diphtheria is one sort of illness; diphtheria bacteria growing on a plate of agar in the laboratory are not a disease even though they can cause it. To distinguish between illnesses according to their causes, as many people do, reflects an appreciation of the significant problems to be faced. But the state of illness must be distinguished from its cause. People may say, for example, poverty is a cause of illness, but they do not therefore consider poverty itself to be an illness.

The English language is rich in words for illness: "sick," "ill," and "diseased" are all acceptable as opposites of "healthy." In ordinary speech, "sickness" and "health" are the broad inclusive terms. They lie at the ends of a continuum, but sickness is the member of the pair to which we give more marked attention. It demands attention in a way that health does not. Someone falls ill and then thinks of the previous state of health, now lost, that perhaps he or she had taken for granted.

It would be convenient if there were a simple criterion of sickness or health to match the clarity of the contrast in speech. Although we may speak of disease or illness in the singular, as though it were a unitary phenomenon, medical writing abounds with different kinds of diseases but gives no simple single definition of "disease." Karl Jaspers pointed this out clearly:

Medical science does not consist in elaborating these normal standards to arrive at a general concept of illness any more than it feels it should discover a single remedy for all its cases. The doctor's function rather consists in ascertaining what precise kind of state or event is presenting itself, on what it depends, how it proceeds and what will affect it. In the great variety of states and events called "disease" almost the only common factor is that disease implies something "harmful, unwanted and of an inferior character." (Jaspers [1913] 1963: 780)

In this respect, it is useful to recall what John Locke wrote in his *Essay concerning human understanding*:

I do not deny but nature, in the constant production of particular beings makes them not always new and various, but very much alike and of kin one to another: but I think it nevertheless true, that the boundaries of the species, whereby men sort them, are made by men; since the essence of the species, distinguished by different names are . . . of men's making, and seldom adequate to the internal nature of the things they are taken from. So that we may truly say, such a manner of sorting things is the workmanship of men. (Locke [1690] 1824: Book iii, Ch. 6, para. 430)

Science directs attention to regularities in nature. It underlies a general view that biological events show regularities and these may, by tests and observations, be possible to discover. The symptoms and the clusters of traits used to identify syndromes or diseases in medicine are abstracted from the many complex phenomena observed in actual cases of sickness. Thomas Sydenham (1742), a friend of John Locke, was very much concerned to discover the regularities of nature when disease was produced, to find the essences of the different species of disease, to distinguish them by names, and to make a classification of diseases adequate to the internal nature of the things they were taken from. Sydenham compared a disease entity to a botanical species and spoke of "specific" diseases. Like seeds of a plant, the disease entity might grow in the body of a patient and develop the characteristic attributes of the species noticeable in the patient's signs and symptoms.

But diseases do not have separate and independent existences. It is a mistake to think of disease "entities" as though they were natural species like plants or animals, when they are actually hypotheses or theories based on certain regularities that are observed in actual entities (i.e., the individual people who are sick) and used to classify them (Kraupl

Taylor 1979: 5–31). Are there really diseases as distinct from individuals or creatures that are diseased? No, the so-called disease entity is a reification. Biomedicine aims at the definition of an impairment, given the nature of the human species, of anyone irrespective of his or her culture. The one-eyed man may be king in the country of the blind but, while perhaps better off than others there, he is nonetheless a maimed man, abnormal by the standards of his species (see Wells [1904] 2004).

The assumption of regularities in nature is the basis for seeking to define the normal range of various human functions. The criteria of normality in medicine are both statistical and ideal; they are ideal in the sense that the proper functioning of different organs is conceived with the help of teleology—scientists try to determine the relationships between different organs, what purposes they serve, what should count as adequate function. Some important physiological functions regulate and integrate the whole. Ideals of integration and balance and of the contribution of different parts to maintain this whole come to be involved in judgments of adequacy. Certain functions vary with age and sex and so the standards to apply vary. However, the appeal of the biological criteria still lies in their objectivity. To say there is something wrong with someone's kidneys is not like saying there is something wrong in telling lies.[1] According to a biomedical view (Campbell, Scadding, and Roberts 1979), signs and symptoms are identified as relevant to disease because they alter the capacity of the individual to survive and reproduce—the essential biological concerns. The spirochete of syphilis depends on precisely set conditions to live. These are given in a human body. It is in terms of its effects on human individuals that we call syphilis a disease. It harms physiological and psychological functioning in an affected individual so as to reduce his or her likelihood of survival and successful reproduction. We cannot say "a society is sick" in any nonmetaphorical sense. Disease, whatever its social repercussions, is not an attribute of collectivities: individuals, not societies, are born, live, and die. Ideally, the characteristics chosen to identify kinds of disease are discriminating and recognizable by objective and explicit means. The aim is to make comparison possible and identification objective.

Should we take the average as a guide to normality? It has the advantage of being measurable. It avoids our choosing between what is

---

1. We do not usually establish or support moral values by appeal to experiment. If telling lies is thought to be wrong, there is no point in waiting to see if the next instance is wrong—we know in advance that it must be.

"desirable" and what is not. However, a purely statistical view of abnormality will end up identifying the abnormal with the unusual. Good teeth are unusual, so is great strength, great skill at snooker, and so on. So we must import ideas of what is relevant and desirable for health: the ideal aspect. But ideals involve what ought to be and resist exact definition. They cannot be identified as straightforwardly as an average can. What is health? Is it "a state of complete physical mental and social wellbeing and not merely the absence of disease or infirmity," as stated in the constitution of the World Health Organization? Health then becomes an unattainable ideal, enjoyed perhaps by Adam before the Fall. The absence of disease and the adequacy of health are less ambitious criteria for determining health than is ideal health conceived in terms of perfection.

Insofar as evolution links abnormality and malfunction, it does not make much difference which of these two criteria we choose in the objective definition of disease. But serious difficulties arise with regard to human diseases because social conditions may so strongly affect both adaptation and what is normal or average. Then the biological and evolutionary criteria lose something of their apparent simplicity and clarity. Adaptive success is bound to time and place, as in a much-cited example, that of the peppered moth (*Biston betularia*). Pale forms of the moth were the only ones known until 1845. By then the effects of the Industrial Revolution had begun to blacken the trees around Manchester with soot. The pale moths' bird predators found it easier to pick them off, and the black mutant forms of the moths—hitherto unknown—became the common form in that altered environment (Curtis 1979: 785). The pale form was ill-fated for survival and reproduction; yet how could we think of calling it a morbid or diseased variant? If certain kinds of change in any living creature may be called those of disease, in a global and longterm view such changes may be seen to result from varied causes, such as genetic change, maladaptation to environment, environmental change, and the predatory, parasitic, and competitive habits of different organisms. The issue of disease may be focused on the individual of a species. However, answers about whether some condition of the individual should be considered a disease are not always absolute, unequivocal, or all-or-none. With regard to the human species, in marked contrast to other animal species, there is great difficulty in specifying "ordinary circumstances." For most animal or plant species, ordinary circumstances are, to an overwhelming extent, outside their control. Adaptation is a result of natural processes by which individuals of the species either survive to reproduce or they fail to do so and the species eventually dies out.

The argument that normality in the sense of average will imply something like the optimal or ideal condition depends also on the environmental stringency of nature in eliminating maladaptive difference. This is how natural selection should work. But with the human species, adaptation to environment becomes problematic because of the ways people alter their natural surroundings. They have often reshaped their own environments so much that it becomes hard to speak of them as "natural environments" (see also Fabrega 1974: 134–37, 267–73). The point of H. G. Wells's story "In the country of the blind" ([1904] 2004) was that there, the one-eyed man could not be king, for the inhabitants had made their towns and their ways so strangely and so peculiarly suited for themselves that the sighted man could not see how to follow them, so he was left bewildered, clumsy, and helpless.

People modify environments to suit their wishes as well as their needs. They use cars, build cities, plant crops, work in factories, and in countless other ways complicate what they have to adapt to. It is not necessarily clear whether a specific attribute then brings advantage or disadvantage; at times, all we can say is something changes. Findings may become average that are not ideal; tooth decay is an example. People learn how to protect themselves so that traits that would otherwise put them at a biological disadvantage survive. Many characteristics are not overwhelmingly or strikingly malfunctional but only relatively so, requiring other stresses to produce evident sickness. Or they may be graded characteristics (like blood pressure or serum cholesterol levels) that fall within an average range on a continuum that begins to be statistically associated with manifest sickness at the upper or lower ends of the common range and beyond. However, the association with sickness is not inevitable; it may depend on other contributory or predisposing factors. In such cases, the identification of standards is very difficult. Studies of the physiology of hunter-gatherers, for example, made biomedical scientists change their view that the rise of blood pressure with age was inevitable. When continuous or graded indicators go outside the normal range, the person affected does not necessarily switch suddenly at some discrete step to become sick: indicators of disease may well have borders or ranges where the decision about whether someone is sick or has some disease must be qualified or uncertain. Sickness is often not an all-or-none, either/or state.

Whether an inherited predisposition becomes evident or not can depend on the environment. A trait may be inherited yet not show itself in a recognizable form until environmental stimuli, such as deficiencies or excesses, expose it. Responsiveness and plasticity are essential to human development of every kind. The distinction between the intrinsic and the environmental, like that between the physical and the mental, is convenient but artificial. The ultimate biological criteria of survival—threat or risk to life and reproductive capacity—may in fact be almost impossible to apply. Instead, medicine concentrates on specific disease theories, not on a general theory applying to disease as a whole.

The assumption of regularities in nature is crucial for specifying normal attributes and for identifying kinds of disease. No simple view of cause and effect is possible if natural forces are thought of as beings with free will (and possibly capricious). If a people believe that other beings or natural phenomena can make them ill but may choose whether to do so, they alter the conditions for finding out regularities or "laws" of nature. They alter the possibilities for predicting the outcome. What may seem critical is to determine the unpredictable reasons why the agent causing illness has acted. The regularity of a link between cause and effect is no longer present: there can only be an appeal against the agent's choice and some hope of averting a bad outcome. To understand the reasons for the illness becomes more critical.

The more the symptoms of a syndrome are definable only in social terms, the less likely we are to find an underlying biological cause for the disorder. Consider some reasons why people may be unable to eat specific food: (a) certain people cannot eat a particular kind of parrot because of a cultural taboo, socially defined in terms of age and kin relationships, that determines its inedibility for them—recognition of the rule and social disapproval stop them from eating it; (b) some people cannot eat pork because their religion forbids it, yet the force of the rule is perhaps felt so deeply they feel nauseous or might vomit on finding they have inadvertently consumed it; (c) other people cannot eat crab or prawns because they are allergic to them and eating them produces nausea and vomiting, even severe shock. The wholly social terms that make the parrot inedible may be changed by place or age. The idiosyncrasy that makes someone allergic to crab or prawns cannot be changed by putting that person in another social context or by convention. Nevertheless, the fact that circumstances may alter cases does not itself make medical theories subjective or arbitrary. The harmful effects of some malfunction may be more or less severe, depending on the environmental or social circumstances of the person affected. The effects are, in other words, relative to circumstances—relative in the sense of being neither universal nor absolute. The absolute is not the same as the objective: objectivity is not bound up with being able to state a rule that has no exceptions (i.e., is absolute). Diet and water requirements vary with age, sex, size, activity, and environment; so do many other physiological variables. Bambrough gives an analogy: "The fact that a tailor needs to make a different suit for each of us and that no non-trivial specification of what a suit has to be like to fit its wearer will be without exceptions does not mean that there are no rights or wrongs about the question whether your suit or mine is a good fit. . . . Circumstances objectively alter cases" (Bambrough 1979: 33).

With almost all diseases, there is some interplay between factors that are internal and external to the patient. What is at issue is the significance of the effects of the different factors. Indeed, a disease theory is unlikely to be useful when its characteristics are largely or wholly dependent on the external or social environment. Although it would make things easier if the biological and the social were sharply separate and unmixed in real life, they are not. Poverty and lack of education may contribute to infection; genetic endowment may have played a part in the crime someone committed. The difficult part is to know how large a part and how directly each played. The answers are almost never all-or-none. The social and the biological components involved in a syndrome interact. Medical theories about diseases are based on a concern to find underlying biological disturbances. The more the symptoms of a syndrome are definable only in social terms, the less likely it is that a medical hypothesis about the syndrome (viz., that the cluster of traits is symptomatic of some underlying biological disturbance) will in fact contribute much to an understanding or explanation of the syndrome or traits. And a strictly biological view of disease leaves out the dimensions of illness of chief interest to the anthropologist or the sociologist—those dimensions related to the social context and significance of illness. Someone's illness is an event, a patch of personal biography, to be understood rather than classified. For biomedicine, it is only by ignoring much of what is individual about a particular illness that the types or categories can be recognized.

The aim of understanding the particular events of someone's illness (how that person has construed them, how the illness constitutes part of an individual's biography) is much more appealing to social scientists because it accords with their interest in the social significance and meaning of an illness. Many problems in medical practice belong primarily to the social dimensions of illness. Clinical practice, not detached scientific study, is the daily preoccupation of most physicians and the raison d'être for medicine. Concern for the patient, skill in interpreting people's be-havior and what they say about themselves, skill in showing sympathy, gaining trust, and learning to giving advice are essential parts of any healing practice. Let me repeat Jaspers's lines: "The doctor's function rather consists in ascertaining what precise state or event is presenting itself, on what it depends, how it proceeds and what will affect it."

It is easy to imagine that an experience of life in which one is directly dependent on one's community and dependent on nature must color at-titudes to illness. Human self-interest has often supposed that nature is animate and has feelings of sympathy and antipathy toward people. Yet we may wonder how some beliefs survive the test of practical experience. There are countless examples of beliefs held to be true at one time or place but not another. Values may constrain the opportunities for knowl-edge. The authority of past great writers has sometimes blinded people to their own experience. Medicine is full of examples of wrong or mis-taken reasons that people thought were good and would serve to justify a course of action. Even so, they are not wholly trapped in the customs and beliefs of their own society. The story of borrowings, the diffusion of the great traditions of medicine, the wandering healers and peddlers of pat-ent medicines, the adoption of cults and rites of healing, the rise and fall of fashionable treatments, the diversity of modes of explanation and of healing now to be found in nearly all communities imply a willingness, even an eagerness, to try alternatives and find solutions that will work. In illness, perhaps more so than in other things, people sometimes feel such an urgent need to escape suffering that they may become impatient with conventional wisdom.

Part iii: responses to change

Ways of accounting for illness certainly vary. Many of these ways are linked to social, moral, or religious beliefs. This next section, Part III, is concerned with changes in response to illness. Chapter 5 suggested that leprosy in biblical times shifted from being a matter of priestly rules, taboo, and exclusion to being one of atonement for sin or guilt. Eventually, the label of "leprosy" came to refer to something requiring treatment wholly within the secular domain of medicine and public health. It was, in effect, an example of medicalization. The beginnings of such shifts in approach and frames of understanding are the subject of the next chapters on Bregbo, witchcraft, and depression.

CHAPTER NINE

Bregbo, a healing center in Côte d'Ivoire

Bregbo is a village on the shores of a lagoon, about twenty kilometers from Abidjan, the capital of the Côte d'Ivoire. The village is a community that became famous as a center to which sick and unfortunate people came for healing and guidance. Some stayed for weeks, others for years. The community grew up around its first leader, Albert Atcho.[1] Most of those who came were from the Côte d'Ivoire, although a few came from farther away, notably from Ghana. The community began to form in 1948; by 1967 it had grown to hold about 900 people. Between Abidjan and Bregbo is a large town, Bingerville, with a psychiatric hospital. In the beginning, it was the hospital that sent patients to Atcho because there was nothing clear it could do for them, and some of the patients were quite agitated. The calm of Bregbo and a kind of security surrounding Atcho enabled many of them to eventually return to their villages. The description of Bregbo that follows is based mainly on *Prophétisme et thérapeutique*, edited by Colette Piault (1975). This is a portrait of the place and the man who founded it from the varied perspectives of six writers, covering a period roughly between 1965 and 1970. As a case study, it may serve to show how in one distinctive setting, perceptions of illness and treatment began to change under new economic and political pressures.

---

1. Albert Atcho died in 1990.

The founder Albert Atcho was a prophet in the Harrist tradition, although he claimed no place in the Harrist hierarchy or priesthood (Augé 1975a: 252). The front of his church at Bregbo proclaimed the Ten Commandments of Harrism in cement letters:

Love your neighbour; Do not work on Sunday; Do not bear false witness against your neighbour; Do not despise your neighbour because you also shall be judged; Do not kill; Do not go naked; Honour your father and mother; Do not steal your neighbour's wife; Do not seek to know the mystery of God; It is strictly forbidden to satisfy sexual pleasure in the open air; Do not eat meat on Friday; Do not eat human flesh; Do not drink human blood; Do not insult the poor because it is a sin—W. W. Harris. (Bureau 1975: 101)[2]

Blessed by Atcho, the lustral and healing water with plants and bark conveyed the presence of God and was similar to the water used in baptism. Atcho instituted a special system of water distribution through his network, a great web centered on Bregbo and Atcho himself.

Atcho had a secretary and clerks who helped in his healing work. They questioned patients to find the roots of their misfortunes. After long interviews spaced over many days or even weeks, a patient would give a confession. This admission of guilt, typed up by clerks, was then read aloud in a public ceremony of confession, with cleansing and treatment or penance to follow. Over 3,000 "diabolical" (*diabolique*) and "ordinary" confessions were collected for study. Here is the beginning of a typical "diabolical" one: "I declare publicly that I am a witch. By my diabolical action I have killed my grandfather Agah Daniel, Koutou Kjarabou, I have killed the unnamed newborn child of Agah Elié, two unnamed newborn children of Assamo Anan. . . . I have killed my grandmother . . . I have killed . . . I have killed. . . . Here are the names of my associates. . . . This is the list of my spoilings and destructions, my evil actions" (Piault 1975: 123). This was the type of confession that emerged from some who came to Atcho due to sickness. They expressed a new self-understanding in the stereotyped terms of Bregbo. He called this healing.

---

2. Admittedly, these are fourteen "Ten Commandments," and they are those of Atcho rather than the Ten Commandments proclaimed by W. W. Harris.

The Annual Chief Festival of Bregbo took place each year on November 1. Atcho's influence was celebrated with great ceremony.[3] He received official recognition for his healing ministry by being named Chevalier de l'Ordre National Ivoirien (Knight of the Ivorian National Order). People came from a widely dispersed network of villages where Atcho's lustral water (for blessing and healing) was distributed. When ministers of state came, it was a further confirmation of Atcho's fame; the same was true when foreign researchers came. He was proud of his political and external links. Monsieur Clavère, Assistant of Atcho, spoke of this in his speech of welcome at the Festival of Bregbo in 1968:

> Agent of healing, great herbalist, Monsieur Atcho, instead of engaging in commercial trade with his healing herb, has given it freely to international sociologists who have come to visit him. Thus for more than four years, we have received the visits of doctors and sociologists, in a word international research workers, without mentioning also the many film-makers who have taken his portrait back with them and a record of his healing activities. (Piault 1975: 69)

What can we make of this man and his qualities? This was the story told of his revelation: the prophet Albert Atcho was born in 1903 and his birth was miraculous. At birth, he held a white powder in his hand. This powder, obtained from a certain tree, made water froth with suds when put in a basin. It was put into a lustral water for washing the sick. Atcho was one of the Three sent by God to look after Black people: his task was to take charge of ills of the body and soul. His father named him Atcho, which means "to bathe," and he told his son that he was destined to serve God as one who washed away sins. The story described Atcho's first act of healing when he was twenty-one years old. Military service then took him away to France. His real work of healing began after he came back. He met the great Harrist preacher Pita Logba, who put him to a test: "If it is truly God who has given you this power, you will remain a healer forever, but if this power comes from yourself, God

---

3. This annual festival lasted for three days. Day 1: Day for politics, with the visit of someone representing the President of the Republic and the awarding of a decoration, Atcho in modern suit and tie; Day 2: Harrist religious celebration, with the Harrist congregation all dressed in white—Atcho as well—and processions, addresses, and hymns; Day 3: The village network celebration, with a return to ordinary dress, music, and dancing.

will take it from you." Albert Atcho triumphed in the test, and Pita Logba said, "Go, it is God himself who sends you to save your people. Go and do your work." Pita Logba prayed. Atcho returned and began his career. Such was the story of the revelation and confirmation of his healing powers (Piault 1975: 27–45).

People sought his lustral water to help in healing at home. Atcho could heal even at a distance. The Chefs d'eau (Water Chiefs) from the villages came regularly to fetch his water. The network of ties to Bregbo could be traced far afield. When Atcho visited the villages, he performed healing and was asked to confirm or reject witchcraft accusations made between covillagers. His role was to recognize or unmask and condemn the sorcerer or witch. However, his work with witchcraft was ambiguous; sometimes he confirmed or rejected witchcraft accusations made by a sick person against someone else, usually one of the sick person's covillagers; at other times, his work consisted of showing the sick person that it was evil in himself that made him ill (Piault 1975: 73–85).

The teaching of Atcho was powerfully, often magnificently, expressed in his sermons. The problem of inequality between White and Black people was explained as God's choice. But it was actually understood and lived in terms of sorcery and witchcraft. In the special terminology of Bregbo, these were things of the devil, of *action diabolique, actions en diable*. Power was seen as a privilege that was evil only when misused:

> The Devil is a spirit whom God loves. He gave him power to visit his people, to see good and evil. It is through the Devil that God has sent his wisdom. The Devil helps to make all that is necessary to man. The whites with their diabolical spirit, they do everything, make everything. You, Africans, you make nothing. The Africans refuse the good use of the diabolical spirit, whence comes death and disease. (Bureau 1975: 105)

Someone with power might transform evil not so much by giving it up as by making it pass into the public domain. To become like White people meant transforming sorcery and witchcraft powers from the world of darkness and night by bringing them to the world of daylight. Devilry of the night was witchcraft and sorcery: devilry of the day was knowledge and cleverness. The transformation required people to take a radically new view of their world.

By custom, suspicions of witchcraft turned on people within the matrilineage who owned more things and kept them for themselves, the powerful and wealthy of the village or lineage; in practice, however, the weak and wretched were more often accused (Augé 1975a: 269). Traditional views aimed to preserve equality between members of the social group. But Atcho denounced this expectation of equality as an illusion and as harmful. The power of sorcery and witchcraft could be used by the envious to bring down those who exerted themselves and who succeeded. Africans would not tolerate inequalities; only White people did. That was where the difference was thought to lie. This Harrist speaker explained:

> With you in France long ago, all the village houses were single storied. Then one day a richer and more ambitious man wanted to build a second floor to his house. His neighbours were jealous. They said, "What? He wants to put himself above us!" So what did the neighbours do? They all built houses with two floors and then the neighbours of neighbours built them with three floors. So that is why your towns have not stopped growing up toward the sky. With us it's the same. In a village one man wants to put himself above the others—he builds his house with cement, a second floor, a staircase. The villagers are jealous. They say, "What? Who is he to put himself above us?" But the difference from you whites with us is this: that man will never live in his house [he will die by witchcraft]. (Bureau 1975: 117)

The traditional view of witchcraft was one of persecution by others, and it reinforced a morality of lineage and village obligation and solidarity. In their theory of witchcraft, the cause of illness was external to the patient. It might come from neighbors or relatives—that is, from other people on whom someone should be able to rely for support but who denied their obligations. Illness was attributable to evil in others who chose to use witchcraft or sorcery to satisfy ambition or greed. The theory involved a view of fraught relations between the individual and his or her social group. Whether things went well or ill with someone depended in part on others conforming to their obligations to support him or her as a member of the group. The village African could see the outward evidence of prosperity in the town (cars, shops, hotels, shining glass, and steel). They saw what was possible for some and aspired to it. But to enter that glittering world required wealth, education, and skills not provided in the traditional setting. People could go to the towns, but that was just a beginning. They risked joining the jobless, mobile, urban population. With signs of prosperity around them, they made up a reserve of frustrated and aspiring people who had little money, no organized voice, who wanted work and would work for little pay. The success of business depended in part on that reserve.

Marc Augé (1975b: 219–36) suggests this as the reason for the official praise of Atcho's work. The mass of people came from villages in which they learned a persecutive theory of misfortune. They believed that ills in life would come to people because of evil in others, especially those they should have been able to depend on. They came to town full of hopes, but many failed to realize them for want of skill and education. If those who failed transferred their traditional understanding of misfortune to their new situation, they might conclude that their failure and misfortune were due to evil in those others they had to depend on in their new surroundings. These others were potential employers, the new conditions of work and life created by those in authority, the government, the laws. In this might lie the seeds of unrest or uprising.

New arrivals at Bregbo went to see the prophet and tell him their reason for coming. Atcho then had to decide whether he could help them. He selected his cases, rejecting people who seemed violent and mad or some with serious organic ills. At the first consultation, he would implant a sense of the need for confession. From a recording of one such interview, J. Lehmann (1972: 355–93) showed the skill of Atcho. In the extract, Atcho suggested only obliquely to the patient that he might have hidden faults to confess. It is noticeable that Atcho accepted the patient's explanations for his illness without comment, for instance, that the origin of his illness was the *poison en diable* (devil's poison, sorcery) used by the patient's uncle. It was possible that the uncle would continue to harm his nephew, but that did not matter any more. It was more important for the patient to think over his faults and to confess and so begin the healing process. That was how the shift in interpretation occurred. Confession might allow the patient to disengage himself from some responsibility for his acts, offering a way to get out of the consequences his actions would have if they were real. The insistence in the subsequent sessions was on total avowal: nothing should be repressed, nothing hidden. The relation of undisclosed sin to illness appeared in the aggravating effect of hiding anything.

But in the end, the written confessions revealed a strongly stereotyped set of wrongdoings: ones involving violations of rules about sexual behavior, others dealing with fetish practices, yet others having something to do with *actions en diable*: sorcery, drinking blood and eating human flesh, murder. The stereotyping was so evident that what was important seemed to lie less in what was said than in the fact of saying it. The completed confessions that were typed out were not guides to the individual problems from which they grew so much as guides to the changed attitudes and ideas established at Bregbo.

Between the beginning (the troubles or misfortune) and the end (the confession), between the spoken and the written, a change was worked: the contrast could be seen in the transcripts, for example, the interviews between Aka Afué, a Baoulé woman, with the clerk eliciting her confession in comparison with the eventual typed "diabolical" confession (Piault 1975: 257–75). In the transcripts of later interviews, she accepted and admitted to her devil killings and those of her associates. However, the transcript also revealed her personal tragedy: she was barren.

CLERK: You have killed all those people. Are you going to speak and tell us about it? Think carefully. Say everything you think, whatever comes into your head.

AKA: If we had sold all we killed, we could have had a million francs. Everything we killed, we destroyed. My father he killed too, and I have to struggle now to get money for my father so that we can eat. Me—I am in a state of sin toward God and I gave my womb to my devil associates so that I cannot have children and my periods have stopped. I don't have my periods any longer and I still have headaches. And I cry out, O God! I am my father's only child and after me there will be no more children. Why haven't I had children? If my friend has a nice dress, that always makes me feel awful. It is some diabolical jealousy. Even when I eat, I never give any food away. I don't even want my husband to have a second wife in the house. I must stay the only one, I have magnetized him so he won't have a second wife. I go to so many places because of my illness, wandering without a penny on me. This illness strikes me down and I have nothing to make it better, and then I think I had better let myself die. Everywhere I go people say to me, "Afué, you have our sympathy. Afué, our sympathy." The illness never leaves me. What shall I do? It's sin. I could stay in a corner and weep. I have friends who have children and me, I don't even have a child with me. It's because of my sin that I haven't been able to have children. That's really because I got into the group of my (devil) friends and I gave things up to them, my associates. It's because of that I have no children. I always say that. (Piault 1975: 261–62)

The clerk then questioned her about all of her *actions en diable*: how she drank women's blood, brought about their miscarriages, displaced their wombs, made labor painful for them, and caused the newborn children to die. In the spoken confession, the first part was marked above all by the theme of her unhappiness at her barrenness and her *actions en diable*. The latter part was about her efforts to give up the fetishes she used to try to bring back her lost fertility; she also spoke about trying to get rid of her headaches. In the end, belief in God appeared as the theme: God alone was capable of curing her, not of her barrenness but of her headaches.

In the written confession, the whole matter of her barrenness was reduced to two sentences. The far larger part was concerned with her metamorphoses into animals that destroy, her killings, what she had wrecked and brought to ruin.

What Atcho did, in the view of Andras Zempléni (1975: 153–218), was to provide patients with a bridge of understanding between old values and the new situation that imposed demands for an individualism foreign to their traditional values. In the new setting, people experienced the demands of competitive self-interest. But they had been brought up with different group values and obligations. The traditional explanation of misfortune was adapted to those group values. They were not necessarily easy to change. The strength of Atcho's appeal may have been rooted in the ambiguous way his message responded to a problem and moved toward a solution. His emphasis on the devil and *action diabolique* involved a relabeling of ideas about witchcraft and sorcery and a new emphasis on the individual's own potential to control his or her own fate. In many confessions, the view of *action en diable* came close to the notion that the patient had a diabolical double that caused harm; what confession offered was a recognition of this. To the extent that patients saw this in traditional terms as a dark or nighttime double of themselves, they were not held responsible for it in the same way that they might have been held responsible for their daytime doings. By confessing, they detached themselves from the dark deeds; by exposing what the night hides, they enfeebled it. The people who gave confessions were not judged and punished in secular terms; instead, Atcho taught that God punished through illness. God also offered a chance of redemption through confession if people wholly recognized their faults and renounced evil.

Is Bregbo unique?

It would be easy enough to suppose Atcho and Bregbo were the products of some unique combination of circumstances and an exceptional individual. Augé argues that Bregbo was unique: "Bregbo, through its intellectual relationship to the persecutive scheme of witchcraft and its links with Harrisme and Power, is unique" (Augé 1975b: 236). Certainly the confessions recorded at Bregbo are very striking, and Atcho seems exceptional. However, Margaret J. Field (1960) had conducted an earlier ethnopsychiatric study of people at shrines in rural Ashanti, Ghana. She recorded many case histories, including confessions of witchcraft much like many of those from Bregbo. The following example is an extract from Case 19, Akosua N., a woman of about twenty-six with three surviving children, married to a catechist from her home town:

> Akosua's present illness. The onset was eight months ago immediately after a four-month miscarriage with heavy blood loss. When she walked about she felt darkness coming over her and something crawling up from her feet. She attended a hospital out-patient department and was given "injections and medicine." She improved physically but continued to brood. Four months ago she started strange behaviour. She sat about weeping and refusing food, was sleepless and walked about at night. She said she had seen people on the wall at night. One night she said she had seen someone with *mpesempese* hair (*obosomfo*'s hair/hair of a priest of an *obosom*) standing in the yard and that it meant that the *obosom* [spirit or lesser deity] under whose protection her brother had put himself had come to "catch" her because she was a witch and had planned to kill her brother. She said she had done a great many other evil things. When she saw people talking in the street she thought they were talking about her.
>
> The teacher-brother wrote down her "confessions." Her mother and mother's brother came to Mframaso [the shrine village] with her, bringing the written confession which the *obosom*'s clerk read before the shrine. This included most of the stereotyped misdeeds of witches—killing her own and her relatives' children and various other people; causing accidents; illness, barrenness, poverty and the blighting of crops; night-flying; harbouring big snakes in her belly, head and vagina; planning further deaths not yet achieved. . . . In spite of all these misdemeanours the *obosom* said she had more to confess and must come back another day. (Field 1960: 183–84)

Witchcraft and sickness

Just as with leprosy in biblical times, some conditions we now think of as sickness were differently viewed in the past—for example, in Europe when demented women were identified as witches. The assumptions dictated public responses. The second part of a textbook of the Inquisition, the *Malleus maleficarum*, "is devoted to what we would call today clinical reports. It tells of various types of witches and of the different methods one should use to identify a witch. To use modern terminology, it describes the clinical pictures and the various ways of arriving at a diagnosis" (Zilboorg1935: 8, 9). The book used the dogma of true faith to fuse insanity, witchcraft, and heresy into one concept and exclude even the suspicion that the problem might be a medical one. In Gregory Zilboorg's account of the blows of the witches' hammer and what he called the first psychiatric revolution, he portrays Johann Weyer as a tranquil but devastating critic of the Malleus (Zilboorg and Henry 1941: 144–244). Like Michel de Montaigne, Weyer wrote against demonology and its cruelties in favor of a medical view of those who were judged to be witches. He accompanied his chief work, *De praestigiis daemonum* (1563), with a letter to Duke William of Julich, Berg, and Cleves in which he says:

> To you, Prince, I dedicate the fruit of my thought. For thirteen years your physician, I have heard expressed in your Court the most varied opinion concerning witches; but none so agrees with my own as does yours, that witches can harm no one through the most malicious will or the ugliest exorcism, that rather their imagination—inflamed by the demons in a way not understandable to us—and the torture of melancholy makes them only fancy that they have caused all sorts of evil. For when the entire manner of action is laid on the scales, and the implements therefore examined with care and scrutiny, the nonsense and falsity of the matter is soon clear to all eyes and more lucid than the day. You do not, like others, impose heavy penalties on perplexed, poor old women. You demand evidence, and only if they have actually given poison bringing about the death of men or animals do you allow the law to take its course. (Weyer 1563, quoted in Zilboorg and Henry 1941: 216)

Weyer went over "in minute detail all the practices from exorcism to the endless varieties and refinements of torture, from the days of the past to his own." He left no doubt that but one conclusion is warranted: the witches were mentally sick people, and the monks who tormented and tortured the poor creatures were the ones who should be punished (Zilboorg and Henry 1941: 215–16).

In the Côte d'Ivoire, witchcraft was (and no doubt still is) used to explain certain events. It informed an outlook on experience. Certain key ideas about the powers of the person provided the potential for a perse-cutory theory of misfortune and illness. Social rules set out an arrange-ment of duties and attachments. Values and expectations were framed within them. The threat of witchcraft sanctioned some of their ideas about responsibility and blame. Thus, guilt or persecution might be an explanation for someone's illness.

Ashanti social rules in the domain of family and kinship also con-strained relationships in ways that could lead to witchcraft accusations (Fortes 1950). If beliefs about witchcraft sanctioned some aspects of be-havior, we might expect the beliefs to persist so long as the same pattern of social structure prevailed. In fact, Meyer Fortes reported that rapid social changes had increased the levels of concern for witchcraft, as did Margaret Field. It is difficult to know what witchcraft beliefs were like before colonial change. In the 1890s, Mary Kingsley noted the strength of West African witchcraft beliefs:

> You will often hear it said that the general idea among savage races is that death always arises from witchcraft; but I think from what I have said regarding disease arising from bush-souls' bad tempers, from contracting a *sisa*, from losing the shadow at high noon, and from, it may be other causes I have not spoken of, that this generalisation is for West Africa too sweeping. But undoubtedly sixty per cent of the deaths are believed to arise from witchcraft. . . . Public feeling is always at bursting-point on witches, their goings-on are a constant danger to every peaceful citizen's life, family, property, and so on, and when the general public thinks it's got hold of one of the vermin it goes off with a bang; but it does not think for one moment the witch is *per se* in himself a thing apart; he is just a bad man too much, who has gone and taken up with spirits for illegitimate purposes. (Kings-ley 1899: 209, 161)

Fortes's analysis (1950) pointed to certain strains and divisions in Ashanti social structure. They help to account for the direction of accu-sation and confession, as well as the disproportionate number of women over men who came to the shrines in Ashanti. With similar social struc-tures and values, similar tensions occurred among the coastal Alladian peoples of the Côte d'Ivoire who made up most of Bregbo's clientele. The lagoon peoples of the coastal Côte d'Ivoire shared many basic ideas with the Akan peoples of Ghana. The experience of colonization, economic failure, and humiliation might have been partly behind the reorientation of witchcraft explanations and an emphasis on guilt.

The West African prophets William Waddy Harris and Albert At-cho perceived witchcraft and fetishes as a source of great harm and evil. Fortes said that among the Ashanti,

> Accusations of witchcraft are everyday occurrences . . . and their vol-ume is increasing as claims based on lineage ties come to be felt as more and more onerous. Side by side with this is found a rapidly growing addiction to cults purporting to give protection against and to detect witches. Illness, death, barrenness, economic loss, and other misfortunes are often ascribed to witchcraft, and those accused are most often close matrilineal kin of the sufferer especially a mother or sister. (Fortes 1950: 275)

Confessions at Atcho's Bregbo community (Piault 1975) and at the Akan shrines (Field 1960) also suggest changes occurred in ideas about witchcraft.

Augé (1975a) took witchcraft to be at the heart of a peculiarly dark view of the world. Certain assumptions guided them, in particular ideas about the nature of the person and witchcraft (Augé 1975a: 120). These shaped people's understanding of events. They looked on things that happened as signs. There might be powers at work below the surface of appearances. Ideas of witchcraft and sorcery allowed people to interpret ordinary experience more profoundly. Augé adopted his surrealist view from André Breton, finding the *surréel* more suited than the "supernatu-ral" to describe the coastal people's sense of their social world and of the witchcraft (1975a: 103, 144). The surrealist approach takes account of real happenings and their apparent contradictions but it attributes deeper meanings to them, more profound relationships in the contra-dictions. Events of daily life, family, and work, may have deeper mean-ings and "speak" to people who can understand: they may indicate things about themselves and their relations with the world and other people. At least this can happen for the person who saw clearly, the clairvoyant or diviner, who sees the meanings and signs as belonging to this world, not as emanations from another or higher world. Breton articulated his notion of the surreal in these terms:

> *La théorie du monde est une théorie du surréel.* [The theory of the world is a theory of the surreal.] The system of causality in such a concep-tion of the world is not less logical than another, but it is condemned to the perpetual making of hypotheses about who or what will be

stronger (*les rapports de force*). The warrior of an Ebrié village, who confronts the coloniser to prove his invulnerability, is not blinding himself to things: he is testing out the truth about himself, and his failure serves as a demonstration and will be understood as such. (Breton 1975a: 144)

The duality of the person appears in many guises in West African thought. Someone's reflection in a pool, in another person's eyes, or in a mirror are images of one kind of double. The shadow is another kind: the shadow needs light, it flits along beside the person who casts it: it vanishes in the dark. Where is that shadow double at night? At Bregbo, *action en double* (action as a double or shade at night) was understood to be *action en diable* (action as a devil in darkness).

Certain aspects recur within a general Akan scheme of ideas about the components of the person. All observers have stressed the Ashanti and Akan belief that witchcraft is transmitted by inheritance within the matrilineage—that is, with the blood (*mogya*)—and that witchcraft works against members of the same matrilineage, most commonly against close matrikin. This is the critical point for understanding guilt and blame: witchcraft strikes within the matrilineage. To hurt people outside it, there is magic or sorcery. Witchcraft harms those who are closest. Sickness may be the outward sign of these complex subtle struggles between doubles, destiny, and individuality.

*   *   *

A number of points and questions have, I hope, emerged from this synopsis: first, the personal success and charisma of Atcho and the political extent of his influence; second the ambiguous shift from persecution to guilt in the explanation of misfortune that allowed for some continuity of beliefs in witchcraft; third, the ambiguity about whether Atcho should be perceived as a prophet or as a healer; fourth, explanations for the extraordinary public confessions of witchcraft, their stereotyping, and the persuasive role of the repeated interviews and the community; fifth, Bregbo and Atcho are not unique cases, and there is a remarkable similarity between some Ashanti shrines and Bregbo in their organization and methods of healing; sixth, there are relevant similarities between Ashanti and the coastal Côte d'Ivoire peoples in social structure, witchcraft beliefs, and colonial and postcolonial experiences; seventh, women and jobless young men seemed to preponderate as sufferers. The two following chapters explore explanations for some of these findings.

The next chapter (on witchcraft or depression) moves from the question of shifting ideas, uncertainty, and ambiguity in Indigenous understanding of misfortune to its role in the psychiatric identification of depression. What part do assumptions or bias play in perceptions of illness? The chapter that follows is about the rise of shrines for healing, misfortunes, and the nature of the healing they provide.

CHAPTER TEN

Witchcraft or depression

Margaret Field (1960) had a special interest in mental illness. She suggested that in certain societies, some people who are morbidly depressed confess to witchcraft. Among those attending the shrine in Ashanti, Field saw women who were anxious, agitated, and miserable. Some accused themselves of fantastic acts of evil and of causing harm. "Some were deluded, some hallucinated, some in morbid fear, others in exaggerated anxiety, and so on. Some believed themselves bewitched, some felt themselves being changed into witches, others thought themselves already witches, mysteriously disseminating destruction. Their compatriots, invited by them to share their beliefs, readily did so: mental illness was not recognised as such, for it wore the garments of traditional ideology" (Field 1960: 13).

She studied shrines in rural Ashanti, Ghana (Gold Coast, as it was known at the time). The confessions of some people who came to them strikingly resemble those later described at the therapeutic community of Bregbo.

Field had been influenced by her own 1930s anthropological fieldwork to propose that "the key to an understanding, not only of witchcraft but of many other preoccupations of unsophisticated people, was Clinical Psychiatry" (1960: 13). She equipped herself to examine it further by getting a medical qualification and psychiatric training. She returned in 1954 to make her ethnopsychiatric study of people at new shrines like those she had seen in the 1930s. Her aim was to study mental illness, so she chose the cases in her book accordingly. She cautioned, "Mentally ill people comprise only a very small proportion of the pilgrims who flock to these shrines not only from within Ashanti but from distant parts of Akan Ghana. The great majority are healthy people supplicating for 'protection'" (1960: 87). She then explained,

> Although the shrine therapists recognise their limitations and frequently tell patients with pneumonia, cardiac failure or pulmonary distress with blood-coughing, to go to hospital, they stand firmly on the theory that the primary vulnerability of the patient to the disease is of supernatural origin and until redemptive ritual has been performed the hospital efforts are futile. When a patient who is already under *obosom*'s (the spirit's) protection comes asking permission to go to hospital this is always given. (Field 1960: 117)

Selection by the healer or the client or the observer?

As mentioned in the previous chapter, some of Albert Atcho's first clients came from the psychiatric hospital at Bingerville. Sometimes he referred physically and seriously sick patients to the hospital. Otherwise, Atcho rarely refused to treat someone who came to him for advice. The case histories suggest that many had already tried other kinds of treatment. If there was some selection, it seems to have been done mostly by the patients and based on Atcho's reputation spread by the distribution of his network and his fame. The most reasonable assumption is that those who chose to go to shrines and spiritual healers believed that spirits or mystical powers might be affecting their lives and health. When people told Atcho or the shrine priest what their problem was and the help they wanted, they revealed reasons or motives for coming. However, it was open to an observer to reinterpret their motives or reasons. This was also evident in what Field wrote concerning the Ashanti shrine priest. The priest's methods were strikingly like Atcho's in terms of style of questioning and insinuation. In Field's medical opinion, many people who complained of sickness suffered from distress of mind rather than organic disease. She related their distress to the cultural concern with bad conscience and ill-will toward others. She wrote:

> The majority of those who come to the shrines complaining of sickness do not appear to have anything organically wrong, but they are

troubled. They complain of palpitations, pains all over, headache, trembling, giddiness, and darkness in front of the eyes. The priest is quick to recognise the patients and comments, "There are troubles in your sickness," or "You are sick because you are keeping things in your head." Often he elicits confessions and fears by employing shock tactics. "What about a certain man? What about a certain woman? What about a certain quarrel?" If the patient looks genuinely blank he tries another tack, but if there is any hesitation or embarrassment, he presses the point till he has elicited either confession or specific anxiety. Adultery on the part of the woman is one of the commonest causes of palpitation and "pains all over." If the patient is reticent, he says, "Go away and come back when you are ready to lay bare what is in your mind." (Field 1960: 113)

Depression and the maintenance of belief in witchcraft

Field accepted that people largely take their own ideas from ideas that are normal in their society; she also agreed that some of the beliefs might resemble those of the mentally ill. But she went further to suggest that the source of certain culturally specific ideas might have come from delusions of the mentally ill: "An active belief in witchcraft . . . is kept alive by that mental illness which Psychiatry calls Depression and the fantastic delusions of sin and guilt which beset patients. Witchcraft meets, above all else, the depressive's need to steep herself in irrational self-reproach and to denounce herself as unspeakably wicked" (1960: 38; see also 317).

The roots of someone's particular response are in the individual, although culture molds it. "The basic predisposition—the 'psychiatric risk'—is probably the crucial factor throughout" (1960: 248; see also 201–3). As noted above, Field said that most pilgrims had good mental health and wanted to ask for protection. Furthermore, "Financially successful men are full of fear lest envious kinsmen should, by means of bad magic or witchcraft, bring about their ruin. Unsuccessful men are convinced that envious malice is the cause of their failure" (1960: 37).

Mental illness at the shrines

Field chose to work at the new shrines in order to find rural cases of mental illness of recent onset. At the time, not much was known about mental illness in African rural settings. Relying on hospital records would give a false picture of the amount and kinds of mental illness, since people did not go to them and there were few hospitals anyway. The ones that existed were in towns; their resources for the treatment of mental illness were scant. For Field, the shrines were primarily places to find psychiatric subjects, and she did find them there. On the basis of her sample, her findings challenged some accepted ideas about depression in African people. Kennedy noted the extreme variety of the prevailing views on depression in Africans (from common to nonexistent) and the impact of Field's work on psychiatric opinion (Kennedy 1973: 1139–45; for a revealing discussion of this question, see also Littlewood and Lipsedge 1982: 68–86).

Depressed Ashanti people expressed guilt, fear, and misery in self-accusation; they accused themselves of being witches and of harming or killing their close relatives. They had fantastic ideas of the evil they had done—fantastic not to the Akan, who could accept the ideas within their understanding of witchcraft, but to the outsider. How can we be sure what self-accusation indicates? Field thought it was the cultural guise for severe depression in Akan women. Colette Piault and others who worked at Bregbo found the confession to be so highly stereotyped as to offer little insight into the individual's particular state of mind and personal history. Instead, the confessions showed the effect of a special form of social pressure and persuasion when they were drawn up. Here, then, are contrasting interpretations.

The relation between individual and culture is reciprocal. Mental illness can provoke feelings of guilt just as local beliefs may provoke morbid anxiety. Do delusions feed on those stories and images? Where are the clear standards for identifying the mental illness? Such standards are needed if we wish to compare its prevalence, variations, and disguise in different societies. There is no discriminating laboratory test for the disease, so we are left to depend on the clinical criteria. To evaluate the treatment Atcho offered, we would need to know what effects he really did bring about. But an answer about the nature of those effects depends first on the accuracy of the diagnosis. The man who is found to have no diabetes after some treatment cannot be described as having been cured of diabetes if he never had it in the first place. It is like the problem of the Indian rope trick: you may expend much ingenuity explaining how it might be done, but if no one can do the trick nor ever could, you would be wasting your time. The moral: you need to find out first whether anyone can do the trick before trying to explain how it is done. The difficulty with places like Bregbo and with people like Atcho lies in deciding what it is you have to explain. Witchcraft could be linked with depression. Ideas of witchcraft might prompt guilt. The curious thing about Bregbo and the Ashanti shrines was that people confessed to abominable acts of witchcraft. It is hard to imagine that anyone would stand up in public to declare that they had done such things. Yet this is not unlike what occurs in England, for instance, when some severely depressed people may feel they are responsible for the misery and misfortunes of people they love; they too may declare themselves guilty of abominable acts. However, a confession of witchcraft and the self-accusation of a severely depressed person might sound similar, but the likeness does not go much below the surface.

Figures of speech and different standards for the display of pain and emotion may be misleading enough to cause mistakes. This can be a practical problem for diagnosis. A suspicion that someone is harming another by hidden means might be the paranoid delusion of someone with schizophrenia. A similar suspicion of occult harm might appear to be someone's firm conviction in witchcraft allegations. The idea that other people can harm one invisibly is a potent source of anxiety. The fixed suspicions of one person may be diagnosed as schizophrenic delusions, the witchcraft fears of someone else seen as superstitions. We are liable to consider both the suspicions and the fears as false, but we see a difference. Paranoid delusions and suspicions of witchcraft are not the same. The first, in theory, indicates something abnormal about the individual; the second notes something about accepted cultural beliefs. The resemblance between them is superficial. In Meyer Fortes's opinion, "Ashanti witchcraft beliefs are customary beliefs, not psychopathological symptoms, though they lend themselves to the self-accusations and paranoid delusions reported" (Fortes 1977: 148–49).

The diagnosis of depression

The diagnosis of depression in psychiatry has long provoked debate about how to define the disease and characterize its clinical varieties. The contradictory opinions about its prevalence in African populations (see Kennedy 1973) suggest that diagnosis is even more difficult when cultural influences change the presentation of the illness. Is the disease or syndrome really less common in some African communities, or is it only that the observers failed to recognize or find the sufferers (Marsella 1978)? If we suppose that the observers fail to recognize it, we cannot tell what the prevalence is on the basis of their estimates.

Grief, guilt, and suspicion are normal reactions in some circumstances. But depression as a mental illness or disease involves more than this. The name implies that a sad or gloomy mood is one sign of it. The textbooks of psychiatry describe the psychological features associated with the disease (gloom, misery, anxiety; self-reproach, thoughts of guilt and hopelessness; suicidal feelings); there are also other symptoms including physical ones (changes of sleep pattern and appetite, constipation, loss of libido, dull, slowed responses, brooding, or agitation) and signs of changed social behavior (loss of energy and interest, neglect of appearance, impaired work performance, social withdrawal, irritability).

The presence of the psychological and physical symptoms together helps to distinguish the disease syndrome from the grief that is a normal reaction to loss. But the expression of feelings varies with personality and culture. Instead of saying he or she feels miserable and worthless or suicidal, someone may complain primarily of physical symptoms—trouble sleeping, change in appetite, energy, or bodily aches and pains. Roland Littlewood and Maurice Lipsedge (1982: 200) suggest that in many Third World countries, mental illness may be seen in essence as abnormal actions rather than mistaken beliefs. Without direct complaints of feeling wretched and worthless, the diagnosis may be missed when depression is not the main complaint. From the name of the disease, the mood sounds as though it should be its mark, yet it is not always.

Within any one society, people vary in verbal skills and in their disposition to examine their own feelings. Misunderstanding is not confined to language. It applies to behavior, gestures, and demeanor. Conventions of stoicism can mislead just as customary patterns for display can. Languages are differently stocked with words for emotions, and their idioms may seem strange to foreigners. The conclusion that Africans often present psychological distress as bodily disturbance might derive simply from misunderstanding their figures of speech. Clichés we use ourselves, taken literally, would put us in a wildly surrealist world: "She was all ears," "I cried my heart out," "It made my flesh creep," "I exploded with rage." The misunderstanding of African distress could have that sort of basis. Nevertheless, we can learn the meanings of figures of speech even with foreign languages.

The difficulties of diagnosis

If we only look for the verbal expression of feelings and thoughts, signs of the illness may be missed. Arthur Kleinman (1980: 150; 1986) notes that Chinese dislike the display of distressing feelings and are taught not to show them. Disapproval and shame make people hide their feelings. He suggested that instead of voicing them, they displace their distress into an awareness of bodily aches and pains.

Andras Zempléni identifies something similar in explaining why diagnosis at Bregbo is difficult:

> It is generally accepted that one comes to consult Atcho because one is ill. What should we understand here by "illness"? There is no doubt that, among the troubles presented in consultations at Bregbo, the competent specialist would recognise both some of the major syndromes of general medicine and some psychopathological disorders dissimulated behind the thick hedge of somatisations that all psychiatrists have noted in African contexts. . . . The complaints which are by far the most frequent are those which could indicate just as well a budding organic syndrome as a diffuse malaise expressed in the "language of the body": "headaches," "body aching all over," "heartaches," "burning feelings, heaviness," etc. And what to say about those people who describe their "illness" sometimes as a diminution of their strength, that is, according to traditional idiom, in one of the constitutive aspects of the person ("I lack blood," "the devil has sucked my blood, I am almost dead"), sometimes as a misfortune put down to the magic of others ("I lack work, someone hates me"). (Zempléni 1975: 156–57)

The phrasing of feelings in terms of body language and imagery clearly requires perceptive interpretation. It is difficult with such examples to distinguish between conventional idiom, idiosyncratic, or poetic imagery, hyperbole, symptom, and sign. The problems of identifying what someone else feels from what he or she says and does have always existed.

Somatization

Kleinman has given much attention to "somatization." He defines it as "the substitution of somatic preoccupation for dysphoric affect in the form of complaints of physical symptoms and even illness" (Kleinman 1980: 149; see also Kleinman 1986). He suggests that the process or mechanism leading to these bodily complaints rests on psychological disposition but with the difference or addition that such a disposition has an ulterior cultural cause or origin. People in a society are disposed by their culture to show certain forms for the expression of illness. He suggests that "the somatic idiom for cognising and expressing depressive feelings among Chinese constitutes the affect as a vegetative experience profoundly different from its intensely personal, existential quality among middle-class Americans" (1980: 149). His suggestion is that "Depressive feelings, then, are not simply suppressed by Chinese and expressed by Americans, but rather are different feelings.... Similarly masked depression with somatization in Chinese patients may not represent substitution or displacement of a universal dysphoric affect, rather a different type of depressive feeling (i.e., vegetative rather than psychological or even a special type of vegetative state). This is a fascinating question for cross-cultural psychology and psychiatry, but not one answerable at present" (1980: 171). By the way they speak, Chinese people shift concern from the affect itself to the specific situation that gives rise to the affect. They leave the feeling vague but define the external situation that maintains it (1980: 149). The Chinese define anxiety, depressive feelings, and the like (dysphoric affect) in extraindividual rather than in intraindividual terms (1980: 160). The style of description differs but that does not necessarily show that the feelings do.

Anthony Marsella (1978: 350) roundly asserts that depression in non-Western societies implies a totally different experiential process. Depression is a disorder associated with cultures that tend to "psychologize" experience. His position is a version of strong cultural relativism. He argues, in effect, that they perceive as bodily discomfort what might have been feelings of depression under other cultural circumstances. However, in the Taiwanese Chinese cases reported by Kleinman (1980: 151–57), careful clinical examinations showed that psychological symptoms of guilt, hopelessness, gloom, and social withdrawal could be found, just as they can usually be found in "masked depression" in European and American patients. An illness felt differently in the radical sense suggested by Marsella would not be merely a question of someone being inarticulate or following a convention or disguising shameful symptoms; it would be a different inner experience.[1]

---

1. The ideas of "depressive equivalents" and of depression so far somatized that depression is not part of the illness are speculative. Indeed, the

The issue is difficult: it is at once the philosopher's question about another's subjective experience: "Can we really know someone else's pain? Or how they see the color red?" It is also a practical problem for the working psychiatrist (as, indeed, for other people). The Sapir-Whorf idea that people who use different languages live in different worlds is a half-truth at best. No one supposes that those whose language has only two basic color terms all see the world in black and white. Littlewood and Lipsedge (1982: 76) suggest that some psychiatrists would record the diagnosis of depression only if their patients actually complained of it by name or if they had delusions of guilt. However, conversely, they also observe that members of ethnic minorities in Britain may believe doctors properly deal with physical illness and that the best way to communicate with them is by trying to talk a suitable language of bodily complaints.

The evidence of the detailed case histories presented by Kleinman and Field seems to correspond to a more straightforward view of depression. They reveal combinations of physical, psychological, and social symptoms. When the psychological symptoms are not obvious from what the patients say about themselves, cultural "masking" seems to explain their absence better than some radical difference in the character of the experiences. There might be various motives for the disguise of symptoms: shyness, embarrassment, reserve, or preconceived ideas of what the doctor wants to hear about.

Description or interpretation

Many diagnostic labels convey little about what precisely the patient complained of or felt or what signs were found. This was an important element of Alvan Feinstein's critique (1964, 1967) of clinical medicine in general and the undervaluing of clinical observation, the move away from the bedside to the laboratory. The physician's attention shifts from the patient to the laboratory findings on fluids, tissues, and tracings taken from him or her. Some diagnoses in fact convey little information about what the particular patient feels or complains of. To know that someone has diabetes, for example, may identify the disease, but it hardly reveals

---

prelogical character of depression without depression might appeal to Lucien Lévy-Bruhl—an illness most apt to the Primitive Soul (Lévy-Bruhl [1927] 1928).

in what way the patient is sick and, in fact, there are many different possible effects of being ill with diabetes.

Feinstein (1964: 1175–76) distinguishes three components in the doctor's examination of the patient. Nowadays, the clinician is tempted to jump too quickly from observation to interpretation to diagnosis. But the diagnosis is an inference stated in the nomenclature of anatomists, pathologists, and physiologists, not a description of what was observed at the bedside. Clinicians often fail to distinguish the three separate acts of clinical reasoning (description, interpretation, and diagnosis); they combine description with interpretation and may fuse all three procedures into a single act of diagnosis. If the diagnosis does not describe what the clinical observer has seen or felt or heard, even less does it describe what the patient felt or did. The position in principle would not differ greatly from that of the Ashanti woman saying she was sick because of witchcraft. She is not describing her symptoms; she has interpreted them. They are masked partly because they have already been interpreted and diagnosed.

There may be a further aspect to difficulties of diagnosis. Some behaviors mimic depression. In some respects, Gnau behavior in serious illness does as well. The purpose of the behavior is not to identify precisely the symptoms experienced by the sufferer so another person can interpret them. The sufferer has already done that for himself: he now acts in a way designed to remedy his situation by calling attention to his need for help. He does not offer a description of his symptoms so much as make an appeal. Clinical encounters are not always run on the same principles. The doctor may assume that the patient's part is to describe what he feels, while the interpretation and treatment is the job of the doctor. The patient's view of the priorities is different: the doctor's primary job is to provide a remedy. The clinical tasks (description, examination, interpretation, diagnosis, treatment, prevention) are not necessarily put in the same order or given the same significance.

Thus, even within the same culture, not only between them challenges beset our efforts to understand illness and what to do about it. Medical anthropology both raises these challenges as questions to be addressed and attempts to point to paths toward providing answers.

CHAPTER ELEVEN

The impact of events

Many people associate change with stress. But the idea of stress is difficult to use. It can be given a precise definition in physics but not in physiology and psychology, where the term gains added meanings and less clearly measurable ones (Richter 1957: 31–33). The word has a double aspect, an outside or an inside reference—that is, stress as cause or stress as effect. Is it the stressor agent or the condition of the person or thing stressed? To quote Michel de Montaigne's example again, "The philosopher Pyrrho, in peril of a great storm at sea, could offer his companions no better example to follow than the serenity of a pig, their fellow traveller, which was looking at the tempest with perfect equanimity" ([1588] 1927: 485).

We should therefore distinguish the state of stress from the consequences of stress. The consequences of stress may be adaptive and valuable to the individual. Without stress, there would be no learning and no individual achievement. On the other hand, the consequences of stress may be maladaptive, leading to neurotic states, psychosomatic illness, and deviant behavior. Claude Bernard ([1865] 1949) was among the first to see disease as the outcome of attempts at adaptation—attempts that, though appropriate in kind, are faulty in amount. The reasoning he applied to physiological responses might sometimes be applied to social responses as well.

Stress and social change

Émile Durkheim's *Suicide* ([1897] 1951) was the seminal analysis of the effects of social circumstances on behavior and mental health. His own ideas were rooted in discussions at the time about the effects of a breakdown in social cohesion. "Since the basic theme of *Suicide* is the ways in which social bonds become weakened and ultimately break down in modern societies, this work has had an immediate and continuing relevance to the study of deviance and the whole field of social pathology" (Lukes 1973: 205). Durkheim, reflecting on the practical consequences of his study ([1897] 1951: 370–92), argued that it was necessary to find a remedy to the dissolution of social bonds taking place in modern society. But why think that people are so innately conservative that change in general must distress them? On the grand evolutionary scale, the species *Homo sapiens* stands out by the ability to learn, to change with astonishing speed, to adapt, to innovate; in this versatility, *Homo sapiens* also has the ability to find the source of biological success.

Must social change cause distress? Jack Goody (1957) doubted whether it was right to take new witch-finding cults as an index of increase in individual anxieties in Ashanti. "We have as yet no euphorimeters. . . . Yet sociologists and anthropologists appear to be increasingly committed to a hypothesis that culture change increases 'individual anxieties,' 'emotional malaise'! Is this not as dubious as Marx's doctrine of increasing misery under a capitalist economy? And is it not immediately suspect as a possible rationalization of the social scientist, sociologist or psychologist, resulting from his vested interest in stable phenomena?" (Goody 1957: 362). Not every precontact society existed in some Arcadian state of harmony and stability. Stephen Kunitz (1970) wryly traces the way social theory has indulged a conservative belief in stability and the supposed warmth and cohesion of the so-called primitive community. If we use the analogy of the organism, then internal stability would appear to favor well-being. Any change upsetting internal balance would be harmful. Claude Bernard's famous aphorism was that fixity of the internal milieu is the condition of a free life. Kunitz traces how this physiological idea was applied to the individual in society through Cannon's concept of homeostasis and Alexander Leighton's work (Leighton 1959; Leighton et al. 1963) on social change and mental health in different societies. Leighton and his colleagues based their hypotheses on the value of social integration, harmony, and equilibrium for both individual and social health.

Functionalism predisposes us to think in terms of equilibrium: each part should serve a function that contributes to maintaining the whole. The well-being of the whole depends on the harmonious integration of the parts. Kunitz elaborates:

> The point is that functionalist theory, which has come to be equated with equilibrium theory, resting as it does on an organic analogy of society, sees change in terms of disequilibrium, dysfunction, and even, at times, pathology. It is in this sense that I would call it conservative. The *gemeinschaft*-like community tends to be static, unchanging and without history. When it undergoes change, according to this theory, it is likely to disintegrate, and this causes psychiatric problems for its members. (Kunitz 1970: 320)

In Durkheim's usage, "anomie" referred to the absence or weakness of social rules. It was pathological, a state of disaggregation. He viewed small-scale societies as having well-established traditional rules, so they were not supposed to show anomie. Many anthropologists since Durkheim have explored how upbringing and social sanctions aim at producing conforming individuals. Deviancy is assessed in terms of the expected patterns of conformity. "In general, all modes except conformity are essentially deviant in nature, and deviancy tends to be measured in terms of the *status quo*" (Levy and Kunitz 1971: 98). But in fact, not all small-scale societies are alike in the ways they stress obedience to authority and tradition. Europeans have not always supposed that the life of those they saw or imagined as their primitive contemporaries were examples of social harmony: witness Thomas Hobbes, for one. As we cannot study precontact society, we tend to fill the vacuum with wish-fulfilling reconstructions. It is "all too easy to attribute the pathologies we can see today to the only cultural reality we are able to observe, that of contact and acculturation" (Levy and Kunitz 1971: 100). By examining long spans of records of homicide and suicide and alcoholism among the Navajo and Hopi peoples, Levy and Kunitz showed good reason to doubt that "deviance was absent from pre-reservation society as well as for doubting that social deviance is in all instances high at present, or even on the increase" (1971: 119). The levels of deviance among the Navajo and Hopi differed from each other, and these levels had remained stable over long periods. The deviance also showed patterns more consistent with traditional cultural configurations than with contemporary levels of stress or acculturation.

The question of increase in mental illness

The prevalence of diseases change. But sources of data, especially in regard to mental illness, are all too few, and it is difficult to assign exact significance to them. For West Africa, nothing sure can be said about changes in the diagnosis of depression in West African patients. Either a real change in prevalence or changes in diagnostic habits could account for the purported increase in recorded prevalence. Raymond Prince (1961, quoted in Kennedy 1973: 1141–42) has given various reasons for shifts in diagnostic findings. For one thing, there was the problem of observer prejudice: before independence, outsiders considered African peoples to be too simple and irresponsible to get depression; after independence, they believed Africans gained responsibility and its attendant cares and burdens. For another, Western doctors did not recognize culturally masked depression—that is, depressed people were not thought of as "sick" in a way that would have made it appropriate for them to come to the custodial hospitals for the mentally ill (such as there were in the colonial era), but now they come to the more dispersed, open hospital and clinic settings. Yet again, the incidence of depression might have increased under Westernization, literacy, and other modern pressures, but there is no satisfactory evidence of a real increase in mental illness, although disruptive changes took place during the colonial period (and also in the postcolonial period).[1] The early colonial phase created a mood

1. Edward Forster (1972) reviewed the patterns of mental illness for the twenty-year period (1951–71) during which he was director-consultant of the Accra Mental Hospital. He was specifically concerned to match the prevalence of mental illness (as judged by the records of the hospital) against the stresses of political events in the country. He divided the events that took place into four five-year periods: "Preparation"—the five years leading up to the independence of Ghana from colonial rule; "Independence"—the period of adjustments in the first five years of independence; "Crisis"— when Nkrumah was frightened and suspicious of revolution, so surveillance and dismissals increased and the country was impoverished and disturbed; "Change"—when the coup d'état took place (1966), followed by major political changes and economic austerities. At the hospital, the largest number of outpatients was seen during the period of crisis, the period associated with the most suspicion and increased violence. Forster considered the anxiety to be justified and the cause of the increase in outpatient numbers. The proportion of women attending the outpatient clinics increased; they seemed most strongly affected by the uncertainties. Many women had great

of resentment and frustrated resistance. The mood was propitious to the emergence of new local leaders and religious cults. William Wade Harris came at the right time to catalyze reaction. He gave his own particular stamp to Christianity in a conversion movement of exceptional sweep.

Disruption: The emergence of leaders and cults

The first part of the twentieth century, in the Côte d'Ivoire was "a time for prophets" (Marc Augé's phrase). Prophets arise in times of trouble and confusion. In West Africa, colonial conquest, the development of plantation agriculture, cash crops, the introduction of schooling and missions touched the lives of nearly all the people in some way. Some of the themes in the sermons of Harris and Atcho could be derived from experience of these events. People asked themselves how to obtain jobs, money, new tools, and the weapons that were so powerful; they speculated on what produced them. The effect was to create widespread desire for things they could not get and to awaken a sense of inferiority and aspiration. If the previous social systems had been relatively self-sufficient, relatively closed to other ideas and ways of doing things, colonization forced them to take stock of other practices and ideas.

This history is relevant to the success of Harris and the mood of the people who responded to his preaching. People had lost faith in the protection of their traditional religion and their gods. They were leaderless. Harris came in 1913–14, offering hope and leadership. When he denounced the traditional pagan religion, asking them to reject it and accept his new teaching, thousands converted. Harris had the distinction of inspiring the greatest Christian mass movement in West African history (Haliburton 1973: 30–37; Webster and Boahen 1967: 249–54).

Ghana and the Côte d'Ivoire both had a history of prolonged resistance and eventually suffering crushing military defeat. In both countries, the people were humbled by invading powers with Maxim guns. Social disruption in the Côte d'Ivoire was possibly more acute than in Ashanti and Akan Ghana because of the destruction of villages, the deportation of chiefs, and the policies of regrouping and resettling villages. But the contrast of Blacks and Whites, socially inferior and superior, was evident in both countries. The forced labor system and the land appropriations

---

difficulty supporting their families on a meager budget during the food shortages.

had enormous impacts on Indigenous Ivoirians. White settler planters were very evident in the Côte d'Ivoire. The demand for export crops—coffee and cocoa—was a strong inducement to West African farmers. The development of cash crop plantations changed local patterns of production and land use.

Harris thus emerged at a critical time. The humiliation of defeat and the disruption after long struggle left people ready to embrace a leader who offered them hope and moral direction. The striking mixture of Christianity, an explanation for Black subordination and failure, and the hope of redemption was fitting for the times. People could come together to fight against witchcraft and fetishes. Recent humiliation, frustration, and defeat provided the favorable conditions for Harris's success.

In 1918, the catastrophic influenza pandemic swept through West Africa with terrible effects that were long remembered (Field 1969: 87, 90; Peel 1968: 60). Both Margaret Field and J. D. Y. Peel believed that some shrines and cults were founded in the wake of this pandemic. Local people themselves recalled the panic and prophecies that circulated at the time. People had apocalyptic visions of doom and the need for a religious revolution or revival. Writing of the Yoruba, Peel (1968: 60–62, 70, 73, 102, 130, 292) notes that a number of prophets gained their fame by preaching about the meaning of sickness.

It was indeed "a time for prophets": their message was more telling in adversity and change. William Robertson Smith's analysis of the Old Testament prophets and the rise of the Priestly conception of sin also illustrated this point (1889). Harris believed in the power of the Bible. He carried it with him and preached from it. He broke traditional taboos and destroyed fetishes, yet no harm came to him because, he said, of what he carried with him: the Bible, the secret of White power (Augé 1975a: 290). Harris did not deny the existence of spirits and magic powers; he disputed their strength and defied them. He set out to convert people of the Côte d'Ivoire in 1913 and had great success in the endeavor. The individual who first gives direction in a time of crisis may gain much influence.

There is no doubt that Harris had exceptional and inspiring personal qualities: he captured the imagination and devotion of people he preached to. He was intelligent, proud, serious, severe, fervent. To the extent that a general change can be ascribed to the influence of one outstanding person, that person's life and the influences that molded him may be crucial to understand his or her actions and achievements. The influences of particular events in Harris's life—his narrow escape of a trial-by-witchcraft ordeal, his opposition to settlers in Liberia, his imprisonment, his vision in prison, his termination as an assistant Episcopalian school teacher—might be traced in his thought and work. They stoked the fire of his preaching. However, the success of his message cannot all be put down to the qualities and charisma of this one man.

In the case of Atcho, what else might have contributed to his success? The village of Bregbo was built around him. Before his influence, it was a small, dim place. The people who came to live there because of Atcho were not, for the most part, descendants of anyone who lived there a hundred years ago. Bregbo became the center of his network. The village, the daily crowd of people waiting, watching, and the weekly sessions of healing bore witness all the time to Atcho's power. He sought a certain glory through Bregbo. The church and Atcho's villa, Ehuyia Thérèse, were new, fine buildings in the modern style made of cement. He welcomed foreigners and embraced the idea that news, films, and books about Bregbo went abroad. The interest of research workers was flattering. The vocabulary and style of Bregbo were modern: it was a "therapeutic community," it had a "secretariat," its clerks used headed notepaper and typed up confessions. Similarly, clerks had been prominent in the early phases of the Harris movement. Perhaps other elements were copied. Ritual forms of the Catholic Church (confession, penance and absolution, baptism, and the use of holy water) were conceivably models for some of Atcho's ritual methods, but the use of ritual ablutions, with special water or herbs for cleansing, and white clays, are widely distributed in West African rituals (Peel 1968: 96, 99; Wilson 1973). Yet in his methods of consultation and treatment, one of the surprises about Atcho is that he did not borrow the outward trappings or labels of colonial medical practice, such as the hospital, doctors' and nurses' uniforms, stethoscopes, injections, and the like—even though he emphasized that he was a healer and Bregbo was a therapeutic community. It would seem that long stays at shrines have been a long-established Indigenous pattern, not an innovation copied from the hospital.

It is not surprising that Atcho's sermons were about inequality and how to get rich and powerful. Atcho's own lifetime (1903–1990) ran almost from the declaration of Côte d'Ivoire as a colony in 1893 through the ethnographic reports in the mid '70s until his death at the age of eighty-seven. It spanned periods of government by soldiers, then by civilians, French colonialists, and on to self-government; it saw the advent of cars, steam engines, and airplanes. Many Ivoirians of his generation had known schooling, a system of forced labor, Christian mission teaching, wage labor. Some got rich in business or professional jobs. The new national capital was built with multistory glass, steel, and concrete buildings. Atcho's generation watched this happen. Traditional knowledge and cultural assumptions brought from their villages did not arm them for the encounter. His generation was made acutely conscious of inequality by the treatment they received from White people by seeing vehicles and machines they knew nothing of at first and could not understand. Some of the White Europeans told them they were inferior, wicked, sinful, or stupid. Sometimes Atcho said that the lower position of Black people was God-given, at other times that it was the result of their own sin and choice of wrongdoing. According to Atcho, Black people misused powers by which they might have become clever, skillful, and rich, but they directed them to do evil. The appeal of his message was that people could change their behavior and thereby could acquire power and wealth. Atcho pointed to Africans who became rich and powerful to prove his point. He himself was an example, with his house, his wives, his celebrity and honors, his businesses. People saw how some Africans managed to cross the social gulf between Whites and Blacks and how government had passed into their own hands. Atcho taught that the powers mishandled by too many Africans by night had to be brought out into daylight, confessed openly, and transformed to bring benefits rather than harm.

The change Atcho demanded was not based on developing the inner logic of traditional ideas but on a blatant repudiation of the past. According to his sermons, Ivoirians blighted their own destiny. Development and progress depended on rejecting past practices and transforming themselves by turning from night toward day.

Atcho presented himself as a healer, not a prophet or a priest. His healing was open to all, regardless of their beliefs. He relied on the notion of the healer as someone who is purely beneficent in aim. Prophets rebuke as well as foretell. A healer, being nonsectarian, is open to all who need his or her help, concerned only with doing good. This is a comforting image. Almost everyone who stayed on at Bregbo had troubles. Some—the failed and wretched—came because they had nowhere else particular to go (Piault 1975: 40–43, 155). For some, it was a halfway house between hospital and home. Others, required to go to Atcho's community to be exposed to the truth about themselves and their own evil, stayed because they were persuaded by what he told them, to do penance and hope for salvation. Atcho and his staff provided that support in adversity by exposing evil, imposing punishment designed to expunge faults, and by offering redemption and healing through confession and cleansing. He also mediated and interceded with God on behalf of the repentant. His work was explicitly concerned with individuals and their particular problems. Atcho stated that his mission was to heal the illness and suffering of people round him.

However, this image of a healer and therapeutic community disguised the other aspects of Atcho's appeal. He was a successful businessman with commercial interests in fishing and other activities. Bregbo provided him with the labor force that brought him wealth. Atcho did not ask for payment for his healing work, but he got something in return. Bregbo was a working community as well as a therapeutic one. Those who stayed for healing were expected to work if they could and to do so for no pay. The community fed itself and ran a market. Modern and successful: the image of desirable change presented by Atcho and Bregbo appealed to African officialdom as well as to the ordinary Ivoirian and the unfortunate. Their interests were like those of the French businessmen who continued to flourish under the government of President Houphouët-Boigny. Judith Lasker (1977: 273) quoted his words: "What the Ivoirian wants is to share in wealth, not to share misery. And to do this we must, before everything else, contribute to the creation of wealth." Atcho was a good example. His relations with the authorities in power were good. The interests of government were well served by docile, unrecriminative people. Was there a kind of complicity between Atcho, his views, and the interests of government? Atcho's teaching turned witchcraft back upon itself, portraying it as sinful so as to shift responsibility for failure to the actor, turning what might have become blame pointed at powerful others into guilt felt by the unsuccessful.

Rural young people were looking for jobs and a golden future in towns but met frustration in their search. They lacked the education and skills needed for the jobs they wanted, the life they dreamed of. New cults and shrines seemed to respond to their need for support. Some among Bregbo's resident population revealed aspects of the community in this light. Barthelémy, a truck driver out of work in Abidjan, fell ill after a series of misfortunes and came to Bregbo. Andras Zempléni had many conversations with him (Zempléni 1975: 173–208, 277–322). Barthelémy had struck a European with his truck and killed him: he lost his job, went to prison, and his illness followed, marked by diarrhea, vomiting, trembling, insomnia, headaches, "pinched nerves," loss of memory, and, above all, terrifying dreams, all accompanied by domestic miseries. Zempléni reflected on Barthelémy and his situation:

If he can, just as an assumption, escape (by being at Bregbo) from the domestic hell he has been through or from the (mental) asylum at Bingerville which he has only just avoided, then that's already something gained. There is no doubt that Barthelémy prefers to live in the shadow of the prophet (Atcho) rather than to sink into madness on the streets of Abidjan. His instinct for survival would be able to find at Bregbo a place of respite. Time to gather his baggage together. For there is also no doubt that sweeping the paths at Bregbo is not the last word on his story, and that he will find himself, sooner or later, back on the real stage for his destiny, that is somewhere on the work-sites of Abidjan. (Zempléni 1975: 207)

Shrines and healing cult centers can provide places of refuge and care. But this, though conspicuous in the context of city life, is not an innovation. Rural shrines provide lodgings for pilgrims and supplicants who want to stay for a time. The organization of Bregbo as a village healing center and community is an example of a more widespread pattern, not a unique invention or a product solely of modern urban life (see Field 1960: 92–94, 105; Peel 1968: 133; Twumasi 1975: 36 for comparable examples). People's needs are obviously relevant to the existence and activities of the shrines and centers. Lack of alternative care and support for the sick or unfortunate person away from home may explain partly why they spring up, why there are so many, and why they are so varied. Medical and welfare needs were greater than the colonial health services could meet, and after independence, the government resources allocated to health continue to be small when matched against the needs of a large, widely dispersed population (Lasker 1977).

What people do when they are ill must obviously also depend on the availability of treatment—whether it exists and is accessible given their means and situation. Dennis Warren (1974: 122–23, 247–50) found Western medical services (government and mission) were increasingly used in Techiman (Ashanti) because they were close by and provided prompt treatment. Both the introduced medical services and the traditional healers continued to practice without conflict. In his opinion, the people accepted the hospital services and used them not because their own values and ideas had greatly changed from traditional to modern ones but because the new forms of treatment were convenient and available. Choice of treatment anywhere probably depends on a complex mixture of need, belief, trust, opportunity, convenience, experience, and curiosity. Situations and methods vary with whether people put trust, to a greater or lesser extent, in the methods, the healers, or the institutions.

Religion in medical change

As the authority of traditional religion was undermined, would-be practitioners had to specialize. Care of the sick was one way. People did not convert to modern medicine with an exclusive commitment. To put stress on an exclusive belief in one system of medicine is to mistake the most obvious character of demands for care in sickness—the desire for a remedy, the hope that a treatment will work. At the same time, people still wanted some protection. The call to purge evil and evildoers had its appeal to people who were uneasy. The move against witches drew support. The promise of relief was tied to identifying who was to blame. An anti-witchcraft movement could rally people to a common cause and, by uniting them, could serve latent or dissimulated political purposes.

Atcho offered more than protection or treatment for profit. His treatment had a strong religious and moral component; he taught a set of doctrines offering the prospect of personal salvation and change. He asked for moral conversion; his patients had to cease from evil. That is what the minister Denise praised him for. One might hesitate to say whether his role was medical or religious. Atcho wanted to call himself a healer, not a prophet. He chose to appear unlinked to the political and economic spheres even though he was actually engaged in them. He could influence elections in the lower Ivory Coast through his network, which put him in touch with small village communities. Atcho's plantation and fishing interests grew along with his prestige. But despite his title of healer, he was not officially recognized as a medical worker or as part of the health services. Atcho knew that hospital and clinic medicine was something quite different from the care he offered. He referred some people to the hospital, particularly the psychiatric hospital at Bingerville (Piault 1975: 63–64), but there is no information about his opinions on official medicine or what he thought of surgery, injections, drugs, and the like. He did not compare his views about the underlying nature of sickness with those of hospital medicine nor did he comment on the introduced methods or explain why some kinds of healing worked for some people but not others.

Why should a traditional religion, disturbed by social change, develop in a medical direction? A first reason is that the new orientation continues a concern it had before. Although ideas associated with religious practice and belief had been used in explaining and treating the sick, illness did not disappear. Quite the contrary: new diseases were introduced, and in some places, epidemics were unleashed. The health care provided by colonial governments fell short of what the population needed. This left the field open for folk practitioners to become even more active; despite their loss of authority in some spheres, diviners, healers, and priests were sought out to deal with personal misfortune and illness. Innovations of method took place.

There is no reason why people should commit themselves to only one system of medicine. The willingness of people in many societies to use both Western biomedicine and their own methods of treatment has been widely noted. They choose from what is at hand. They seek relief, not consistency for its own sake. Their trust is not based on belief in the system as such. It is only in a loose sense that we can say that treatments as varied as pharmaceutical drugs, surgery, psychotherapy, radiotherapy, and advice on exercise and diet fit coherently or logically within a single system. It is more accurate to see them as a highly syncretic mixture of treatments with diverse styles and origins. And in reality, the practice of introduced medicine in the developing world does not often meet ideal conditions. There may be a fine, well-staffed hospital in the capital, but perhaps outdated penicillin, fake tablets, colored candy, and steroids are being sold as modern remedies in rural markets; local people may see both as treatments introduced by Western medicine. People do not have to accept a particular body of knowledge or beliefs to swallow a tablet or inject someone in the arm; they need only the equipment. In practice, pluralism is made up of this mixture of old and new that people use based on pragmatic choice without insisting on a unified system.

Pluralism may mean the mere presence of alternatives. The new treatments and the new places for medical care are not necessarily seen as competing with customary healing methods; some are too strange to be seen as analogues or replacements. Instead, they are something novel to add or try out. It is perhaps more typical of the providers of biomedicine to perceive a conflict than it is of the people treated with it. We may think that it is pluralism that is curious. On the contrary, experience shows it is the common rule. Most people are primarily concerned with effectiveness, with practical considerations, rather than with explanatory consistency or logic. Both medicine and religion involve matters of belief and practice, but the emphasis of each is different. At Bregbo and the Ashanti shrines, the powers—whether of spirits, humans, or medicines—were used to secure particular benefits and obtain relief from illness. The approach was often more magical than religious.

Peel's study (1968) of the Aladura churches in Nigeria, despite the points of similarity to Bregbo and the Ashanti shrines, provides a contrast, showing a predominantly religious attitude toward illness. The Aladura Christian churches take an extreme line based on a view of illness as punishment for sin and on a central doctrine of the potency of prayer. They believe sickness is caused by sinful deeds and that God answers prayers. If petitioners confess their sins, God will heal them. Illness thus becomes a test of faith and abstention from medicine the sign of commitment. Medicine and divine healing are seen as rivals. The founders of the Faith Tabernacle and the Christ Apostolic Church opposed the use of medicine as an attempt to interfere with God's arrangements. This was not because they thought that human medicine could not be effective but because using drugs and other human remedies would represent a weakening and compromise of faith in Christ. If God wishes to heal, he well. It is a tough faith to follow and live by (Peel 1968: 119–35).

In a religious attitude toward illness, belief about its significance is what matters. In contrast, in a medical attitude toward illness, the main focus is on remedial action. The Aladura churches take sickness as a vital test of faith. The religious meaning of illness is what concerns them, at least in principle. The orthodox Western medical view is not concerned with the moral or religious significance of sickness but with the practical problem of what can be done to prevent or remedy it. In Atcho's explanatory scheme at Bregbo, the ties between sickness and sin were still evident. The traditional views integrate the natural world with a moral interpretation of it.

The history of medicine shows that the relations between science, technology, and ideas do not conform to grand theories about methods in the advance of science. Ziman explains:

> Sometimes a technique precedes a science; at other times, a new technology grows from a series of discoveries motivated by idle curiosity. Some techniques develop in close connection with parallel pure sciences; in other cases, practice and theory may separate for many, many years, and live almost independent lives, until they recombine fruitfully. . . . The lesson is, perhaps, that the history of science and technology is of sufficient diversity and richness that it cannot be summed up in an abstract formula. (Ziman 1976: 35)

The writings of the Greek anatomist Galen lasted centuries as the authority before anatomy turned again to practical dissection. It was a long time before the study of morbid anatomy brought any direct benefits or improvements in the practical treatment of the sick. Should we be surprised to learn how recently it was that doctors began to examine their patients (Reiser 1978), to expose them to touch, palpation, percussion, and observe their outward appearance and manner rather than just talk to them? Innovations in chemistry, lens-grinding, and electricity altered possibilities of knowing what was going on inside the bodies of the sick. A particular discovery in another field—for instance, the thermometer or the electrometer—led eventually to particular developments in medicine, sometimes significantly altering the old perspectives. A traditional system of explanation may give illness meaning in religious terms. Western medical treatments can be fitted into it necessarily subverting its ultimate or core beliefs. But as treatments at the level of symptoms and signs become more effective, the importance of treatment on the religious or moral level seems to lessen. People recognize new possibilities for controlling infirmities.

The experience of introduced Western medicine in Africa has been short. Religious and magical beliefs have been relatively resistant to change. For all the authority attaching to science and medicine in industrialized societies, many alternative beliefs and practices live on in popular esteem. As Keith Thomas concludes in his great study of *Religion and the decline of magic*, "If magic is to be defined as the employment of ineffective techniques to allay anxiety when effective ones are not available, then we must recognise that no society will ever be free of it" (Thomas 1971: 668).

Part iv: treatment

Part IV is focused on belief in treatment and on questions of efficacy. Healing activities can have various functions even when causality (in our terms) is not at issue. In the hope of relief, a great variety of things have been tried as treatments. Some are ready to believe in miracles; for others, experience brings skepticism. Different aims and different expectations guide judgment. Questions of therapeutic efficacy—of cause and effect—are almost always difficult to answer. Compliance from patients normally requires their willingness to believe a treatment might work. Also relevant is the question of trusting in someone else's judgment, skill, or knowledge, or in what has been done in the past. The shared beliefs and opinions of other people in the same community and the advice of specialist authorities are further potential influences.

CHAPTER TWELVE

Healing actions

Treatment takes many forms. According to the dictionary, the verb "to treat" means "to deal with, to act or behave toward a person with a view to a result"; the aim is not focused, as it is with "healing" and its etymological implication of restoring soundness and wholeness to the body. "Care" may be a part of treatment that is missed by the word "to cure." In common usage, "curing" has connotations of success; someone is either cured or not. However, Arthur Kleinman (1980: 82) suggested using the verbs "to cure" and "to heal" to fit the distinction between "disease" and "illness," so that we could speak of the "curing of disease" when we refer to establishing effective control over disordered biological and psychological processes, while using the "healing of illness" to refer to the provision of social and personal meaning for the life problems created by sickness. This distinction might alert the reader to think about the criteria used to identify the benefits from treatment.

Even with a view of benefits confined to biomedical aims and the sick person—ignoring others upset by his or her sickness—there is room for differences of aim: whether the removal of symptoms is a good thing or the maintenance of normal social adaptation a far better thing; whether to search out a cause to satisfy the doctor's curiosity or to search only to the extent that the patient's well-being demands; to be rational or empirical in treatment; to be satisfied with recovery or to aim at ideal health; to be quickly but only partially effective or to seek completeness and say one is "cured." Without knowing the aim, the criteria for determining success or failure remain unclear. We also need to know who made the judgment, for it is obvious that the sick person is judged beyond dispute of whether he or she feels better or not. But this view may not be the same as the healer's or physician's nor that of the sufferer's family or community.

Various elements may be thought to contribute to effective healing: the personal qualities of the healer; the correct and skillful performance of therapeutic or ritual actions; the effectiveness of the herbs or drugs used. All three elements play some part in most treatments, but at one extreme is the charismatic healer whose ability to heal is perceived as a unique individual gift; at the other extreme are therapeutic drugs or herbs with properties that are intrinsic to them, so they can be used by anyone who knows how to use them. Somewhere in between come therapeutic performances that involve mixtures of individual skills, learned techniques, and forms of complex action such as surgery, behavioral routines, rituals, spells, and magic.

Verbal techniques and moral persuasion in treatment: The healer

In the late nineteenth and early twentieth centuries, Pierre Janet (1919) did outstanding work on psychological healing. Henri Ellenberger compared his achievement to "a vast city buried beneath ashes, like Pompeii. The fate of any buried city is uncertain. It may remain buried forever. It may remain concealed while being plundered by marauders. But it may also perhaps be unearthed some day and brought back to life" (Ellenberger 1970: 409). I have plundered it a bit, especially *Les médications psychologiques* (Janet 1919), his huge historical, psychological, and clinical study of methods of psychotherapy. He wrote particularly on the healer–patient relationship and those forms of treatment depending mainly on talk, personal influence, and psychological effects. Janet was interested first by automatisms, unreflective actions such as those that could be produced through suggestion and hypnosis, both of which represented special forms of influence or persuasion. The conditions for suggestion to work in the waking state were those in which the subject's thought was depressed, as if numbed. The field of consciousness was narrowed by preoccupation with one idea, and thinking was slow, uncritical, and not easily roused or alerted (Janet 1919: 249, 279). In the case of hypnosis, there were various special ways to induce the state using fatigue, exhaustion, surprise, and shock. Some parallels can be seen when patients are anxious, weakened by their illness, and ruminating on their sickness.

Certain powers of the mind observed in connection with hypnosis and hysteria have fascinated observers. Despite suspicions about diagnoses or methods and the whiff of deception that so often came with them, they have inspired fertile speculation about mental processes and possibilities (Ellenberger 1970; Jaspers [1913] 1963: chap. 6; Kraupl Taylor 1966: 233–95). During Janet's day, such phenomena pointed to powers of the mind over the body, a chimerical diversity of signs and symptoms that could result from mental causes. They gave support to the prevailing dualistic view of mind and body. They served as models for the process of psychogenic causation, ideas of psychosomatic illness, and somatization; they have also inspired theories about the unconscious in psychoanalytic explanation and treatment.

Self-verifying convictions can result from autosuggestion. Unconscious self-deception is sometimes implicit in them, taking many forms. More varied and extreme are similar phenomena resulting from the influence of others, whether charismatic individuals or leaders or particular social groups. The role of hope and expectations in deception and self-deception, the powers of the mind over self and others, the malleability of people in response to prestige and collective pressures—these make it plausible to attribute to the emotions and the unconscious mind (as well as the conscious mind) aspects of both harm in illness and therapeutic benefit. If symptoms and signs of illness can sometimes be caused by the mind, then it seemed plausible to Janet that they could sometimes also be cured by the mind. We know the placebo effect ascribes a beneficial therapeutic effect to the expectation of benefit and the persuasions of faith. But the problem is to identify the range and limits of such effects and define them more precisely.

One component of the placebo effect is the impact on the patient of the doctor's or healer's own belief in the efficacy or value of a certain treatment. This, combined with interest and attention to the patient's condition, may influence both parties. They lean toward assuming that any improvement is due to the treatment, but any worsening must be due to the illness. Their belief seems justified to them. They attribute benefit to the independent properties of the treatment rather than to their own convictions or to the natural remission of the illness.

Nevertheless, better reasons than mere possibility are needed before we assume there are psychological causes for signs or symptoms to appear or disappear. The variety of allegedly hysterical signs has perhaps encouraged us to be uncritically ready to put illness in preindustrial society down to psychological mechanisms. It is perhaps paradoxical that we should think this about complaints of illness in individual cases when we also know about the high prevalence of malnutrition, parasitic and infectious diseases, and the often demanding environments in which people in such societies live. Perhaps there is also something paradoxical in the contrast of Denis Diderot's and Jean-Jacques Rousseau's portrayals of the classic harmony of the Noble Savage with these other pictures of the Ignoble Savage fallen victim to fears, psychological stress, and noxious emotions.

Janet studied the skills and insights of the old magnetizers, hypnotists, and folk healers. In his view, psychotherapy was not a scientific procedure and had much to learn from the art of other practitioners. He laid great stress on rapport in moral influence; it depended on a direct and personal relationship between a healer and a sick person in which the healer as an individual was perhaps more important than the method used. The healer's qualities of personality, the particular relationship with its peculiar intensity, the patient's attachment to the healer and need for direction could lead the patient to set exceptional value on the healer's words and understanding. As Janet put it,

> People act unceasingly on each other and social influences are among the most powerful causes of health and illness, depression and excitation. . . . Ever since the development of behavior and ideas about individuality, personality, and freedom, people have attached great value to the individual, to penetrating individuality, to the conquest of the individual; they have invented intimacy, i.e., special relationships determined by the particular character of two persons face to face, "*parce que c'était lui; parce que c'était moi*," and these delicate and perfected relationships are among the most powerfully exciting that society can offer us. . . . Direction is precisely the therapeutic use of this particular form of social action by people on each other. (Janet 1919: 417–19)

Albert Atcho achieved something similar in his treatment (or moral direction) when a patient who came to him had to review his or her life, the roles and relationships that he or she had been involved in, and then reconstrue them. Some healers, like Atcho, seem to have exceptional personal qualities, which they use to create confidence. Bonds of attachment and dependency grow between the patient and the healer. A sense of urgency or anxiety over the troubles of illness might be strong motivating factors behind a patient's readiness to respond. Atcho's work strikingly exemplified many aspects of verbal techniques of treatment. He had high authority and prestige; material signs of his success surrounded the patient. He gave moral direction and advice that was phrased in terms of values and ideas he and the patient shared. Although his message shifted notions of blame and guilt, it was not so radical as to deny all the former constructions of good and evil and responsibility. In his initial interview with patients, Atcho did not confront and challenge them so much as listen to their stories with sympathy and offer them encouragement, reassurance, and help. He hinted at an interpretation but then left it open for the patient to develop and explore in later sessions. In the first meeting, he assessed the patient's suitability for treatment. In the verbal interchange recorded by J. Lehmann (1972), Atcho insinuated a doubt, suggesting a reinterpretation of the moral situation to the patient. He then set up the plan of treatment through interviews and confession, established the patient's readiness to comply, and indicated the clerk who would carry it out. The clerk gradually elicited, reinterpreted, redirected, and wrote up the confession for the public rites of healing in which Atcho again acted. The elicitation of the confession might have taken a month or more of almost daily sessions with the clerk. The reliance on clerks to work with patients had come about as Atcho's success had grown and he elaborated his procedures. Atcho himself acted at the beginning and the end, but in the middle his clerks carried out the main work—that of remolding conscience and belief—which was so remarkably expressed in the written diabolical confessions. They testified to the power of moral direction and persuasion exercised at Bregbo. The eventual confession contained a great modification in the patient's personal construct of the significance of roles and relationships he or she had been involved in. The guided self-reexamination was a sort of indoctrination that led patients to adopt—or at least confess to—changed assumptions about themselves and their relationships.

The stress on a detailed review of all one's past actions, accompanied by the demand for total avowal and the repeated sessions with a clerk who directed the interpretation toward revealing acts and feelings (hidden and even barely remembered or acknowledged), inevitably recalls some kinds of psychotherapy, especially psychoanalysis, which are similarly based on avowal and confession as a means to insight and health. The meaning of past events becomes changed in the process. As at Bregbo, it is striking how people undergoing psychotherapy are willing to adopt wholly different elaborate explanatory frameworks and meanings through such a collaborative reinterpretation. The element of encouragement and support reinforces the desire of a demoralized person to accept the interpretation. It takes time for the intimacy of the personal relationship between sufferer and therapist to develop and for moral redirection to sway the patient. The frequency and duration of interviews are notable as a preparation for the culminating public act of confession, an "act of termination," as Janet called it. One aspect of diagnosis and therapy has always been to give an explanation and meaning to the symptoms the patient experiences. When the symptoms are distressing and mysterious, an interpretation of their cause and significance—sometimes just being able to give them a name—may help tame the anxiety and suffering they cause. People may then be able to make decisions with a more coherent picture of the situation; they can act with a clearer aim. But it would be a mistake to suppose that the mere explanation or naming of unhappiness and personal problems is necessary and sufficient for relief.

Atcho's treatment resembled a process of cognitive restructuring that culminated in the public act of confession. The rationale was that there was a sort of nighttime double of the self; this allowed the patient to dissociate (perhaps to distance or exculpate) himself or herself from this other self. But the analysis tête-à-tête with the clerk was not enough by itself. The private acts of self-assessment would lead up to the punishment and reward of the public act of confession that shamed the subject (as well as being a self-dramatization) before others, especially Atcho, the respected and admired prophet leader. The confession of horrifying deeds released emotion after the penances or tasks decreed by Atcho as punishment or expiation had been fulfilled. As a catharsis or purging to break the spell of evil, it gave the self-dramatization of the confession a point of release and termination, ending with the prayer and blessing by Atcho when he powdered the left foot of the patient with kaolin and gave him or her some of the lustral water (Piault 1975: 125–29).

In the end, the treatment moved from words to action. Atcho's work was an example of verbal therapy akin to other forms of psychotherapy, based on an idea of the remedial value of moral insight. Words, ideas, and meanings are the basis of verbal therapies like confession and psychotherapy. Voice, gesture, eye contact, and positioning play a part in the effects of therapy. The relationship between a patient and a therapist is crucial for its success. In the case of Bregbo, Atcho's role as well as that of the clerk who elicited the confession has to be borne in mind. The relationships involved elements resembling those in the relationships of priest to penitent, parent to child, friend to friend, trainer to trainee. In its typical European form, Christian confession a private act of self-accusation that is usually made to someone in authority and has public consequences. Without a moral authority figure, the guilt that provokes confession might not be generated. Christianity stresses the free moral and religious nature of confession by contrast with the confession extracted by coercion, torture, or threat. The confessions at Bregbo reflected these Christian influences.

Confession as a mode of treatment is not found only in societies influenced by the ethical doctrines of a major world religion. Some of the most striking descriptions of therapeutic confession come from studies of hunting and gathering societies (Hallowell [1955] 1967: chap. 14; Rasmussen 1931). The common principle behind a range of treatments is that guilty actions may harm the person who has carried them out, even when they are hidden. In some cases, exposure is said to destroy the power of evil or witchcraft. People may purge themselves of guilt by revealing their actions, by punishment, or by the humiliation of public exposure. When we focus on the elements of purging, control, and guilt, we can find a continuity of principle running from therapies based on nonverbal actions to the essentially verbal techniques of confession. If illness is specifically linked with a breach of a taboo, sickness can expose the cause, just as a sin may be exposed by particular signs of sickness. Over time, these associations may change. As I discussed in chapter 5, the history of concerns over leprosy suggests that they shifted from notions of taboo to those of sin, from emphasis on the collectivity to emphasis on the individual, from cleansing by sacrifice to notions of contrition and confession. The shift is expressed in Psalm 51: "For Thou delightest not in sacrifice, else would I give it: Thou hast no pleasure in burnt offering. The sacrifices of God are a broken spirit; a broken and a contrite heart, O God, Thou wilt not despise."

The influence of the group

So far, my focus has been on the relationship between therapist and the patient. But the group is also a powerful influence. Bregbo had the atmosphere of a therapeutic community. There was the village and the spectacle for the new arrival, who was a spectator *and* invited to take part. During the public séances when residents commented on the cures to visitors and new arrivals, a sick person could tell his or her own story or listen to it retold (Lehmann 1972: 360). Rapport connected the individual to the group. For some, the community at Bregbo provided a long-stay refuge, a place of reassurance and support, increasing rapport. The confidence of the community in the healing methods could also sway the sick person. Such an influence is a factor of special force in settings where treatment is highly public and dramatic. The group lends support to the sufferer through its shared belief and enthusiasm, its hope that he or she will get well. An improvement reconfirms everybody's faith.

People are susceptible to the influences of others. Shame, ridicule, praise, and sympathy are social responses. Readiness to imitate, to learn by example, to accept teaching, and to follow others are all necessary for participation in social life. The effects of crowd solidarity arousing emotions through sympathy, the mass of people, the noise and cries, sometimes drum beats and musical rhythms have long been exploited in practice. Heightened group feelings may also underlie the susceptibility of an individual to respond to treatment. The organization of treatment often gives a patient's family and others a satisfying way to express their concern; it may mitigate gloom or worry over serious illness. The coordination of action in distressing circumstances, the effort of acting, the arousal of hope, may contribute to reducing anxiety and may help the participants in a crisis by giving them a sense of coping with the situation.

The beauty and magnificence of some healing rites and the noise, drumming, and singing that accompanies them act on the participants and on the sick person who is their raison d'être. At Bregbo, confessions that were not public would not have had the same power to shame or to absolve patients from the guilt that led to their illness. They may have felt the force of the wish of the group that they get well, especially when the group members believe their own well-being depends on it, so sufferers may yield to the wish or try to meet their expectations. Similarly, Victor Turner's account of Kamahasanyi's illness (Turner 1964) exemplifies the shared motivation in a healing rite. It is vividly conveyed in an extract Turner quotes from his field notebook (1964: 260–61). His account of the Ndembu cults of affliction is an outstanding example among many that indicate how joining a cult or community may bring benefit through the moral support provided by other members, including those who also suffer or have suffered from the same problems as the new candidate for membership. They offer shared understanding and experience and give living proof that the illness can be overcome or lived with.

But dramatic, complex forms of treatment require preparation and organization and have a cost in time and labor. They cannot meet most needs. There must be some selection of the kinds of illness for which they are appropriate, a selection favoring chronic ailments. Acute illness cannot wait for them; much illness declares itself and begins to clear up spontaneously too soon for an elaborate healing ceremony to be got ready. Rest and isolation, nursing care, support and dietary measures, and a range of simple household remedies are at least benign in their effects and so ordinary that I have scarcely referred to them. They provide the mainstay of care for illness. But we tend to give our attention to the occasional, the uncommon, in exotic treatments. I stayed for nearly two years in Rauit, a Gnau community that then had about 350 people. In that time, there occurred one major healing rite lasting for twelve weeks and about twenty public healing rites that took a day to do; all the other forms of care were limited to nursing care and brief private therapeutic acts, including treatment I provided. During that time, the men and women exposed to risk of illness numbered 195 (I am excluding children from this assessment) and those who fell ill spent all told 2,447 days incapacitated to some degree by illness (G. Lewis 1975: 117). To present the major ritual treatments as the full subject matter with which to assess the Gnau methods for treating illnesses would grossly misrepresent the actual situation. The simpler forms of care must also be examined.

Isolation in illness: Gnau behavior in 1968–69

Gnau behavior in illness is notable for its social isolation. It is marked by the contrast with normal life, a social eclipse, and by the display of apathy; the patient looks dirty, neglected, he or she is silent, socially withdrawn, passive. It is a way of showing illness, isolating the patient, and eliciting care. When asked, local people might say they mean to show the afflicting spirits that their threat or punishment has been effective. Some sick people feel as ill as they look, others in part mean to deceive. The extreme is the inert patient lying alone unwashed, naked, in the dark of a closed hut. He eats little for fear of various mystical dangers in normal food; the sick man or woman may use nettles as a counterirritant to pains or as a stimulant. Apart from the nettles, they have few other physical remedies to use in ordinary care, with no comforts except the fire kept going beside them. If a sick man has moved from the communal men's house to a separate house, his mother, wife, or daughter may sleep on the ground beside him. A sick woman will usually have the company of her daughter, the wife of one of her husband's brothers, or some other female in-law. Alternatively, she may decide to go back to her natal hamlet.

The reduction in talking to others or being talked to is striking by contrast with normal life and sociability. If outside, the sick person sits or lies, not moving much, showing little or no interest in what is going on all around. He or she does not look for distractions or conversation. Soothing by touch or bodily contact is not part of caring for a sick adult. The Gnau do not use massage, manipulation, or rubbing, apart from the nettles with which patients stroke themselves. People now ask for liniment that they like to daub on aches; occasionally, they will prepare a poultice for an aching joint. But most of their time is spent lying alone in darkness or asleep in the silence except for the sounds of movement and activity in the village outside. Unless there is a gathering in sympathy, the village is almost empty during the day, with people gone away to work in the gardens and only one or two adults who stay, nominally to watch over the sick person but in fact to keep an eye on the small children left behind. The night brings no comforts.

Moping in the dark is miserable. The isolation and the opportunity to brood on one's illness perhaps prepare the patient for treatment as a sort of incubation. The sick person is left to ruminate on their pains, their hopes, and their fears. The isolation and darkness serve to heighten the contrast and shock of a treatment if it is done in public. The length of illness is noteworthy. Long isolation and immobility, food avoidances, neglect, and dirt are undoubtedly debilitating. An element of deliberate self-degradation is also involved, either to deceive an afflicting spirit or to match the outward self to an inner feeling. Coping with a long illness contrasts with short-term illness. The seeming apathy and passivity of the Gnau in serious illness resembles prescribed helplessness, as if they knew they could do little in illness except wait and see. The stereotyped pattern suggests giving up: a numbed reaction, limpness, dejection. The behavior is meant to be registered by other people; it is up to them to act.

Treatments observed in 1968–69

During an illness, people come to give treatment to the sick person, some on their own impulse, others called. The same kind of treatment may be done more than once for different reasons or by different people during an illness. But usually each one who provides treatment does so in a single session, completing it in a few minutes, and that is that. The caregiver is not by occupation a specialist in healing. Although in most cases the healer is a man, the person to act, being determined by relationship, knowledge of some spell, or by particular circumstances, may occasionally be a woman.

The method is what matters rather than the individual who performs it, except in those cases when a certain person is required because of having a particular social relationship to the patient. Personal rapport is not in general a striking feature of these short treatments. In theory, the timing of the treatment might be important for making connections between cause, treatment, and effect, or for pacing, as it were, the effort to help. But in practice, interventions are often so unplanned or contingent upon opportunity and impulse that no consistent pacing effect seems likely. Some suffer long periods of inattention; Wolai's illness (described in chapter 3) was a poignant example of that. The passivity of the patient is striking. Most short treatments are private in the sense that, although one or two members of the family may be there to watch and assist by supporting the patient or fetching betel nut or doing something needed for the treatment, others do not crowd around to watch. It would be ill-mannered to come just out of curiosity. The private interaction between healer and sick person is both direct and oblique. When the therapist asks the patient, for example, where the pain is felt, an attendant member of the family is likely to give an answer instead. The therapist may gaze intently at the patient but eye contact in which the patient returns the gaze is rare; instead, he or she looks downward, listless. If the therapist asks a question, it is repeated to the sick person or answered by someone in the family; if required, the patient's arm is lifted for him or her. The behavior of people receiving treatment sometimes gives the impression of a passive human doll being moved rather than moving, suffering treatment rather than seeking it.

Treatment takes place in the day, usually early in the morning or late in the afternoon rather than at night. These are the times for brief social calls—before people go off or when they get back. Someone in the patient's family fetches or helps him or her to the porch of the hut where there will be enough light to see (their houses have no windows); occasionally, the healer goes inside. The reasons for doing the treatment may have been discussed beforehand with the family but not with the sick person, especially if the patient is a woman or a child. She or he does not ask for explanation but submits to it. Action is taken as though on an object with little or no direct exchange of speech between the one who is sick and the man performing the treatment. The choice of healer is defined by the situation, kinship connections, or the particular event rather than by special skills. He is someone familiar and fallible as others are. Such confidence as the Gnau have in their treatments seems to be placed in the method rather than the healer. It is confidence in general; often the attitude to particular treatments is less a strong conviction than simply trying a shot in the dark because they have some reason to think it might work. The treatments do not put in question or challenge someone's personal claims to possess good judgment or skill. Although the sick person shares the same general assumptions as those who perform the treatment, his or her understanding of the particular reasons for doing it may differ from theirs. Wolai's case exemplified discordant views on the cause: Whose magic? Sorcery? Was it his own fault? A breach of taboo? His anxieties about himself were all not shared by those around him, and nothing was done to calm them. It is not difficult to find discordant views just by asking several people what they think about the same situation.

After treatment, there was rarely any immediate change in the demeanor of the patient, except in some cases when objects were extracted from the patient's body. More people were present in these cases, anxiously excited and watching. The extractions seemed to calm them. One woman stopped trembling after treatment, another began to speak again after having been almost mute for two hours, holding her hands over her ears, which she kept bent forward to cover her ear holes. Few people said of their own treatment that they felt suddenly different or relieved after it. They expected to have to wait for a few days to notice improvement, but for how long was uncertain. The healer's concentration during the treatment was matched by the spontaneous declarations of some who said they had put effort into doing it and felt tired or weakened by it. Some said they felt that there was risk in carrying out a treatment, a risk posed by the spirit concerned. One man said he was threatened by the spirit in his dreams after he had treated someone and he took to his bed to make the spirit think it had punished him already and need do no more.

The manner of the healer is contained and his attention concentrated. He does not chat or comment on what he is doing. Many treatments have verbal elements, muttered or choked spells with special noises or trills, accompanied by spitting, blowing, or puffing onto things being used or spat directly onto the patient. The spells are very low, suppressed, secret noises just audible to the patient. The therapist may also speak in a strong voice directly to the afflicting spirit or to spirits of the dead, stating the intention of his treatment, reproaching the spirit for harming the patient, and telling it to leave. The therapist may strike the patient on the chest, head, or arms with the nettles or materials he is using; the blows are intended to startle off the spirit. They are given with sufficient force to cause the patient to jolt or wince. Other forms of treatment involve firm stroking of the affected part with nettles, the movements repeated downward and distally as though to gather together the harm, to bring it into a little pile, and sweep it off at the end into the nettle. The harm is then thrown away by the therapist with a curious overarm gesture. There are other more complex extraction procedures, such as the removal of "arrowheads" described in Maka's case (see chapter 2). The mime, the obvious symbolism of the gestures—removing, sweeping away, sucking out, jolting off, throwing away, cutting free, scolding, sending off, offering valuables, washing—convey what they hope for and an idea of their assumptions about the process of healing. The aims are also stated in the appeals and prayers that precede and counterpoint the action.

The private treatments are usually short; they rarely involve more than five minutes of interaction between patient and therapist. They end with the patient being told (and here the speech is direct) to shake and stamp, to shake off the harm. Water is spat in a fine spray on either side of the patient, which is a form of asking for a good outcome. The patient may be given the betel quid to chew that the therapist was chewing during his action. Alternatively, the patient's arms are jerked to make the joints crack or the fingers pulled and bent to make the knuckles crack. These are taken as signs of a favorable outcome. The patient then sits down or goes back or is helped back into the hut and left alone; the others turn away and go without further comment or inquiry about how he feels.

Treatment gestures and symbols

Some elements in Gnau treatments have distinct names: there are the special materials called *geplagep* (dry or shredded plant substances), *wa'agep* (the cooked preparations like a thick soup or a stew in consistency), and nonmaterial elements such as *belyigap* (spells). These terms identify three types of things that activate or concentrate mystical power (see G. Lewis 1980: 154–58, 171–73). Knowledge of them is esoteric rather than open. The plant preparations have distinctive smells or tastes, using ingredients such as marsupial scent glands and ginger roots and herbs. Spells are transferred into them during their preparation. These ingredients are peculiar, as are the sounds and words of the spells and the song verses used in many treatments. Their special power and quality—peculiar in the intransitive magical or sacred sense described above as "mystical"—are signaled by the rules governing their preparation and the oddness of the sounds and vocal techniques used, for example, choked noises, trills, chanting, and allegedly archaic language.

In many societies, the magical power of sacred words often harks back to the past, to an occasion or a time of revelation (Tambiah 1968). The Gnau see it like that, too, and quite explicitly, as I heard in comments they made during ritual performances about the fixed, just-so origin and quality of what they had to do (Lewis 1980: 50–67). Magical words are something revealed, already set, arbitrary, to be learned, not something to be discovered by reasoning and observation. They use verses from their great songs as spells, adding secret names; they link performance of the verses with the presence and attention of spirits. The songs and spells concentrate their presence, attract them or call to them, as do things from the places and the plants the spirits are specially attached to. People treat the spell sounds, the words, and the secret names almost like objects that can be transferred by speaking or blowing them into substances, leaves, or a person to be healed. The objects then serve as vehicles for transferring an influence, acting as surrogates for the words (Skorupski 1976: 130–59). They are used as if they had an active creative power.

Breathing and blowing spells, as well as spitting betel juice or water, are characteristic techniques of many Gnau rituals and treatments. They involve both communication and transfer. They blow or spit onto objects, onto the patient's skin, or into his or her mouth to transfer an effect. Words and spells may be addressed to thought or objects, to spirits or people; some utterances have fixed forms for repetition, other forms are free and discursive, more like speech or appeals directed at a listener.

The Gnau have various verbs or phrases to refer to these special forms of action and gesture, techniques of the body used in treatment and ritual. The phrases have precise meanings in context; they are, in effect, a technical vocabulary for identifying the elements and distinctive actions of which rituals and treatments are composed (G. Lewis 1980: 43–50). The prayers or speeches in free form, delivered aloud to the spirit or the ancestral spirits, are said to be given in a "loud voice" (*nunt bu*), in contrast to spells and secret names, which are given in a "small voice" (*nunt seki'in*). The spitting and invocation addressed to the spirit "set up" their

Figure 14. A sequence of fieldwork photos shows Dukini healing a feverish child by using a simple treatment ascribed to the spirit Panu'et. From left to right, top to bottom: He waves bespelled nettle leaves over the child; he calls on the spirit to leave the child; he strikes the child over his shoulder blades with the bespelled betel nettles to drive the spirit out; he ends the treatment with a gesture throwing the spirit off.

request and command its attention. The Gnau refer to the invocation by a verb that ordinarily means "to stand something upright." They speak of "bringing" a spell and "throwing it down" into something, "blowing" it in, or "laying it out" over something.

There are different techniques of spitting: ones used with betel juice, saliva, herbs chewed in betel quids, or water to spray during cleansing or the end of a ritual; ones specific to blowing spells into objects, onto skin, or into ears; ones for spitting spells directly into the mouth or for

Figure 15. During a Panu'et rite for a young man's hunting success, a senior man stands before a wooden image of the clan spirit attached to the main post of the men's house. He spits betel nut juice and herbs filled with spells onto the image and smears it with blood from a cassowary just killed in a hunt. The spitting attracts the spirit's attention so it will hear the appeal to bring success to the young man.

transferring them with nettles and blows. The techniques involve different details: whether the patient confronting a spirit should identify him- or herself by having the betel quid with the spirit's special herbs or flowers already in his or her mouth; whether the person extracting magical arrowheads should be thinking of what he is doing; how much the concentration of effort in performance exhausts the healer; whether the healer clamps his lower lip between his teeth to block his breath and force his blood down into his arm as he strikes the patient with the bespelled nettle and treatment materials; and so on. Despite this long list, I doubt I learned all the refinements and nuances of the many techniques.

The commonly used gestures are odd and distinctive; they identify the peculiarity of certain treatments as clearly as special trills and archaic language do the spells. There are verbs and phrases for the repertoire of special gestures: a type of patting that strikes hard and gathers up the

Figure 16. In the Panu'et treatment for hunting, the senior man, standing, prepares shredded ritual herbs (*geplagep*) to give to the younger man, seated. A green *lyimungai* banana leaf with two red hibiscus flowers lies ready for use. As in most rites, the procedure involves an invocation for success uttered over the leaf, which is held above the subject of the ritual, marking the culmination of a critical stage of the rites. (Color image available at www.haubooks.org/pandoras-box.)

illness (*na'abepeda*, "strike-striking him/her with it"); a light, tapping sort of patting (*nagelilapeda*, "blink-patting"); a kind of brushing; just touch; a patting that marks out an area or measures off and surrounds the patient (*nasila*, "peeling"); a way of waving something over the patient so its influence falls on him (*ne'aiya*, *ne'aiyeda*), almost the converse of the harmful influence that falls on someone from overshadowing or "stepping over him/her" (*nauwererapen*); a gesture for "throwing away" the illness and the spirit (*nitawa wilep*); another for sending it off (*nasubla*); one for making the finger joints crack (*nagelapen bigep*); and the like.

The types of special preparations are few. Plants considered necessary for the *wa'agep* soups include six to ten types. The lists of plants associated with making images and masks of spirits are longer (fifteen to twenty items). The same plants may be used for varied purposes, especially those with strong scents (which, as a set, are called *silwi-silwok*, used to scent many rituals). Other materials (such as water from special pools, blood, silt, mud from pools, bark, or termite nest powder) may be needed for different preparations.

Other elements used in treatments act on different senses—sight, touch, hearing, smell, and taste. They may be material objects, sounds and words, scents, the taste of betel quids containing *geplagep*, ginger, and hunting-ash "salt" in *wa'agep*, the sting of nettles, touches and blows, special gestures, the colors of leaves and red hibiscus, red betel juice, and so on. However, the media used for treatments do not involve a complicated technology, and many gestures are simple and clear. Elements of the small private treatments can be combined and elaborated in large-scale rituals for illness.

In long treatments, an imagery of release may suggest itself, as in the example of cutting the creeper wound around the patient's body. There are reiterated assertions that the patient will get well. The performance is ended by an action or sequence in which the spirit's body image is destroyed and the spirit is sent off. There is an element here of make-believe, of wish fulfillment, of stating and acting out what is hoped for. It is almost like the performance of a play. The analogy suggests a number of questions about the form of treatment and how closely the analogy holds. Plays involve a plot, direction, cast, settings, and an audience; so do the complex treatment rituals, with their clear imagery of confrontation, appeal, and release. The first actor—the (passive) protagonist—is the hidden patient waiting to appear at the climax of the drama. The second is the spirit at the center of the drama. Then comes the cast of kin and supporters, led by the senior men who organize and stage it and act

Figure 17. In preparation for healing a patient, a senior man spits bespelled *ge-plagep* herbs and betel nut juice onto the hand of the masked figure of the spirit Malyi before it leaves the enclosure. (Color image available at www.haubooks. org/pandoras-box.)

as chorus with the young men, who also collect the materials and make the "props," and the audience of women, children, and visitors.

Who is the recipient of the benefit? There are various ways we might respond: the patient, whose physical state or moral improves; the patient's family and friends, who desire to help him or her and have the satisfaction of doing so by organizing the treatment and watching; the healer or group of people, who gain prestige or other rewards by carrying out the treatment; or the community, which gains a sense of solidarity and self-reliance. Perhaps belief is affected by this heightened activity and the visible presence of the images of spirits and beings—the point

Figure 18. The large masked figure of the spirit Malyi emerges from its enclosure to meet the patient and perform its healing. (Color image available at www.haubooks.org/pandoras-box.)

is that sickness is a conspicuous trigger for religious activity in this society. Indeed, sickness is a catalyst for the performance of major rituals throughout this region, the Lumi Subdistrict of West Sepik New Guinea (McGregor 1975; Mitchell 1978).

Performances

In Gnau healing performances, the intentions of the actions are explicitly expressed in the accompanying invocations and appeals. The performance involves driving out or extracting the harm, first with a statement, then with an enactment of the wish to be fulfilled. In the appendix of this book is a transcribed recording that conveys the character of a performance: the talk and the levity, people's worries about getting it done on time, the banter between the men, the alternation between off-handed remarks and serious comments, the cues and concern with order and detail. The transcription gives a better sense of Gnau attitudes and understanding, the diversity of opinions, and the complexity of a performance. In general, the plot of the longer treatments is revealed by the sequence of actions. The meaning is clear in outline but not in the details. Obviously, an insider's ability to catch hold of unstated assumptions and associations is more acute than an outsider's. The significance lies in what can be seen as well as in what is said. The interplay of the verbal and the visual allows for both reinforcement and discord, for example, in the contradictory mixture of appealing to an apparently powerful spirit, followed by "killing" it, or in the gesture of throwing a spirit away but also requesting it to stay nearby to benefit their gardens or bring hunting success.

The necessary preparations give the patient time to build up hopes in the treatment. In major rites, much more is invested in the time and labor of staging them. The masks or objects used and the singing and slow pace of some rites create a greater sense of power and mystery. Many people participate in them. For the patient, direct involvement may be confined to one brief exposure to the spirit or, in long rituals, to a series of brief exposures. The brevity of this direct contact between patient and spirit conveys the quality of a shock or of repeated shocks of confrontation. The patient is told to expect to get better and that the spirit affliction will be destroyed and depart from him or her. In the long ritual for Dauwaras, which lasted over three months, the pacing was drawn out as it became distressingly clear he was not getting better. The sequence of acts in the ritual should have corresponded with a pattern of improvement, but they could not be made to fit the reality of his deterioration. People waited, hoping for a change that did not come and, in the end, bleakly accomplished the performance to the sad counterpoint of his worsening state.

In a long ritual, the narrative sequence brings the spirit to confront the patient and release him or her after various exchanges, and then the spirit is sent off. The sequence should depend on the patient's signs of improvement, these serving as cues for the next act in the sequence. But if those cues do not appear, even after waiting for a period, the sequence still must be completed so the dangerous spirit, whose presence is

Figure 19. The patient Dauwaras, carried on a platform, confronts the spirit Malyi for healing. He shows the spirit which knee is the most painful. Malyi will next touch him with the nettles, betel, and spells fixed to its arm while the gathered crowd sings verses selected from the spirit's long ritual song. (Color image available at www.haubooks.org/pandoras-box.)

concentrated by the ritual, can be sent away. The ritual sequence does not allow for a variety of endings and outcomes. The response to a particular case can be adjusted in terms of hastening or delaying the next move, but the timing is more apt to be determined by contingencies such as other demands on the performers' time or the presence or absence of people needed for the ritual. Responses are not finely adapted to the illness.

Changes in social attitudes toward work and the division between weekdays and weekends are gradually appearing in Rauit. By 1985, gatherings to show sympathy for the sick had become less immediate, less

Figure 20. Photos, assembled from 16mm film, showing how Dauwaras, by then severely debilitated, creeps back into the solitude of his wife's house.

pressing, and less obligatory than in what I witnessed during my first visit in 1968–69 or the second in 1975. Visiting because of illness became less frequent; when it did occur, it was more often fitted in during weekends. If this reflected a changing attitude toward time and scheduling, it seemed strange to me. There was scarcely any reason for it in the village, since no one had to follow a strict schedule except the schoolteacher, who came from elsewhere, and the schoolchildren. The changing attitude toward illness and gatherings of sympathy suggested that the Gnau were beginning to leave illness more to the individual, to his or her family, and to the aid post and people specially trained to provide care.

CHAPTER THIRTEEN

A Sepik performance of treatment

Some performances for healing the ill are more elaborate and complex than others. Among the Gnau's more elaborate treatments, the Panu'et ritual was the one I saw performed the most times. This chapter describes it as viewed by an outside observer. The appendix contains the transcript of a recorded performance, giving a more direct idea of the atmosphere of the event and the participants' points of view.

The performance takes up a full day (G. Lewis 1975: 169–80; 1986). Men must go to find the plant materials to make an image of the spirit at the place where the patient was supposedly struck. Materials for the *wa'agep* soup and the Panu'et image must come from where the spirit was actively present. The men set off in the morning to a garden, sago grove, or pool. As they go, they collect the plants and materials associated with the spirit and needed for the ritual: ginger root, sweet-smelling and decorative herbs, mud from a pool by sago palms the spirit nurtures, and the special flower of Panu'et.

The first act, as it were, is set in garden land. The sick person's male relatives and neighbors look for materials to make a basic image and persuade the spirit Panu'et to return with them to the village. The women of the hamlet may need to go to the gardens to fetch food for entertaining the visitors and participants, but they must return ahead of the men. Women are excluded from collecting the ritual materials, which underlines the point that men act on behalf of all in relation to the spirits. The men reassemble at a prearranged garden site after they have found what

Figure 21. A sago stand with mature palms. It is a place associated with the spirit Panu'et.

Figure 22. A sago worksite where women are chipping out the pith from a felled sago palm.

they need. By whistles or ululation, they warn any women still in nearby gardens to clear off. Women stragglers who pass by after that get rude remarks. The men are in control of the ritual, which they see as a duty.

At the garden site where they have assembled, they make a body image for the spirit. Its outward shape is a bark-wrapped cylinder tapering at the ends, about a meter and a half long. It has an internal anatomy composed of leaf and vegetable equivalents, specifically chosen to stand for the spine, ribs, heart, lungs, liver, bowels—an internal vegetable anatomy hidden from sight when the completed image is wrapped in its long cylinder of pinkish bark, its "skin." When the men have tied the skin in place, they prepare a meal that includes sago jelly. In striking contrast to everyday practice, the men themselves "turn" the sago (i.e., mix sago flour and boiling water to make *hatwara* sago). They then eat together at the garden site and, with invocations, place some of the food, betel, and coconut, on a makeshift offering platform at the place where they have made the image. The invocation prayers to Panu'et draw attention to their offering and ask the spirit to come back with them to the village to heal the sick person (a woman named Milek in the case I will describe). They carry the image back to the village where the sick person lies, and the second act begins.

Figure 23. Men make an image of the spirit Panu'et at the sago grove where it struck the patient Milek. They fashion the body of the image by using sago leaf fronds for its rib cage, a wild yam tuber for its heart, and two upright cordyline leaves for its lungs.

Figure 24. The patient's husband crouches beside the undecorated Panu'et image, now with bark for its skin and the two leaf lungs marking the front of the image.

Now in the village, the plain bark image is decorated. The men speak of pleasing the spirit so it will enter the image. They do not hide for it at this point but expect women and children to keep clear of where they are working. They prepare some paint and cut a sago-palm leaf base into a triangular shape for a brush, then paint a face, eyes, and ears on the head. The face is bound in place on the image with shell ornaments and pig tusks. After the face is done, male ornaments and a headdress are added, allowing the long cylindrical object to take on the shape of a human form. Up to then, only the two large red cordyline leaves (the "lungs") sticking out of the bark "skin" showed which side was its front side and which end was the head. The shell valuables and male finery decorating the figure render it worthy to receive the spirit. It must look splendid before the men call on Panu'et to enter its image. Through invocations and spells blown into its vital center, face, ears, headdress, and onto the stinging nettles tied around its base, the spirit is cajoled to enter its image. They say the image then feels heavy with it. They call for Milek, the sick woman, to come forward. She has not been evident until then.

Figure 25. Senior men wait back at the village while the junior men collect the materials and make the Panu'et image at the sago site.

Figure 26. Once back in the village, the junior men paint a face for the Panu'et image, using a sago-palm leaf base as a brush.

The entry of the patient to confront the spirit marks the beginning of the third act, the climax of the performance. People gather around and their attention is focused on the action. The patient is given a betel quid with *geplagep* herbs in it to chew. The men surround her and start to sing Panu'et verses. Over her, they hold a bespelled *lyimungai* banana leaf, with two red hibiscus flowers attached, so she is in its shadow, and someone brings a bowl containing cooked ginger *wa'agep* soup and holds it in shadow as well. The leaf is like a long, pale green parasol splashed with scarlet. Milek declares herself before the spirit and begs it to leave her. One man holds the image horizontally with the stinging nettle base toward her. He brushes it against her, "peeling" around the areas that hurt and then brushing her limbs and trunk or just beside them so as to mark out her whole body, brushing and stinging her.

This sequence ends when he passes the image briefly between her legs, lifts the whole image over her head, and waves it in an arc over her. While this is done, the surrounding men sing relevant verses from Panu'et's song; the singing is part of making the spirit present. One of the men flicks her with a sprig of stinging nettle leaves. The man holding the image then jabs the base of it down to strike the earth at her feet with a jolt. The presence of the spirit and the confrontation ends with the jolt, dislodging the spirit from the image. The singing stops and the image is laid on the ground, as though it were dead. They say they have "killed" it—the verb they use means to kill, hit, or shoot.

With the spirit dislodged, the men cut the image open where the red cordyline leaves—its lungs—stick up through the bark. These mark the surface position of the image's vital center, but they refer to this action as "opening its pouch" (using their word for a marsupial pouch) or "letting the cold in" to cool the hot power. They extract some of the vegetable insides, including its tuber heart and lay them on the *lyimungai* banana leaf with some feathers and fur from the finery. The leaf with the vegetable bits of the insides is again held over Milek. An invocation and spells are sung as tobacco smoke is blown across the leaf, across the hearth ashes and the bowl of soup, and across her as she stands. The leaf is torn down its midrib so that the bits taken from the image spill down over her and fall to the ground.

All the senior men now treat Milek to expel the spirit. They give her some of the ginger *wa'agep* soup and pick up fallen materials from the image to extract the harm. They use spells and spitting as they address the spirit Panu'et, explain to it about her illness, and call on it to recognize who she is and to leave her. They address the image as if it were

Figure 27. A banana leaf filled with spells is held over Milek and she is brushed with the nettle-covered base of the Panu'et image. The men surrounding her sing verses from the song belonging to the spirit.

a person, giving it reasons why it should relent. After speaking their spells into it, the senior men give her more soup. Some put shreds of the cooked mixture directly in her mouth, others give it to her by hand over their right shoulders with their backs to her—a gesture recalling the way a mother pulls her child up onto her back to carry her. They pick up bits taken from the image in a nettle leaf and use them to brush her skin, as if to gather up and remove any illness left inside her, catching the harm with the leaf and brushing it off. Some men strike her sharply as if knocking out the illness. As they do so, they call out loudly for the spirit to leave her and go away to the bush belonging to others. They then throw the harm away with an overarm gesture, as if throwing it far away in the direction they want it to go. They tell her to stamp or to shake her head to get rid of the influence. After all the senior men involved have done this, she goes to sit down.

Next, some women bring hot water heated in green bamboos. They gather around her to bathe her, first with hot water and then with cold, cleansing her body to remove the dirt and illness. It serves as an ending, an act of termination. The treatment is over. Everyone can now sit down now to a meal that the women bring. The sick woman does not eat with the others, instead going back to her house. The meal with everyone eating gathered in groups is a part of all Gnau ceremonies.

On a few occasions, I was struck with how patients who had appeared frail, tremulous, and weak-voiced when they first confronted the Panu'et image changed after the treatment and began using a more normal voice and posture.

The effort of support

A great deal of effort is involved in organizing a treatment for someone who is ill. The senior male relative closest to the sick person—husband, father, or brother—is usually responsible for mobilizing a network of kin and neighbors. He gets support from older men who live in his immediate hamlet and who are likely to be lineage or clan kin. Whenever people gather, they hear about an illness and begin planning it and sending messages. In the transcript in the appendix, the cast of people who speak most often includes members of the patient's husband's hamlet (Watalu), her brothers from the hamlet of Wimalu, and her married daughter and son-in-law from Pakuag. There are some other men present who have come from a fourth hamlet, Bi'ip. They belong to the same clan as her husband and have come in solidarity with him.

Watalu has a mixture of clans. The patient's husband, Purkiten, has strong ties to the other senior Watalu men—notably Maluna and Tawo, who live in the hamlet but are not of the same clan. The senior men from Wimalu have come to take part in treating Milek, the patient, because they are her brothers (i.e., Marki is her brother and Silmai is her collateral brother). They are expected to show concern for her and her children. Silmai, once Wimalu's *tultul* (government village official), wily and forceful in character, plays a conspicuous role with gusto, telling others what to do. He directs banter at the junior men doing the hard work. By contrast, Milek's husband says little; he is busy in the background making sure the necessary food and materials are ready. He holds the finished image for the confrontation between his wife and the spirit, touching and stinging and marking her out with it, while the others sing. Galwun, their son-in-law, helps energetically with the preparations. Two of the junior Watalu men, Walei and Waleka, paint and decorate the image, with assistance and advice from others. Milek's sons are boys still, so they have no responsibilities for this treatment. Very little is heard at all from the women, who keep apart while the decoration of the image is going on; some are cooking, others have come as guests. They include the wives and families of the men from other hamlets who are helping to perform the treatment. Some of the women sit near Milek. Her daughter Dauwanin has to do much fetching and finding, besides giving her mother support. She is the eldest, a busy daughter with her own family to look after, who has been cooking, fetching things, and helping her mother during her illness.

The presence, gathering, and noise of all these relatives and friends are evidence of their support, perhaps an encouragement to the patient. The pattern of seated groups and the movements of different people as they fetch food or materials needed for steps in the treatment reveal aspects of control and the division of responsibilities. The separation of men and women is expressed spatially and in their different tasks. The conventional picture of authority, with the senior men directing the junior men, dominates in the casual mixture of their voices reiterating what to do next.

The movements in the performance from the village to the garden and back to the village mark transitions and intervals in the acts. They link the different settings that involve a contrast between the public focus of treatment in the village and the privacy and exclusiveness of the junior men as they fashion the image in the garden. Spatial shifts of focus are matched by shifts of attention, intensity, and grouping. The early part of the day, when the men search for materials in the garden, seems quite casual, involving just an expedition. Their attention heightens as they get ready to construct the image. They check that they have all the materials needed for it and the *wa'agep* and *geplagep* preparations, and then they begin making the figure. Once they have wrapped and tied it up, they can relax a bit. They eat at the garden, make the offering, and persuade the spirit to come back with them to the village. The return journey is often a cheerful trip, faintly resembling a return from a successful hunting trip. They reenter the hamlet with the figure, which is the cue for the next phase—the decoration in the village.

These various entrances and exits lend a pattern and rhythm to the treatment. They focus attention and act as cues to the groups and categories of participants. Timing, space, movement, grouping, effort, attention, and concentration contribute to the effects of the experience. As the Gnau see it, the men go out to find the spirit and return with the image, accompanied by the spirit. However, the spirit has yet to be persuaded to enter the image. Many entries and exits take place: the entry of the image into the village, the entry of the spirit into the image, the entry of the patient, matched later by the dislodging of the spirit, the "killing" of the image, the removal and casting off of the harm, and the sending off of the spirit. These are brought to an end with the cleansing of the patient, the act of termination. In the transcript, the participants bluster about the right order of actions, having things ready, and getting the treatment done in time, with daylight going and the evening frogs starting to pipe. Though much of it hardly sounds serious, it gives the scene a sense of urgency and exhilaration.

The patient has not seen all the fiddling and painting and fixing needed to make the image; it will be revealed to her as a finished figure. Until then, she has been apart, mostly silent and alone. By the time she comes forward to confront the spirit, the junior men have already done their bit. She looked tense and tremulous. The senior men surround her, calling out to the spirit, chanting the verses. The tempo of different actions and the calls speed up, and the intensity heightens as others come close to watch. Everyone focuses on what is happening. The press of people, the calls, and the mixture of actions make it difficult to see exactly what is being done. Different people are doing different things at the same time. Items like the decorated image and the banana leaf stand out visually. It is dramatic when the image is thrown down with a jolt, when the leaf taken from its insides is torn up and the bits showered over the patient, and when the senior men call out and trill spells as the illness is gathered up and thrown off. These actions catch everybody's attention in the flurry of activity. From the start of the confrontation to the point of

Figure 28. Milek stands while her brother Silmai strikes her with nettles. Her husband Purkiten holds a bowl of a special soup of herbs (*wa'agep*) for her. After this, the base of the Panu'et image will be banged on the ground to jolt the spirit out of it.

throwing away the harm, the scene is one of the people gathered around the patient and concentrated on her. The idea that the spirit is present is reinforced by appealing to it in loud voices, addressing speech and song to it, moving the image around, and waving the leaf over it. When it is over, the pace suddenly slackens and the central focus is lost as the men disperse to go and sit down. The patient moves to the side, and some women come with water to wash her, but people do not gather to watch this. After the treatment, no one seems to pay much attention to the patient any more except her immediate family. But they also have to entertain the visitors and the people who have done the work. For those assembled, it is a time to relax and chat.

Form and effects

There are some final points to note on the form of Malik's treatment. The reason for holding it was because the diagnosis attributed her illness to Panu'et. The aim was to persuade the spirit to desist from causing harm to her and to make it leave. These intentions were clearly expressed in words addressed formally to the spirit and in comments made by participants to each other during the preparations and performance. The method of achieving the purpose followed from the Gnau theory of illness and their diagnosis of this case; the performance expressed and interpreted these concepts. The spirit was made visible in an image, the harm extracted, the spirit "killed" and sent off, and the harm thrown far away. The treatments they perform are logical, given their belief in certain notions about sickness and spirits. A few details depend on particularities in the case (for instance, which garden site the materials must come from, which people will act as organizers and participants), but there are not many other variations dependent on the precise circumstances of the case or on particular clinical aspects of the illness. The response is not specifically adjusted to the individual case other than identifying where and when the spirit struck. If the diagnosis is made, the form of treatment follows according to a set pattern.

We might ask, then, whether the treatment strengthens belief in the theory behind it. "As imagination bodies forth the form of things unknown, the poet's pen turns them to shapes, and gives to airy nothing a local habitation and a name" (Shakespeare [1595] 1992: 3.4). Logic or a rationale does not necessarily have practical effects. The analogy with the performance of a play can be taken only so far. The treatment seems to confirm a theory of illness by making the cause visible. It is make-believe in the sense that the spirit is given form, made present to sight, hearing, smell, and touch. Ideas are objectified; gestures enact the extraction of illness and its casting away. Public representations also teach the young and help to convince spectators. The excitement and interest of a performance bring the ideas alive.

The treatments of illnesses in other societies embody their theories about illness and express their hopes of healing. They might be analyzed or compared for symbolic transparency to see to what extent the actions of treatment convey in nonverbal terms a statement or revelation of the theory of illness that lies behind them. On the question of efficacy, there are different points of view to consider: that of the individual who is ill, those of the other participants, and that of onlookers. In many cults, the patient is the actor at the center of a drama. He or she may be expected to speak the name of the afflicting spirit or need to enter a trance. The patient enters into new relationships with a group, the leader of the cult, and the spirits. Crowds, noise, excitement, fatigue, or exhaustion enhance the effects on the patient. In the Burmese exorcism described by Melford Spiro (1967), the exorcist engaged a spirit through the patient in arduous, protracted negotiation and persuasion. At first, the patient's trembling fingers were pressed together, then they separate in a sign that the possessing spirit who loved him was ready to release him. The patient in trance tried to give a handkerchief (a love symbol) to the spirit but was stopped from doing so. He tried to leap through the window to stay with the spirit. Among the Sinhalese, the ritual for healing illness caused by Sanni demons (Kapferer 1983; Obeyesekere 1968) is performed after midnight with flares by masked dancers reenacting the symptoms caused by the demons, who then suddenly startle the patient. The dancers then portray a series of tableaux in which the patient is shown there is less to fear; the demons are diminished by ridicule and insults and finally subdued, their weakness exposed when confronted with the force of good—the Lord Buddha. In all these examples, the treatments include diagnoses in the sense of defining the illness, giving it a label and a shape. The actions make a diagnosis public, displaying the agreed-upon nature of the illness. The agent of the suffering—the cause or the illness itself—is embodied and objectified. The imagery confirms an idea or suspicion; it may show to the young what older people think. The ideas serve to justify the treatment; in turn, the treatment helps maintain the ideas. The performance of the treatment plays a part, too, in promoting learning and belief.

For the Gnau, illness is a spur to reflection and action, a reminder of forces present but unseen. As elsewhere, it triggers the performance of rituals that give visible and public shape to their ideas. The stand individuals may take concerning the reality of a spirit and its image reflect their experience. With Panu'et, some will know what the image is and how it is made; they have done it and seen it done many times before. They can remember some of the sufferers who got better, others who did not. The gathering includes people who have been through the treatment themselves. Some of those present are close to the patient and deeply hope for a cure. Nevertheless, there is no reason for them to analyze exactly what is going on when they call on the spirit to enter its image. The various actions of "killing" the image, extracting the harm, and sending the spirit off only suggest ideas of localized illness, the nature of spirits, and the presence of harm in the patient, but they do not present them in explicit terms. The question of their reality may not arise for participants. The collective effort and conviction give encouragement and support to the patient and satisfaction to others. Those who have made the Panu'et figure may perhaps see things differently from the patient, who is alone and waiting to confront the spirit. Exposure to the sight, stings, noise, singing, the tastes of betel, ginger, and herbs heightens the patient's shock while in the spirit's presence, but it is acted out in a protected space. The patient is surrounded by the senior men and by friends who are calling out on her behalf, urging the spirit to leave her, striking it, "killing" it, taking the illness out of her, and throwing it away. They show how the illness may be overcome through the process of removing it. The invocations begin with appeals to the spirit and end with commands for it to leave her and assertions that she will be well. The final act of washing her implies the illness is ended.

The words exposure, shock, modeling, and protected space may suggest possible parallels with behavioral conditioning techniques used in the psychological treatment of fears and obsessions. The ideas of acting out a wish, expressing fantasies, or learning in some safe setting how to cope with fears, playing another role or status, trying out different relationships to others or to one's own past—all of these have appeared more or less explicitly in some modes of psychological treatment. The methods used in such therapies have various names and theories behind them, such as drama therapy, modeling, psychodrama, or desensitization. They share some features with the "exotic" treatments described above: acting out in a safe place, making assertions of what is wished for, expressing desires and fears in order to come to terms with them, modeling behaviors to defuse anxiety, overcoming distress through simulation and practice, and perhaps the (almost magical) hope that by enacting something in anticipation, it can be made to come about. But without full, vivid descriptions like those of Bruce Kapferer (1983), Gananath Obeyesekere (1968), Melford Spiro (1967), and Andras Zempléni (1966), it is vain to speculate on the way such treatments work. We cannot just assume they do. The Gnau treatments are not systematically repeated nor do they involve intense exposure or long-lasting effects, so it is not plausible to argue that they must work in the same way as treatments elsewhere or that they are effective for the same reasons. Treatments in other societies include examples in which the intensity, exposure, or repetition may suggest closer parallels to conditioning techniques. Suggestion, persuasion, catharsis, reward, and punishment are all possibly involved in some. Amulets and charms, drumming and dance, or cults of affliction can serve as means to evoke past associations that are presented again in the treatments. The social and collective support displayed during the performance may also be a benefit for the patient.

Milek's illness caused by Panu'et began with a fever and headache, a vague backache, and some discomfort with urination. Malaria may have been behind her symptoms, but I treated her for a urinary infection. Although her fever ended, she still did not feel well. Her illness began on May 30; it was not until June 26 that she felt sure she was well and finally washed. Early on, she had received various treatments: from someone whose spells she thought might have made her ill by mistake; the medicine I gave her; and a small private version of Panu'et performed by her husband and her collateral brother, Saputem. This small version on June 5 was followed by the full version for Panu'et on June 9, the one that I have described in this chapter and the appendix. In the days afterward, she said that she felt she was getting better, but she remained as someone ill, with dirt and ashes covering her body. She still felt "heavy"—a bit stiff, aching, and feeble. She thought this came because a woman from Mandubil had been killed on the spot where Milek's house now stood and where she slept; the woman's ghost weighed on her. For a week, she moved elsewhere to sleep. At last she washed. The problem is to know what difference the treatment made.

In judgments of the relation between cause and effect, timing matters, whether from the point of view of looking forward or of looking back. In a priori reasoning, we need an idea of what to expect without treatment in order to tell whether the treatment makes a difference. If several treatments are all given at almost the same time, we cannot distinguish which worked. Benefits are easily mistaken. A gift for timing—close to the improvement—may tempt us to link an improvement to what was done just before it, especially when considering the case a posteriori. The lack of a prognosis or a wrong one confuses the assessment of the benefits. Right or wrong, prognosis can create or contribute to both favorable and unfavorable judgments. The pacing of treatment is an art. It can be used to help to sustain hope; it may clarify or confuse the evaluation of effects.

To know how long some effect lasts or how often it is produced requires us to follow up on patients who receive a certain treatment and those who do not, those who come back and those who do not. What this involves is, in short, implicitly an echo of the skeptical statistical approach used in biomedicine. The cases described in this book have included successes (such as the treatments at Bregbo) and failures (such as the attempt to heal Dauwaras). Often a simple answer about success is hard for anyone to give. A treatment seems worth a try at the time, but afterward people's attention may shift to reveal other diagnoses. The Gnau approach some treatments almost experimentally, as a trial conducted in the hope of benefit but done casually, without resolve to scrutinize the result. They sustain hopes by remembering how in the past, some people got better, not by identifying which treatments failed. They preserve, at least on the surface of daily life, an optimistic view in general of their own ability to do something about suffering. If an illness continues, this suggests to them that other agents are at work, and their focus of attention shifts forward rather than backward; they do not accuse an earlier treatment of failure or deny the first diagnosis. Belief in someone's ability to control an illness influences the decision to seek treatment and the response to it. If the link between treatment and result is obvious—as it was in Rauit, for example, when the health post workers gave griseofulvin pills to treat a long-standing, disfiguring fungal infection known as *grile*—people are keen for it and great demand soon follows. They seize on the evidence and act on it. The fungal infection in question was distinctive and much disliked. The contrast in their responses to other biomedical treatments—for example, the drug treatment for leprosy—was striking. The links between the signs of illness, the perception of need, and the evidence of therapeutic effects may be so attenuated that a specific treatment might be little appreciated, reducing demand for it. If it involves Western medicine, the Gnau prefer something they are already familiar with, something they know is "strong": an injection, a linctus with a powerful taste, a lotion with a smell to make one's nose tingle. The varied nature of diseases adds to the difficulty of deciding what to do. Many everyday illnesses are bearable or trivial and do not pose such serious problems of meaning or cultural interpretation as those that have occupied this discussion. But illness can sometimes prompt questions of people's convictions and the meaning of events. There are examples in which the introduction of a treatment—a vaccination, an injection of penicillin against yaws, or the like—has removed a form of disease that may have been central to some set of beliefs. The effect of treatment was to destroy the meanings they involve. More broadly, the impacts of bio-medicine may play a part in the decline of magical practices and cultural beliefs.

CHAPTER FOURTEEN

Faith and the skeptical eye

Some wish for miracles to heal them. My subject is the art of healing, a subject in which miracles have played a part. Pierre Janet, one of the great students of the healing arts, wrote:

> It is clear that the principal difficulty . . . lies not in the interpretation of miraculous facts, but in their observation. It is not a question for endless debate . . . to know if the rapidity of cure is a sign of a miracle, or if the Holy Virgin in healing must leave or not leave a scar. Quite simply it is a question of knowing what did happen and that is extraordinarily difficult, the knowledge that we have of these facts comes to us from reported evidence and we know how defective people's reports are as a source of information. (Janet 1919: 32–33)

The first question is deciding what it is that needs to be explained. Answers to that question depend on accurate observation. Janet further explained:

> But there is no smoke without a fire: so many peoples would not have preserved ways of religious and magical healing for centuries if these treatments had had absolutely no influence. Medicine now, scientific or would-be scientific, has improved on some procedures of religious or magical medicine, made them a little surer, but in doing so it only continues them: it could never have been born if they had not already

imposed themselves on mankind because they were effective and useful. (Janet 1919: 34–35)

W. H. R. Rivers also saw certain continuities between Western and non-Western forms of healing: "From the psychological point of view the difference between the rude arts I have described in this book [*Medicine, magic and religion*] and much of our own medicine is not one of kind, but only of degree" (Rivers 1924: 51). Janet realized that there are many similarities in healing rites even though they may be separated by centuries or found among quite different peoples. He had religious healing, miracles, and faith healing in France particularly in mind:

> The practices to prepare for the miracle always stay the same: the sick person arrives from afar after a long and painful journey. The local inhabitants do not easily benefit from the miracle cures which happen on their doorstep and for that reason there are still sick people round Lourdes, which seems curious. One does not let the sick person go straight, and without preamble, to touch the relic or drink from the sacred spring: one imposes a propitiatory novena on him first, long waiting at the door of the temple during which he listens to sermons, repeats prayers, and above all during which he hears tell of miraculous cures and sees the innumerable ex-voto, in brief, he must enter slowly into the temple and he must prepare himself by a special incubation. If the miracle happens the sick person must still thank God in public, decorate the temple with clearly visible signs of grateful recognition: everything happens today at Lourdes as formerly it did in the Asclepion. One could besides make the same remarks about animal magnetism, the mysterious practices around the seer who speaks while sleeping, the rites of initiation, the hermetic teachings present us with the same preparation of the patient under another form.... These observations show the miracle is not as arbitrary or as free as one might think. Miracle though it be, it submits to some laws which have always stayed the same. The God who does these miracles does not heal just anything, nor does he heal just anyhow. Don't go and ask in one of these sanctuaries for God or the (magnetic) fluid to make a cut-off leg regrow, or the scars of wounds to disappear. (Janet 1919: 36–37)

His general point about similarity would seem to apply to much dramatic religious healing and to healing cults. The journey and the foreignness have to be replaced by the creation of strangeness or mystery through masks, trance, esoteric knowledge, special sites, or time of performance. The rites divest officiants from their familiar roles, as do the costumes and special forms of speech.

There have been many attempts to compare treatments (some of the earlier sources include Ackerknecht 1971; Bouteiller 1950; Clements 1932; Ellenberger 1970; Frank 1961; Janet 1919, Rivers 1924). Most often discussed have been questions of treatment—therapeutic efficacy, rationale, the role of the healer—rather than methods for the promotion of health, the prevention of sickness, or rehabilitation. From Rivers and Janet onward, writers have noted similarities; they classified them in various ways, such as by method of training, principles, and techniques (Bouteiller 1950) or by theories of cause and the logic implicit in responses (Clements 1932; Murdock 1980); they suggested reasons for similarities, such as in psychological effects (Ellenberger 1970; Frank 1961) or for their distribution (Murdock 1980; I. M. Lewis 1971; Rubel 1964). Some looked for biological universals of physiology and pathology to suggest plausible explanations; others identified discoveries of herbs or drugs or methods, considered questions of diffusion and spread, or explored the influence of literate traditions or the great regional systems, such as Asian medicine (Leslie 1976); yet others analyzed the effects of political forces, of colonial and commercial interests, and of migration, transport, and poverty on the dissemination of cosmopolitan medicine (Melrose 1982; Morley, Rohde, and Williams 1983).

Hopes and disappointment

Pain, uncertainty, and anxiety make people seek relief in illness. The sufferer looks for help. There is pressure to do something rather than nothing, to try something in the hope that it will work. Many physicians know how difficult it is to practice "masterly inactivity." Talcott Parsons (1951) remarked on this demand for positive action in his original analysis of the medical system and medical practice in society.

When someone undergoes great distress and uncertainty, the bet on treatment, like Blaise Pascal's wager on God (that faith offers the hope of Paradise and disbelief offers nothing), is loaded in favor of belief if the choice is between possible relief or continued suffering. The hope of release or victory over illness is a frequent theme in rites of healing. What interests me is the willingness to believe. The medical past offers its spectacle of optimism and belief, its history of panaceas, theriac, and bloodletting. Testimony is most often testimony of cures, not failures, for "sorrows," wrote Sir Thomas Browne, "destroy us or themselves. . . . To be ignorant of evils to come, and forgetfull of evils past, is a mercifull provision in nature, whereby we digest the mixture of our few and evil dayes" (1977: 311).

There is value in that optimism as a spur to action and a sustainer of morale. A Gnau hamlet organizing a major rite for someone's serious illness—the distribution of tasks, the sequence of days devoted to its performance, the gatherings, the singing, the communal meals—was a scene of energy and activity and hope. It stood in great contrast to that same hamlet weeks later when the sick man was hidden in a house surrounded by barriers, the villagers waiting, demoralized by the sense they had exhausted all they knew to save him and had to abandon hope. The few visitors who now came did so to weep over him. For anyone who had seen the change, it would leave, I think, a strong sense of the social value of the hope that sustains treatment.

Uncertainty over what to expect can make it hard to tell when treatment helps. Equally, it can make it hard to detect harm from treatment. Medicine is full of lessons on how people believe their reasoning rather than the facts. To the Eddystone Islanders in the South Pacific, the fluttering of a butterfly seemed to resemble epilepsy, so by a certain logic of analogy and sympathy, they used a butterfly in treating convulsions (or to cause them; Rivers 1924: 33–34). Similarly, in France and England, physicians let blood relentlessly when a theory of the humors or purification required it. Firm convictions about some reason for illness—as firm as the reasons a Zande has concerning witchcraft—may make a response seem quite rational to the actor. But the fact that an action seems rational does not necessarily make it effective. Empiricists long contended with rationalists in the schools of medicine.

The sick person may view the matter differently from those who watch or apply the treatment. At one point in a performance at Rauit to heal an affliction by the spirit called Malyi, a creeper was wound around and around the sick man's body and tied to the tall, masked figure of the Malyi. They said the spirit had struck him down. He could not walk. He had to lie there; his pain was such that he could scarcely even crawl. They said he was like a tree cramped and stifled by creepers and vines. As men might come to cut the vines so the tree could grow and its branches spread, in the ritual they came and cut the creeper that bound him to Malyi. They cut it into many pieces so he might be able to get up and walk and move without pain. Here, I quote directly from my fieldnotes at the time:

Treatment with creepers, October 22, 1968

There was a bigger gathering of singers and singing throughout the day. Sometimes they spoke about the newly returned plantation labourers being able to learn the songs. None of the *pinistaim* labourers took on the mask and danced outside. At about 3:40 p.m. they got out a long vine creeper and the special leaves to make the *dugi* (navel cord—the name given to the creeper when used in this rite indicates another path of symbolic association: the patient is tied to the spirit Malyi as a baby just born is still tied by the cord to its mother). Saibuten, directing the occasion, unrolled the creeper (*lambet_tamodat*) and hung it on the side of the enclosure fence. He called to the junior men to come and tie the decorations on it. They tied on scented and coloured leaves and some moss. Meanwhile Saibuten split bamboo to make foot-long knife-blade lengths. On each of the three, he tied some scented *dyu'elbi* leaves and coloured cordyline leaves. These were to serve as the knives for cutting the "navel cord." The long creeper was then fastened onto the top of the headdress (*waipet*) of the tall mask and wound round and round its body. Parku got inside the mask to dance for this bit as Malyi. Then people began calling out for Dauwaras (the sick man) to come down from Pakuag. They waited. It wasn't until 5:30 p.m. that he came down, carried in the palm spathe "chair" that Dabasu and Walei had made for him. Dauwaras was in a tense and wretched state, finding all the movement and jolts very painful, holding out his arms to have the *dugi* fastened round him and his outstretched arms trembled, his legs and thighs too trembling. I thought these tremors, easily visible, were from extreme tension. He scarcely looked up at the people so close to him, mumbling in a high-pitched voice, deeply dejected, complaining of his pain, looking down at his feet. His misery affected everyone so that as they wound the *dugi* around him, they looked at him with pity, drawn faced, unsmiling and silent. The *dugi* was tied around his right big toe first and then brought up between his legs, around his neck, then down around both thighs and then wound round his chest a number of times. Saibuten brought out the bamboo knives and, taking the upper end of the *dugi*, cut him loose from Malyi. He passed the knife to Samo who unwound the creeper a bit more from Dauwaras and cut. They called on the men, including many of the younger ones, to come and cut it, unwinding it bit by bit, undoing it from him.

As they were cutting through, Dauwaras thinly complained of his pain, and when they had finished and the bits of cut *dugi* were lying at his feet, he was still speaking of his pain in a little broken voice, almost in tears, still with his head bent down. He stopped. They carried him back to Pakuag. It was a dull grey, after-rain light, twilight. . . . Dauwaras was not getting better. It was a depressing evening. Disillusionment.

The logic implicit in the treatment was coherent—but it did not work.

The skeptical eye

If we are tempted to think no one was as shrewd or as skeptical as we are now, Michel de Montaigne, writing in the sixteenth century, shows us how wrong we would be. To understand what follows, we may suppose that Montaigne was thinking of an imaginary case—namely, that of an elderly Frenchman with a melancholic temperament who is afflicted with epilepsy. The question was: How did the physician discover it could be cured by a preparation of elk's horn applied to the finger during winter and the conjunction of Venus and Saturn?

> Galen tells us that a leper happened to be cured by drinking some wine out of a vessel into which a viper had crept by chance. In this example we may discover the means and a likely guide to that kind of experiment, as also in those to which the physicians say they have been led by the example of certain animals. But in most of the other experiments to which they say they were led by fortune and had no other guide but chance, I find it impossible to believe in the progressive course of their investigation.
>
> I imagine a man looking at the endless number of things around him, plants, animals, metals. I cannot think where to make him begin his experiments; and if his first fancy should light upon an elk's horn, which would need to be a very pliant and easy faith, he will yet find himself equally perplexed in his second operation. He is confronted with so many diseases and so many circumstances, that before he has arrived at any certainty as to whither the perfection of his experiments should lead him, human wit will be at the end of its tether. And before he has discovered, among that endless number of things that it is this horn; among so many diseases, that it is epilepsy; and so many constitutions, the melancholic; so many seasons, in winter;

so many nations, the French; so many ages, old age; so many celestial changes, the conjunction of Venus and Saturn; so many parts of the body, the finger; being guided in all this neither by reason, nor by conjecture, nor by example, nor by divine inspiration, but solely by the movement of chance, it must be a chance that is perfectly artificial, regular and methodical.

And then even should the cure be effected, how can he be assured that it was not because the disease had reached its crisis, or that it was not the result of chance or that it was not due to something else he had eaten or drunk or touched on that day, or to the power of his grandmother's prayers? . . . Besides supposing this proof to have been perfect how many times was it repeated? How often was this long bead roll of changes and coincidence strung anew, to infer a certain rule therefrom? Should it be inferred by whom? Among so many millions, there will be but three men who trouble about recording their experiments; will chance have lighted upon just one of these three? What if another or even a hundred others have had the contrary experiences? We might perhaps see some daylight if all the reasoning and all the decisions of men were known to us; but that three witnesses and those three doctors should lord it over mankind is against reason. (Montaigne [1588] 1927: 235–36)

With such acumen, he distinguishes nearly all the issues. The French physician Pierre Louis, writing nearly three centuries later in 1835 on the subject of bloodletting, observed:

Physicians . . . witnessed a few fatal cases where no bloodletting was employed, and thereupon jumped to the conclusion that this process would have saved them. Other practitioners noted a few cases where death followed a resort to bloodletting, and denounced the practice as the whole cause of death. In neither instance did they employ any check or test of their sweeping conclusions. "*Quels faits!*" exclaimed Louis, "*Quelle logique!*" We must, instead, know how often venesection aided and how often it impeded recovery. . . . Their numerical estimates were of the vaguest character. In the difference here between exactitude and vagueness lay all the difference between truth and error. (Shryock 1948: 136)

Pierre-Charles-Alexandre Louis, a nineteenth-century doctor who conducted research on the effects of bloodletting, impressed the medical historian Richard Harrison Shryock in some ways as the most significant study ever made in medical method, declaring that it placed the crown on medicine as a science.

The diversity of healing practices

The things done in the name of treatment are extremely varied. A list of kinds of treatment inevitably suggests both similarities and differences. The same processes of disease may occur anywhere. Perhaps that is a partial explanation for some of the similarities. But there are problems in deciding which procedures can fairly be identified with each other and when the differences are more significant than any resemblance.

There are many forms of treatment, including guidance on diet, "hot and cold" foods, the balance of humors, regimen, food as therapy; herbs and poisons, the use of drugs; physical treatments involving cutting, surgery, the management of bone and joint injuries, sores, wounds; scarification, counterirritation; exercises and manipulation, ointments, liniments, poultices, heat therapy, sweating and sweat baths, massage; washing, cleansing, purification; talk used as psychotherapy aimed at gaining insight, moral reeducation, indoctrination, persuasion, confession; suggestion and hypnosis; dream therapy and incubation, relaxation, meditation, sleep therapy; religious therapies and treatment rituals; behavior therapies that make use of drama, shock, catharsis, acting out, the gratification of desires, release from frustration, exposure to feared objects, emotional flooding, desensitization, operant conditioning; social therapies involving group support, noise, music, dance and trance, voluntary associations, self-help groups, cults of affliction; and so on and so forth.

Just as difference is a matter of degree and quality, so is similarity. For instance, in an account of the Iroquois's theory of dreams and their dream therapy, which Jesuit priests first recorded in the seventeenth century, Anthony Wallace (1972: 59–75) suggests that the Iroquois came strikingly close to psychoanalytic intuitions and assumptions:

> They recognized conscious and unconscious parts of the mind. They knew the great force of unconscious desires, were aware that the frustration of these desires could cause mental and physical (psychosomatic) illness. . . . They had noted the distinction between the latent and the manifest content of dreams, and employed what sounds like the technique of free association to uncover the latent meaning. And they considered that the best method for the relief of psychic and

psychosomatic distresses was to give the repressed desire satisfaction, either directly or symbolically. (Wallace 1972: 63)

Wallace's approach picks out the similarities. The psychological language identifies them so that we can recognize them stripped, as it were, of exotic cultural qualifications. But when the cultural particularity is put back, the likeness of Iroquois notions to psychoanalytic treatment almost vanishes:

One man, to satisfy the dictates of his dream, had himself stripped naked by his friends, bound, dragged through the streets with the customary hooting, set upon the scaffold, and the fires lit. "But he was content with all these preliminaries and, after passing some hours in singing his death song, thanked the company, believing that after this imaginary captivity he would never be actually a prisoner." Another man, having dreamed that his cabin was on fire, "could find no rest until he could see it actually burning." The chief's council in a body, "after mature deliberation on the matter," ceremoniously burned it down for him. A third man went to such extremes of realism, after a captivity nightmare, that he determined "that the fire should be actually applied to his legs, in the same way as to captives when their final torture is begun." The roasting was so cruel and prolonged that it took six months for him to recover from his burns. (Wallace 1972: 65–66)

As I shall try to identify some similarities in forms of treatment and responses to them, I mention this caution to the reader. There is a risk of deceiving oneself into seeing a similarity where there is none.

What place is there for an anthropologist?

When Max Gluckman posed the question of "closed systems and open minds" (1964), he applied it to the writings of anthropologists using ideas from economics, psychology, and psychoanalysis. What place is there for a medical anthropologist to judge the efficacy of treatment? Biomedicine is specialized and rather suspicious of outsiders. The blunt question raised is this: How can an anthropologist make observations that would be adequate and pertinent to scientific medical thinking if he or she attributes the efficacy of alternative treatments to their putative physiological or psychological effects, or to the pharmacological effects of herbs? Medical people are almost bound to ask them for relevant evidence.

In a famous paper on the efficacy of symbols, Claude Lévi-Strauss (1963) plunges into these problems when he discusses a healing chant used by the Kuna people of Panama as a treatment to aid delivery in difficult childbirth. For all the appeal of his essay, his wonderful explanation of the treatment seems to take its efficacy for granted. It is the idea that matters, not the evidence. First, he interprets symbolism in it that is appropriate for childbirth. The interpretation shows why the song might be a way of treatment. Then he goes into questions of psychological and physiological cause and effect to explain how a song might help in difficult labor. He takes for granted that it works (i.e., aids a delivery delayed or obstructed for unknown reasons—and of which he has no evidence) and suggests how it would do so.

Is the symbolic meaning of the chant recognized equally by the shaman, the patient, and the anthropologist? The analysis suggests that the effect of the chant depends on understanding its meaning. Could the specific meaning discerned by the anthropologist from the text have an effect if the patient were ignorant of that meaning? If the shaman knew it, it might justify his action even though the patient did not know the esoteric meaning. But then, if the patient were unaware, how could the song have its effect? Lévi-Strauss argues that the effect of the song is to make the distressed sick woman relive the initial situation with pain, reveal to her the causes of her distress, and bring to a conscious level conflicts and resistance that have remained unconscious; by implication, this does something to make her uterine contractions stronger or dilate the passage for birth. He says that the specific symbolic meaning has organ-specific effects on the birth passage. Such symbolic imagery can only work on the emotions, he implies, through eventual conscious understanding. But what should we think if the sick woman denied that she thought the chant had a particular meaning? Or if she denied that the chant brought her relief? Or if we found the chant was not followed by her safe delivery?

A detailed ethnographic study by Norman MacPherson Chapin (1981: 394–441) found that Kuna shamans interpret the birth ritual and its mode of action differently, for they consider that its effects work in a spiritual domain separate from the woman's flesh and body and the material world. To Kuna specialists, the curative action of the chant is not aimed at the physical body of the woman but works through two conceptual parallels: a first between the spiritual essence or "soul" of the pregnant woman and her physical body; and a second between the woman's soul and the spiritual cosmos. Kuna specialists distinguish between these different conceptual levels, and the chanter is concerned with controlling events in the world of the spirits. The chant is directed not at the pregnant woman but to the inhabitants of the spirit world. The chant is sung in the language of the spirit world, which is unintelligible to the patient. "The chanter is the sender of the message, the spirits are the receivers, and the woman is merely an uncomprehending part of the audience" (Chapin 1981: 435). Lévi-Strauss neglected the midwives who are vital participants in the birth event. They are familiar with the chant and pay close attention to its progress. They supply the chanter with information about the patient's condition, and they may do certain ritual actions in synchrony with the chant.

> Changes in the woman's physical state provide indications as to the condition of her "soul" (*purpa*), and in turn serve as crucial evidence of the progress of the shamans as they bring the spirit of the fetus down Muu's river . . . the chanter of *Muu Ikar* is concerned with controlling and directing events as they unfold in the world of spirit. The midwives, on the other hand, are involved in a much more earthly task. They are working directly with the pregnant woman's body, massaging the baby into proper position, administering medicine, and bending all of their talents to coax the child from a woman who is convulsed in pain, bleeding, and in acute danger of losing her life. But while the chanter and the midwives are focused on different orders of reality, they are also attending to each other's activities and exchanging interpretations of how things are progressing. In this way they work together, in unison, filling crucial complementary roles. (Chapin 1981: 437–38)

These observations point out several issues: Whose standpoint should be taken—the actor's or the observer's? Is a literal meaning or a metaphoric meaning intended? Who consciously identifies it? Who gives the reasons for action or belief? What is the effect on the woman and her body—delivery of the baby after obstructed or delayed labor? What is the cause of the obstruction or delay (e.g., cephalo-pelvic disproportion, transverse lie, breech position)? What is the effect of the treatment on the mother's mind (e.g., relief from pain, confidence after anxiety)? What do the shaman and the midwife say?

Relativism or double standards?

Criteria of successful treatment may indeed differ from biomedical ones. But I would question how we are to use different or double standards if asked to explain or comment on the efficacy of treatment. For a practicing physician, there are obvious moral issues. We apply critical standards to our own treatments and we expect certain standards of safety and tested efficacy. In judging efficacy, should we apply different standards to the treatments used in other societies—in effect, certain standards for them (perhaps appropriate for them but not for us) and keep others for ourselves (those of biomedical tests and facts)? Should we use double standards in this sense? We may record and understand other people's criteria for successful treatment, but if we want to explain why and how their treatments work in biomedical terms, we enter a different field. If we adopt the strong relativist position, we might argue that we are not justified in applying external criteria to what people in other societies do, perhaps even arguing that the practicing physician is not justified in interfering or intervening. This position would hold that it is inappropriate to subject alternative views to scientific criteria because these only make sense to someone who is already conversant with science and accepts its methods.

For the relativist, "Truth is different on the other side of the Pyrenees"; scientific views about the facts can change. So, it might be held, anyone who is sensitive to cultural relativity should see that one must use the standards given in that society. This sounds like an argument for using different standards according to each context. If rigorously followed, it would make comparison across cultures impossible.

However, we may say that biomedical standards are universally applicable, but this does not mean that only those standards are valid. Describing as well as identifying the views and aims of other people and the criteria they use is one thing; evaluating these by biomedical standards is another.

When we do not understand why a treatment has efficacy, one answer might be, "Well, they say it made them feel better." But is there a link between what they did and their feeling better? "Perhaps the herbs they used were effective," one may say; another might refer to the power of suggestion to explain it, the placebo effect, psychosomatic efficacy, or symbolic efficacy. Whose explanation is at issue—the actor's or the observer's? Did the disease just end in its usual way or get better by itself? Half the time we do not know what was wrong with the patient in medical terms or, indeed, if anything was wrong. The "placebo" or "suggestion" explanations risk creating an impression that much in their illness is imaginary or emotional. Are these other people really so suggestible? Walter Cannon's essay on "voodoo" death (1942) might seem to give some authority to that view.

Perhaps we are more willing to credit the mysterious powers of psychological and psychosomatic forces when the cases come from distant places and concern Aborigines or Africans. It goes with a certain romanticism about exotic people (their witchcraft, their spirits and magic, their "superstitions") and persisting assumptions about their emotional lability. This example from a government settlement of Aborigines in central Australia illustrates the problem:

> Attitudes and behaviours of the nurses at the Yuendumu hospital between 1969 and 1971 varied greatly. Some were very willing to co-operate with a medicine man and to enlist his aid, particularly if a patient requested that he be consulted. For example, there was some doubt about whether a very sick man in his thirties [Jungala] was suffering from a blow on the head or from a psychosomatic disorder produced by the knowledge that he had been "boned" and "sung" following his wife's recent death. A medicine man was asked to come to the hospital to treat Jungala. . . . On 1.6.70 Jungala, Nungarai's husband, died in Alice Springs Hospital from a cerebral abscess after a sickness of a week's duration, during most of which time he was on the settlement. . . . It was rumoured that he had been "boned" and "sung." Everyone on the settlement, including the nursing staff, felt that his illness might have been the result of this rather than the after-effect of a blow on the head received during a drunken brawl in Alice Springs. (Middleton and Francis 1976: 135, 41)

Anecdotal evidence

One difficulty is the anecdotal nature of evidence in most of such cases; another is how to provide appropriate or adequate evidence in the particular circumstances. How do you test for ghosts? As in the case of the Indian rope trick, it is worth making sure the trick has really been done before spending time trying to explain how it was done. But often the reporters resent skeptical requests for more detailed descriptions of exactly what happened, how often, and who witnessed what. Such resentment is quite common when shamanic healing, paranormal or psychic phenomena, or new cures for cancer are at issue. Rare cases and uncommon medical events are bound to be difficult to investigate. In the history of Western medicine, the concentration of patients in large hospitals and the dissemination of published information (Shryock 1948; Ziman 1976) helped to reduce some of the problems of rarity. But for some of the most striking cases anthropologists reported (e.g., suspected "voodoo" death or success in dramatic rituals for healing), it was unreasonable to expect detailed investigations at such times and in such places. Such an attempt would alter the circumstances; the investigative techniques and equipment could disturb and disrupt the event. Moreover, some of the problems could not be answered unless appropriate methods for tackling them were available. This is different from saying, as the strong relativist might do, that such phenomena are intrinsically unsuitable or inimical to scientific investigation. That sounds more like the evasive defense of the spirit medium who says the spirit will not manifest itself in the presence of a skeptic.

It is rare to find examples from anthropologists who record the frequency of therapeutic failures, do follow-ups, or find out how many people do not bother to come back to the healer next time. It is difficult enough to assess the efficacy of treatment in a highly controlled hospital setting; the difficulties outside are far greater. A simple assertion, however confident, that a treatment might work psychologically, psychosomatically, by suggestion, or through symbolic efficacy rings hollow. The double virtue of Kaja Finkler's (1980) and Arthur Kleinman's (1980: 311–75) studies of healing is to have studied the patients' perceptions of their treatment carefully and to have also done follow-ups. Earlier I quoted Janet's remark that the difficulties lie not with interpretation so much as with observation. But the chemistry of laboratory tests, the numbers needed for statistical significance, the equipment, the invasive and specialized procedures for investigating pathology—these are not our province as anthropologists. So what aspects can we tackle, given our means and limitations?

Outcome expectations

The aims of treatments in different societies are varied. We would mistake the aims if we set a medical frame around the biblical instructions for cleansing the leper. They were not a treatment to heal so much as a rite of passage for readmission to the community.

By classifying a problem, the diagnosis may set expectations about the outcome. Conversely, the results of treatment may cast doubt on a diagnosis or a causal explanation. Treatment, in effect, puts hypothesis to test. Prognosis had a high place in Hippocratic medicine because it was held that the physician who could forecast the natural course of the disease would not merely gain in reputation, but he would be better able to treat the disease (Brock 1929: 83–84; Lloyd 1979: 16, 30, 170). Diagnosis was the art of reading signs—the practice of semiology in an old sense. From signs, the physician might be able to tell the past, the present, and the future or if the natural processes in disease were regular and had a pattern that could be recognized. We may separate the notions of diagnosis, treatment, and prognosis, but other people do not everywhere make these sharp divisions. Knowledge of what to expect is a source of strength and confidence. The art of healing also lies in giving advice, in identifying the illness, the problems that gave rise to it, and those it may lead to. Judgments of the success or failure of treatment depend on what was expected to happen without treatment. And so prognosis—or the lack of it—can be critical to the formation of opinions about treatment. In practice, the outcome of an illness is often uncertain.

The Gnau people would say that illnesses caused by the spirits or by sorcery and destructive magic were ones that could lead to death unless they were stopped by treatment. They might say this casually and without qualification. To think that most illnesses, if untreated, will lead to death is to provide a strong basis for belief in the benefits of treatment. The Gnau might attribute serious and mild illnesses to the same cause if the circumstances suggested it. For example, they supposed one particular spirit afflicted a young child who was acutely ill, as I thought, with meningitis; on another day, they made the same diagnosis for an old man with an aching hip after he had been gardening. The same treatment for that spirit might well have very different outcomes.

I have described one panic when a spirit attack or sorcery was suspected, the case of Maka (see chapter 2). In theory, perhaps, the outcome of a certain treatment might have identified or confirmed one of the diagnoses made about her condition. In practice, the villagers' efforts at treatment and their confusion took up all their attention until they saw she was not dying. The pressure for a diagnostic verdict then evaporated. What was left was the satisfaction that they had responded energetically to an emergency and that it was over. On the other hand, the prolonged illness of Wolai made quite different demands on them (see chapter 3). The nature of his illness, its slow rate of change, and the different treatments given concurrently altered the possibility of identifying whether one treatment in particular worked or whether one diagnosis in particular was right. In practice, people at Rauit were little concerned to say what they thought would happen in particular cases or to predict how soon a treatment should be effective.

One strength of saying so many illnesses might be fatal if left untreated is that most people, in fact, get better. The value of treatment seems to be confirmed. The gestures of prediction—for example, cracking knuckles, making a *langit* leaf curl up—were perfunctory. No one seemed to bother about the result once such actions were taken. The serious techniques of divination I saw used were done after death or in desperate situations. Such divination was not for prediction. Although in theory the outcomes of treatment might serve as tests of their speculations about the cause, people at Rauit gave them only fitful attention.

The pastor's dilemma

Illness may be accepted as a derailment of nature, but it has more often been understood in religious or moral terms (e.g., as sin, atonement for guilt, affliction, a test or challenge to the self, a sign of weakness, loss of control, retribution, just deserts, attack, revenge). Treatment, reflecting one or another of these assumptions, might then be rather like a struggle for survival or a battle, a contest against an attack on the patient as a victim, on the one hand, and on the other, the disease, an agent, or a person as the enemy, the inflictor. The illness may be seen as an ordeal or a trial of the self to be endured and overcome, or it might be considered as retribution, a punishment to be suffered, a sin to be expiated, exorcized. The patient may have to be purified, cleansed, refined by suffering, or made whole, put back in balance, restored to harmony, strengthened. Alternatively, an illness can be viewed as a sign, message, or warning, and the treatment a process of adaptation, learning, accommodation, a path to insight and understanding, reeducation; or a quest, a journey, a pilgrimage, a rite of passage. Such connotations are not necessarily explicit, although sometimes the course of events in an illness brings them out.

Explanations and responses to illness, suffering, and death have had a central place in many religions. But in industrialized modern societies, the questions prompted by these events have been increasingly seen as the responsibility of biomedicine to answer. Faith in science has come to supply or replace answers that were previously given by faith in religion.

Biomedical practice then may challenge a religious belief, pose doubts, or lead to a dilemma of duty to self or faith. In the particular area of the Sepik where I did fieldwork, the nearest local evangelical mission was associated with outstanding medical work. But for one of the Indigenous pastors, his own illness represented special problems in the case that follows. For him, they had less to do with the introduction of biomedicine than with the status of his former beliefs and ritual allegiances. His case illustrates the complexity of moral issues sometimes provoked by decisions over the choice of treatment. In this part of the Sepik, performances of the major traditional religious festivals or rituals of the sort called *singsings* in Tokpisin were usually triggered by someone's illness. Some of the major rituals were supposed to have been acquired originally to heal someone. Perhaps that association between religion and healing gave a sharper point to the problems I shall now describe.

In 1985, a *singsing* was going on in a neighboring village. The man for whom it was being performed was the local village pastor, thus a committed Christian prayer leader. The crux of the matter in this case was whether the ritual to be performed was a medical or a religious activity. If it was religious, that meant it was "heathen" and wrong for a Christian to take part in. But if its purpose was to heal him, did that excuse his participation? His village was the same as that of the aid post orderly (APO) who had come to work in Rauit. The APO told me the story (in Tokpisin). It presented problems for him. He, too, was a Christian and someone who owed his medical training to the evangelical mission, especially to the first missionary doctor there. The pastor became ill, the APO said, and no one could not find out what was wrong with him. He went to the Wewak and Lae hospitals for tests. The doctors there could not determine the cause, yet he continued to feel ill. He kept dreaming of fish and spirits of the dead, who said he must do a *singsing*. So, against his will, he said yes. His dreams predicted he would have diarrhea for three days after the ritual started, and the watery stools would remove the sickness from him. His main trouble had been pains in his belly and a feeling that his feet were going to take off and he would fly. This, said the APO, was what made the doctors at Lae concentrate on his previous motorbike accident and bangs to his head, even though he had not felt pain in his head at the time. When he returned to the village, people held the *singsing* for him despite his reluctance. Some of the people in his village who were strong converts said it was wrong to hold the *singsing*, a sin God would see. Some of them left the village for the duration of the ritual (either in protest or to escape God's wrath or the mission's disapproval). Soon after it started, the ill pastor had diarrhea and then felt better. Ever since then, he has danced in *singsings* and stays well. The APO pointed out to me that the *singsing* made him better (given the evidence of the prediction and the timing), so it was possible that bad spirits of the village made him ill. Furthermore, the doctors at Lae could find nothing. Perhaps the accident had harmed his brain, he said. Then, speaking for himself, the APO wondered what was right: he himself was a Christian, he believed God could see everything and everywhere, holding *singsings* was a *pekato* (sin), yet the pastor was a strong Christian and had prayed fervently. Why hadn't God healed him? Why did he then get better with the *singsing*? I thought the APO was genuinely perplexed. But I was also aware of his ambiguous position toward me, a doctor, someone who knew the missionary doctor who had trained him. Was it calculated a little by what he thought I might tell the mission people?

Ten days later, I was going through the village where the *singsing* was still being held. A missionary Bible translator who had been working for years on Au, the language spoken in that village, had just come up the hillside to see the pastor who was healed. I found them sitting on the ground in the porch of the pastor's house. They were talking in Au. I understood nothing, but afterward the linguist told me what was said: he had gone to see the pastor who, he heard, was deeply upset, conscience-stricken about allowing the *singsing* to be performed for his illness. The pastor said he had allowed it only at the heavy insistence of his relatives, after all the investigations and much prayer. He told the linguist that he was annoyed the *singsing* was going on so long and that he had repeatedly urged them to end it. He had prayed until he was exhausted. Then his relatives from another village turned up to dance and he could not refuse them. While the *singsing* was going on, he said he could not lead or take part in any Christian services. He prayed but felt in the wrong.

From the linguist, I learned that his illness consisted in dizziness, ringing in the ears, feeling light-headed. It had been diagnosed as Menière's syndrome. He also had migraine with visual aura. He was taking some pills prescribed by the doctor at Lae for his symptoms. But the pastor said they didn't help; only the *singsing* did. On that day, he looked well, neatly dressed in a white shirt, clean shorts, boots and socks, and a wristwatch.

Later, however, he seemed different when he came to Rauit for a ceremony celebrating the birth of someone's first child. I quote from my fieldnotes:

He sits down to chat. They offer him the mash of yams, coconut and taro. No, he can't eat that, tubers come from the ground. Then a lot of chat about all the things he cannot eat because of the singsing. All food that has an association with the ground, ground-living birds and animals, fish, even tinned fish: he speaks about these food avoidances as a committed believer. He told me he used to have belly cramps and pains after food, feel pins and needles running about his skin, his guts twisting and turning. You could hear them making noises like sago grubs inside the trunk of a palm. He felt unsteady on his legs, but things didn't seem to turn round outside him. He had a small, high, ringing sound in his ears. Both the ringing and the dizziness have left him since the singsing. He intends to keep the food avoidances for a time and then try tiny amounts of the foods, waiting in case any of his symptoms come back. What strikes me now is his cheerful and sincere conviction that the singsing helped. In this setting, I would never guess at his perplexity or his pangs of conscience.

An unswerving commitment to one set of beliefs is the demand of monotheism, asserting the truth is single and exclusive. But local patterns of belief in Rauit were not at all like that. In many cases, the stated belief was "Because that's what everyone says" or "Because someone who knows says so." If enough people said so, something might become the truth. For example, it was often hard to tell in advance the day on which a ceremony would happen, a hunt would take place, or a party would set out on a visit. One or two people might say, "Oh, yes, the day after tomorrow," yet the event would not happen then. But if many people said, "Yes, the day after tomorrow," then it would happen. With scandalous gossip, the victim had to deny it quickly and vigorously, loudly and publicly, before too many people gave it currency and credence. People might repeat something as if it were a fact when they had only heard a rumor. Would it be accepted or contradicted? Some of these assertions were actually surreptitious experiments or tests to see if, by trying them out, they would pass muster and take on a stronger status as the truth. How often does truth or fact turned out to be or to depend on what everyone accepts or says it is? As an explanation for belief, it is not so far from the analyses offered by Peter Winch (1970) or Thomas Kuhn (1970). One can believe many things without ever having to put them to any test. But that is not always the case with medical treatments. Treatment involves doing some action to remedy suffering, and the result might challenge expectations or the beliefs behind the action.

Quesalid's story: Of belief and doubts

Belief or disbelief in a treatment, a healer, or a remedy does not have to be fixed or certain; it is not a matter of an all-or-none commitment. Franz Boas recorded the story of a Northwest Coast shaman named Quesalid who began to have doubts about his treatments. The texts by Boas (Boas and Codere 1966: 120–48) on shamanism include personal accounts of the initiation and practice of Kwakiutl shamans, with a perceptive commentary by Boas on reasons for shifts of belief in them. Quesalid's story became well known when Lévi-Strauss used it in his essay (1963) on the nature of the sorcerer's belief in his own magic. Boas knew Quesalid for over thirty years, and between 1897 and 1930, he recorded four accounts Quesalid gave him of the same events. Quesalid (Qaselid) was, in fact, George Hunt, Boas's Kwakiutl friend, coauthor, and close collaborator. After Boas taught him to write, he wrote Kwakiutl texts for Boas as well as being, in the most literal sense, a participant observer and ethnographer of Kwakiutl life (Boas and Codere 1966: xxviii–xxxi). The texts provide direct insights into his personal beliefs and experiences. Boas discusses the shifts in Quesalid's attitude to what had taken place at his initiation to become a shaman in 1870 or 1874. His beliefs in the theory and practice of shamanism reflected conflicting pressures on him: his identification with other shamans, his membership of a secret society, his own experience of "fainting fits," the constraining authority of older shamans, then of missionaries, his fear of getting into trouble with the government if it found out about corpses being used, and a desire to show White people that he was critical about things in which he knew the Whites did not believe.

Boas notes the possibility of imagination and contradictory attitudes altering the recall of long past events—and Quesalid's pride in Indigenous culture, his wish to impress Boas, and his perception of Boas's interests. As to the flickering quality of Quesalid's skepticism, which Lévi-Strauss brings out so well, Boas also discusses the brilliant development of illusion and trickery in Kwakiutl ceremony and art. The winter ceremonial contained a profusion of spectacle and great ingenuity devoted to stage tricks, illusions of decapitation, trap doors through which monster spirits appeared and disappeared, and masks with second hidden faces. A society that values and competes in such arts of deception must encourage the skeptical spirit that is such a fascinating element in Quesalid's story and that indeed runs through Boas's whole account of shamanism, for instance, in the account of the "dreamers," the "creatures of the shamans" who are their "eyes" or their spies; the pretense of sickness and dying through self-starvation; the theater of ecstasy; the arts of belly wobbling and jaw trembling; the trick of transforming a piece of quartz into a starfish; the illusion of sucking disease out of the body and showing the illness in the form of a bloody worm in the shaman's hand; or the ability to vomit blood in public. But the shamans match these deceptive acts with the sincerity evident in many vivid personal accounts of dreams, visions, and experience of sickness and healing: Tlebeet's account of sickness and of being outside his body, when, he said, "I arose and saw my body lying on the ground groaning"; or the shaman affecting sickness with smallpox, coming back to consciousness, thinking that many wolves were near him and that two were lying by his side licking his body. "The principal inference to be drawn from these accounts," writes Boas, "is that notwithstanding the knowledge of fraud, a deep-seated belief in the supernatural power of shamanism persists, even among the sophisticated" (1966: 125).

Beliefs may shift over time. There are also blurred areas where it is hard to know whether someone means something literally or not. The treatment of illness is rich in the ambiguity of instrumental versus expressive action. Discussions of ritual and belief in magic have made these questions prominent (Beattie 1966; Horton 1967; Leach 1968; Skorupski 1976; Tambiah 1968). Consider another one of the Kwakiutl examples in Boas and Codere (1966: 360): If a woman is pregnant for the first time, she gathers four pebbles on the beach, which she puts under her garments. She lets them drop down and prays, "May I be like these!" She does this to secure an easy delivery. Boas argues there is no evidence (unless presumably she were to say so) that would show whether she is performing an act from which she thinks an easy birth follows as a necessary, causally determined result or whether she believes that the symbolic act is a prayer to a supernatural power residing in the stones or the act. The line between magic and religion, as these are distinguished by convention, is fluid. "It is not even the same for all individuals in the same society. For some, the relation between two happenings may be purely mechanical; for others, it may have a religious significance" (1966: 162). He then points out that the Kwakiutl use medicinal plants with healing properties that have been discovered through careful observation. Nevertheless, they make prayers to these plants, which gives them a religious connotation. They imply that the plant becomes efficacious on account of the prayer addressed to the plant. When used without the prayer or any other indication that supernatural powers are involved, the act would be analogous to one based on experience. He gives a parallel:

> The difficulty of drawing a clear line between causally determined and magically determined may perhaps be illustrated by an example. If, in doing some woodwork, someone spoils his work repeatedly when using particular knife, he may say, "That is an unlucky knife" and refuse to use it. The word "unlucky" implies, no matter how weakly, an uncontrollable "supernatural" power. If he should take it up some other day and say to it, "I hope this time you will behave better," it may be merely a linguistic form, but it may also imply the idea that on account of his expressed wish (or prayer) it will be more willing to obey his hand. I feel certain that a clear distinction between happenings whose interrelation is understood purely as those of cause and effect and others that imply or express explicitly the presence of something supernatural cannot be sharply drawn. (Boas and Codere 1966: 162)

An effect? What did they really think?

In certain treatments, the Gnau extract arrows shot into people, but the arrows are not all of the same kind. Surely they must see some difference between symbolic surgery and literal surgery; it is implausible to suppose that they consider all kinds of treatment to be similar in principle. There are three kinds: (A) I described Pauwarak's and Maisu's attempts to remove "arrows" (*sigap*) from Maka (see chapter 2). They did it in a careful but prosaic way (even though at the same time the procedure looked like a bit of "magic"). They both seemed to have had trouble finding any of the arrow points after the extractions and were not sure whether they had got any in the end. The "arrows" they looked for were tiny spicules that could easily be confused with fibrous shreds or splinters in the dust where they searched. A skeptic might say that they could easily find what they were looking for in the dirt, that the mixture of selective attention, expectation, and error would meet no difficulties here in sustaining belief (Jahoda 1970: 33–52). (B) I also witnessed the successful removal of larger *minmin* sorcery "arrow points" from Maka a few months later—the largest was about four centimeters long, made of white wood, and looked like bone. The man spat it out with what looked like a gout of blood into a half-coconut shell filled with water (he had been chewing betel before he did the extraction). (C), there were still a number of men in the village who had been wounded in fighting in the past and had had arrows cut out from their wounds; they could describe doing such surgery or having it done to them. Some of the arrows they made had tips designed to break off in a wound. Similar methods were sometimes used to remove splinters embedded in someone's foot or hand.

The three kinds of arrow removal suggest that those removing the arrows would take different positions on the question of the match between what they are *actually* doing, what it *looks* as if they are doing, and what they *say* they are doing. Gnau do talk among themselves about fraud and sleight of hand, and they say that some people produce arrows by tricks but some are genuine. It is easier to imagine the actors in (A) doing the extraction with complete sincerity and conviction than in (B), where the size of the arrows extracted makes it much harder to believe. It is also difficult to challenge people directly about the sincerity of their actions without appearing to suspect them of fraud or tricks. As Boas's commentary on Quesalid's accounts made plain, even when you know someone well and imagine you have put the question tactfully, the answers may leave you wondering how far they said what they really thought. From her fieldwork in China, Emily Ahern (1979) noted how magic and medical treatments are often not practiced with the certainty they will work; the attitude of mind in doing them may be like that of a supplicant or a petitioner and may range from wishing and hoping to expecting, requesting, or imploring, even to commanding—there is a whole spectrum there. She likens some of the Chinese attitudes to those they take in their dealings with officials, bureaucracy, and legal institutions. She suggests that these gave them experience of the uncertainty of desired outcomes and models for ways to express hope and to seek attention and help from superiors. Belief in the efficacy of petitions is not something one would normally think of characterizing in terms of "literal" or "symbolic," binary terms that seem inappropriate.

Questions about sincerity of belief become more insistent with accounts like that given to W. Lloyd Warner by a Murngin Aboriginal sorcerer:

> Her large intestine protruded as though it were red calico. I covered my arm with orchid juice. . . . Little by little I got my hand inside her. Finally I touched her heart. I pushed the killing stick with my thumb up over the palm, which pressed the stick against my fingers into her heart. . . . I turned her over, her large intestine stuck out several feet. I shook some green ants on it. It went in some little way. I shook some

more on and a little receded. I shook some more, and all of it went
in. Everything was all right now. There was no trace of the wound.
(Warner 1937: 199–200)

What kind of surgery is this? Could I have been the man who said
that? What conceivable experiences could lead me to tell such things
and believe them? Were they fabrications or fantasies? It is striking that
surgery in the imagination could be so vividly described and so ambitious when surgery was in fact so rare and limited.

Introspection tells us that belief in a treatment is quite often in an
inconstant state. Interests and emotions may affect it, so it is inappropriate to pose the issues solely in cognitive terms. Belief implies an attitude
toward what someone asserts. Our very use of the word "belief" rather
than "knowledge" to describe what people think suggests the stance we
take toward what they say: a stance of doubt or disbelief.

Compliance? Or the rejection of advice?

In the changing medical situation of the Sepik over the course of my
research in 1968–69, 1975, and 1985, the introduction of new treatments
brought forward various problems of trust and compliance. Compliance
can, of course, at times be an issue with respect to medical advice anywhere, and the issues range from ignoring relatively trivial matters to
rejecting necessary treatment, even to being forced to comply.

The problem for the public health authorities in New Guinea concerned the long-term treatment for people with leprosy. In chapter 5, I
mentioned how the earlier segregation policy for lepers blighted the life
of the first man in Rauit to show signs of lepromatous leprosy. He was
sent to prison for absconding from the hospital, then sent far away for
treatment when he absconded again. He was newly married in 1968; his
wife had no children and, in his absence, had an affair with his brother.
This led to much family misery, fights, and punishment for other people
as well. The local hospital was originally set up with a separate ward
for lepers (according to government public health requirements, which
were later revoked). By 1985, the health center was no longer manned
by a resident doctor, and a missionary nun, a nurse specialized in leprosy, came to take charge of the services for leprosy and tuberculosis. The
segregation policy had long been ended. Concerning compliance with
leprosy treatments, opinions differed, as my notes attested:

The Nurse: The specialist nurse at the Leprosy Mission said that P. [the patient in question] was not taking his treatment. He should be on three drugs because of the high risk of bacterial resistance, given his long history of intermittent treatment. He didn't come for his check-ups. When he did come, she said, he was perfectly friendly, they got on well, joked together. But he was quite unreliable and she didn't believe he took his drugs. He hadn't come for months. She doubts whether anyone in the village is taking their leprosy treatment as they should. They are certainly not coming to follow-up appointments nor have they come to get further supplies of dapsone [the drug used] at the right times. P. [with his lepromatous leprosy] is a real hazard to others in the village. What can she do? He won't listen. They won't listen.

The Aid Post Orderly (APO): The APO in this village is someone of considerable reputation in the subdistrict; he was once the health education orderly for the area. When he had that job, he did a lot of patrolling, explaining about leprosy and finding cases. The aid post work he has now is not arduous the way he does it. He has known P. for years—since P.'s childhood—and he first spotted and diagnosed his leprosy. Years ago, he also had to report him to the *kiap* [government patrol officer] when he absconded and would not follow the treatment. He says he has talked and talked to P. in the past. He can't get him to take the treatment now. Telling him about how it spreads to others has no effect. P. has been taking the drugs for so many years and can't see the point of still going on with them. He no longer cares about getting sores and injuries. It's true that people with leprosy should come to the APO to get their fresh supplies of dapsone, but not many do. He's fed up with telling people to do so. He lists the people who have come regularly and those who have completed their course of treatment. Most others have taken only part of the course of treatment; they have pills moldering in their houses. He leaves it up to them now. The sister [the Leprosy Mission nurse] gives them three- or four-month appointments, but they don't go. They are *bikhet* [uncooperative, obstinate, they do as they like]. I asked what happened if they didn't go. Nothing, it's not like before, they can't call the *kiap* and get him to send a policeman. When he was doing the health education and leprosy work, he [the APO] used to go around to find people who were defaulting on treatment or absconding. But the leprosy control people can't do it all the time. Now really the only thing the sister can do is to ask the village *kaunsil* [councilor] or his *komiti* [chief assistant] to try and persuade someone to come. That doesn't work.

A Young Man in the Village: A number of the people I questioned about completing treatment said they had been told to stop because they had finished; that did not fit with the impression I got from the sister. Other people commented on P. and his treatment (but only because I asked). One young man said most people took the medicine for leprosy for a while and then threw it away but told the nursing sister they were taking it, or else they didn't go back. The older people felt they needn't bother because they would die anyway and clear off that way. I asked who really felt like that and he cited P.'s aged mother, who in fact had suffered from leprosy, too, but had died for other reasons. But, I said, that cannot be true of Delen [the other man who has lepromatous leprosy]. The young man spoke more seriously now. People like Delen think they have eaten the medicine, they can't feel anything wrong, so they think it must be enough and they stop. Or they look at their skin, think the lesions are not significant, and wonder why they should bother about them. Infected sores are worse.

The Patients: Delen is a calm, dependable man in his mid-forties. I know him quite well. I broached the topic of his treatment with him. He said he takes them as he was told to. He put his hand into his *bilum* [string bag] and brought out the tin of dapsone to show it to me. I had been there for five weeks; I just happened to ask him that morning. He says he takes them and has more in his house. His manner is unbothered. I can't see why I should disbelieve him; I have no grounds to doubt his word.

As for the patient P., I didn't see him for nearly two months after my return in 1985. He lives in the hamlet most distant from the main village, and he had shifted his house to an outlier of the hamlet. For most of the time, he had been quite far away from the village at a bush site, Saikel. So I didn't see him until a day on which most of the village gathered for a boy's puberty ceremony. P. and his brothers arrived late, when there was a crowd already gathered in the *warkao* [the day house where people gather] (Fig. 30). P. came in discreetly and sat at the back of the *warkao* on a *garamut* [slit gong] (Fig. 31). I did not speak to him at first, partly because I was involved in conversation, partly because I wanted to see whether he would make a move. He saw me stare at him from time to time. He couldn't have supposed I didn't recognize him. Then, after half an hour, I got up and pushed through to speak to him—a very public move, given the crowd. I sat down beside him on the *garamut*. He smiled. I asked how he was. He said he was well and that he had been staying at Saikel. Can you do everything you want to? I asked. Yes, I can hold a bow and arrow, I can shoot. Can you do gardening? Yes. How about your hands and feet? (He was wearing plastic sandals to protect his damaged feet.) He showed me his hands and feet, he said they were all right. How could he go up and down steep slopes with those sandals? He said he takes them off on steep slopes. Abruptly, unfairly, I asked about his medicine. He said he is taking it, he has four bottles for four months' supply and takes the pills every evening before sleep.

Since my visit in 1975, he had stayed in the village and did not want to have to leave it again. We talked a bit about when I had been there before. He cheered up, especially when recalling the dispute over the Saikel bush, how old W. nearly got speared. I told him he ought to make sure he saw the nurse sister regularly about his treatment so that she was clear he was taking it. He had depigmented scars on one elbow, which I think are from burns. His hands were obviously affected, with right little and ring fingers deformed and clawed from contractures. His appearance showed his disease more obviously than before: thickening of his eyebrow ridges, no eyebrows, fleshy ear lobes. His eyes look all right. His toes are damaged, with the loss of part of one. I didn't try to examine him. This was what I could see as we talked.

One important factor behind what people do is the information they have, the nature and sources of that information, and how they evaluate it. The following episode gave me a little insight into these matters:

A Shrewd Observer: I am sitting by a garden in the bush called Namelim with Tilpetau, a man in his early thirties. His wife died some weeks before in the hospital at Vanimo on the coast; she had been sent there from the local health center. Her death is a calamity for him and their two children. Tilpetau, looking through his *bilum*, takes something out, wordlessly holds it up for me to see, as if challenging me to guess, just as he did before with his wife's family-planning card. This one is also a crumpled card. It states that he is on dapsone, 100 mg a day, and it has a note saying, "for sandals and gris." What is the card for? I ask. It is because of the holes in his feet, he says, and shows them to me—hard to see them on the soles of his feet, about four tiny punched-out holes, approximately 3 millimeters in diameter. They hurt on strong pressure. Yes, he knows it is a *sik lepro* card. They gave him medicine to take every day because other people in the village have *sik lepro*, but he doesn't have it. The medicine he has is "for something else" (*beiya menamdem*), it is for

Figure 29. Visitors who have come for a ceremony rest in the *warkao* day house. The man seen standing has brought a set of bow and arrows destined as an initiation gift for his sister's son.

Figure 30. A log slit gong used to accompany ritual dances and funerals and to signal to people in other villages or distant gardens. This slit gong is housed in a lineage's day house, but most lineages keep them in their men's house.

his feet. He took it for a while. He still has a lot left, but he hasn't been taking it since he went to the hospital at Vanimo with his wife. He only started it at the time his wife was ill in the health center. What he was taking, he said, is not the same as the "big medicine" they take for *sik lepro*, because that kind they eat on Mondays and Thursdays. Yes, he knows they say he has leprosy, but he does not believe them; what he has is not serious. The only serious cases in the village now are P. and Delen. He points out to me that he doesn't have any skin marks, not the kind that involves a loss of feeling, and he hasn't swollen up anywhere. He just has these holes on his feet. But he wants to get the plastic sandals. So do a number of men in the village.

I was struck by the way he didn't reveal at first how much he knew about leprosy: about the other (two-day) treatment schedule he had observed at the health center (a multiple drug treatment to stave off resistance to dapsone), his conclusions about the types and severity of the disease. He and other villagers make a clear distinction between the kind of illness P. and Delen have and the other *sik lepro*, which is what most people diagnosed have. This is the tuberculoid type, which shows up as painless marks on the skin. In the views of one young man, "People don't think leprosy is serious. It is not a bad disease in the sense that you could die from it. Leprosy is *wuyinda* [good, mild in quality], the signs are just marks, they don't harm or incapacitate you. People don't believe what the health education people tell them. What those people tell them or show them in the pictures isn't what they have." The skin lesions that villagers see look much like other skin troubles they know well: *gapati watelila* or *gadu'et wanu'en*, which are benign fungal infections. They are used to putting up with *grili* (an unpleasant fungal disease). Leprosy doesn't even itch or hurt or smell or scale off. Scabies, infected sores, abscesses, and wounds are worse. The swelling kind of leprosy, the kind P. and Delen have, is different. People might die from it. The villagers have expanded the category to include some quite different serious illnesses, ones accompanied by painless swelling of limbs, face, or body, which they suppose are true cases of *sik lepro*.

On the one hand, there are the villagers' doubts that people diagnosed with leprosy really have a serious disease. On the other, there is the nurse sister's conviction that the villagers are not taking treatment, that the main fault lies with them. When I followed up answers from some of the villagers who said they had been told to stop their treatment, I found they were right. The cards kept by the sister showed that in 1978 and 1983, a number of them had at some point been told to discontinue treatment. The diagnostic questions are medical matters. The health authorities may have misconceptions about the patients' extent of defection and apathy about treatment. But when villagers express some doubts about the seriousness of what disease they have, even about whether they have real leprosy, I think they are sometimes right.

Response to innovation

Leprosy stands out as an example of a disease for which the people of Rauit did not ask for treatment; it was imposed or brought to them. With leprosy, compliance was a matter of persuasion; in the past, it was something closer to enforcement for someone with lepromatous leprosy. The call for treatment came from the providers (the public health service officials), not the recipients, who were passive or simply tolerant. Initially, they were unaware of the diagnosis, and many are still unconvinced of its seriousness. If they really believed in the benefits of treatment, they would act differently. They complied willingly with griseofulvin treatments for *grille*, a disfiguring fungal skin disease.

Just about everyone in the village knew that the aid post had a white powder (procaine penicillin), which was meant to be dissolved for injections, could be sprinkled directly onto an infected cut or sore to clear it up quickly. When the APO was not looking, adults and children would surreptitiously pick up half-used vials. They kept them *bilong was tasol*—that is, "just in case" they might need it. The APO said he knew they should not put the penicillin powder directly on sores; he knew about resistance and skin reactions. And he said all this with his brother-in-law's twelve-year-old son sitting on a bench beside him in the aid post, wearing nothing and clutching two half-used penicillin vials in his hand. He had just snatched them for his father. This use of penicillin was an innovative misuse of the penicillin powder; they observed that it worked well. Someone must have experimented first. It seemed suitable to them because it was so like their former use of silt or termite dust to dry up cuts quickly. It was also like the sprinkling of lime or *kaona* lime on cuts.

But any long-term treatment, as with leprosy, is liable to put its own merits in doubt because of the delay in improvement and lack of obvious results. In Rauit, the time between any treatment (cause) and an improvement (effect) was expected to be short. The longer the time gap, the less likely they were to consider a treatment effective. They did not see that some forms of treatment take a long time to work. The need to continue with a repeated treatment undermined belief in its value. There was scant chance that someone diagnosed with leprosy would complete a full course of treatment.

When health patrols justified the need for treatment of leprosy, they did it by referring to the dangers of future harm to the infected person and of spreading it to others. But it is notoriously difficult to convince people that something worse in the future has been stopped from happening. Leprosy was new to the villagers. They were told they might spread the disease to their children and family through "germs." But germs were not visible. The idea of germs (*jiem* in Tokpisin) had already taken strong root in relation to some illnesses, though not to *sik lepro*, except for the bad swelling sort. The ideas they now learned about infection and contagion—that invisible agents can make an illness pass or jump from one person to another—were familiar. The new agents of illness, *jiem*, behaved rather like their own spirits.

With something common like infected cuts and sores, villagers knew what to expect and could assess the benefits of a new treatment. Patrol officers, missionaries, and health patrols had advised or ordered them to dig latrines, to improve their water supplies, to dispose of corpses through burial because, as they kept saying, flies and germs spread diseases. But the villagers had always had rules of their own about washing, hygiene, and food, as well as ones for the disposal of excrement and rubbish. Yet they often seemed to neglect scabies and sores. They acknowledged that bandages and penicillin injections made infected sores better. Flies settled on open sores; dressings kept them off. Their traditional leaf bandages and bark dressings were rarely to be seen by 1985. The new dressings from the aid post had displaced them, but the villagers had to depend on the staff for them. They had become less self-sufficient. Whether someone sought treatment depended on its availability and distance. But the common reason they gave for neglect was that most sores got better anyway. They were used to putting up with them; the aid post had only been there for a few years and was not always staffed. The neglect was a kind of learned tolerance. At the distant hunting camps where people would stay for two weeks or more, traditional methods for treating sores were occasionally used. I watched the grandfather of two young girls make a mixture of yellow sap, crushed vine creeper, and lime to put on their sores. Most children were used to putting up with flies, scabs, and pain—but they did not have much choice.

*   *   *

If the definition of health goes beyond the mere absence of recognizable diseases, as it does in most conceptions, it is associated with social values and personal ideals. Ideals for health cannot be comprehensively defined except by taking values into account. Many of the choices and answers must lie with the community and individual conscience. In some way, every society has made care of the sick a collective responsibility and not left it solely to the individual. In Gnau, there is no word meaning "disease" in general, but there is a verb for saying "he is sick" (*neyigeg*), which can be used for any state of illness. It is a form related to the word *neyig*, meaning "he will die" (G. Lewis 1975: 136–39). The added syllable seems to modify the meaning rather than intensify it. I learned its meaning of being sick without noticing or realizing the morphological connection with "to die." Yet years before, Rivers (1924: 4–5) had defined medicine as: "Practices by which man seeks to direct and control a specific group of natural phenomena . . . affecting man himself which lower his vitality and tend toward death." This referred to the phenomena we call *morbid*. The very word for being sick in Gnau pointed to its connection with death. One chief object of Rivers's book was to discover the nature of the concept of disease among those who fail to distinguish medicine from magic and religion and the steps by which medicine has become differentiated from other institutions and acquired independent existence. There were many peoples, like the Melanesians he studied, for whom medicine, magic, and religion were so closely intertwined that disentangling each from the rest was difficult or impossible. He gave preeminent importance to

> the great mystery of death as the most important motive in the development of the religion of mankind, the connexion of religion with the art designed to meet disease, the harbinger of death, would have seemed especially natural. . . . That running through the history of mankind there has been in action a process of specialization of social function stands beyond all doubt, and I should have been keeping strictly within the truth in regarding the increasing distinction of medicine from magic and religion as an example of this process of specialization. (Rivers 1924: 56–58)

In biology, an organ is said to be specialized when, although it is efficient in one respect, it lacks the capacity to perform other functions that are satisfactorily performed by similar organs in other animals. The differentiation of medicine from its initial confusion with magic and religion did not easily take place. Criteria of medical progress are now largely set by medical specialists. But the experience of illness and the practice of medicine are hard to separate completely from religious and moral values. We are too quick to take our present medical system and practices as the standard by which to judge progress in treatments. If we extrapolate from the notion that specialization involves the loss of capacity to perform other functions that were satisfactorily performed by comparable entities elsewhere, we have grounds for taking an interest in other people's ways to care for the sick. Medicine is concerned not just with life expectancy and population statistics but also more directly with the illnesses of individuals and with providing care for their suffering. As Rivers wrote, "I believe that there are now becoming apparent in many departments of social life (I recognise it especially in that of science), indications that specialization can be carried too far, and that with further advance we may come again to those close interrelations between the different aspects of human culture which are characteristic of its earlier stages" (1924: 115). In the final analysis, this may offer a justification for the comparative study of medicine in different societies, not just focusing on our own.

Transcription of Milek's healing

This treatment was recorded on June 9, 1969, in the middle of my first fieldwork visit among the Gnau. The patient, a middle-aged woman named Milek, had been ill for about ten days with a fever, malaise, vague backache, and some discomfort on passing urine. For these symptoms, she had already received several treatments: one to counter a spell, a treatment from me, and a small version of Panu'et. Since these afforded her no relief, a large version of the Panu'et healing rite was held four days later, from which this translated transcript comes. The transcript starts in the second act, back in the hamlet of Watalu, when the junior men are preparing the face, painting it, and decorating the image under the supervision of the senior men. Their concern to do it well—in the sense both of doing it correctly and of doing it beautifully—appears in many comments, teasing, and criticism. For the treatment to be effective, they must please the spirit, they say; otherwise, there is a risk of it doing more harm. Another feature of this section is the high number of instructions contained in the comments and criticism. There is a continual barrage of banter, prompting, reiteration, and rhetoric in which all the senior men seem to want to have their say. Many of their statements involve instructions about technical details of what to get or what to do, many of which are contradicted by competing instructions. Reasons for doing something and snippets of information are scattered throughout their discussions. Things are done in the wrong order and corrected, opinions are loudly asserted and contested. It is a way of learning. It is lively, a bit chaotic. There is no reason to expect that the details they argue about here (for example, the position of the pig tusks) will come up for dispute next time. The translation below preserves the continuity of the recording. It is a full translation (I have cut out only a few asides.) I think the way they talk and comment gives insight into the style and mood of the ritual performance as well as revealing directly how they express their ideas. It is the text of an event.

Cast of characters

From Watalu Hamlet

> MILEK—the patient, a woman about fifty years old
> PURKITEN—Milek's husband

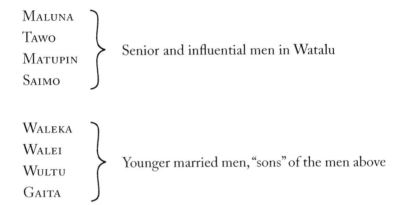

> MALUNA
> TAWO
> MATUPIN
> SAIMO
>
> } Senior and influential men in Watalu

> WALEKA
> WALEI
> WULTU
> GAITA
>
> } Younger married men, "sons" of the men above

> WIVES AND CHILDREN (not much is heard from them in the recording)
> OTHER MEN (only those with something to say in the transcript are listed)

From Wimalu Hamlet

> SILMAI—Milek's "brother," collateral line, former *tultul* [assistant to the headman]
> MARKI—Milek's full brother, older than she is
> MAITATA—a younger man, married to Milek's step-daughter (i.e., Purkiten's daughter by a previous wife who had died)

From Pakuag Hamlet

DAUWANIN—Milek's eldest daughter, wife of Galwun
GALWUN—Dauwanin's husband, Milek's son-in-law

Others

MAISU—a senior man from Dagetasa Hamlet, of the same lineage as Galwun
DAUWARAS—younger married man, from Bi'ip Hamlet, of the same clan as Purkiten
WANI—father of Dauwaras

Preparations for the performance: Painting the image's face

SILMAI: You think it's like the *nimbalgut* nut pattern. The line should go down like this, then make it go up, like this. Then around and along like this—there! Draw it like that and up—here . . .

MARKI: Get a betel nut for her. I'll prepare it for when she has to spit in front of it. (*This is done to identify herself to the spirit Panu'et.*)

SILMAI: Bring me the stuff. We've got to do the face, decorate it, and put the spells into it.

MATUPIN: Do the jaw line—down and then going up.

WALEKA: Do the jaw line, then draw the face for me.

WALEI: See if there's some water. Isn't there some poured out for doing the painting?

SILMAI: Draw the line straight down the middle for the nose. Right. Now go on down until it joins the jaw line. . . . There! That's enough for the jaw. Give us some more [paint] for the eyes, both sides. Enough. That one goes down there. That one turns and goes up there. He's brought a [sago-palm] leaf base for painting on.

DAUWARAS: No, no, I came alone. The leaf base was too slippery-surfaced, so we put breadfruit sap on it so we could paint on it (*the sap serves as a primer*).

MARKI: Dauwanin, bring some betel so I can get it ready.

PURKITEN: And some ash salt. And bring some ginger. For spitting over the things.

MARKI: Like that. Carefully now. Will you need two betel nuts prepared?

MALUNA: Just split one. What would you want two for? There's some of the Eagle wood (*to be added to the* geplagep *herb scrapings*). You should take some and put plenty in so that the betel has some kick. To give spice to the ash salt.

PURKITEN: Dauwanin, get them some water.

GALWUN: Hurry up.

PURKITEN: Pour it over the ginger.

DAUWARAS: Break off some of it. Cut some cordyline.

(*They need the cordyline to make a stiff sort of paintbrush out of its stalk. Purkiten and Marki pound* geplagep *herbs to mix with the ginger and ash salt. Later, they mix these into the* wa'agep *soup mixture, which they have partially cooked in the garden, where they added beetle grubs to the mixture.*)

MALUNA: Cut some cordyline and bring them at the same time. Fetch a leaf so we can cut it. . . . Make the line, one side like that and the other like this, so they come together. (*He makes a wedge shape like the fork of a tree to indicate the line of the jaw.*)

WULTU: He's tearing it off at the stalk, he's tearing the stalk off.

MALUNA: That's right—the stalk.

WALEKA: Hold it up and I'll tear it off.

WALEI: No, you hold it and pull. Yaopei, get a knife!

WULTU: Keep the stalk with it.

WALEKA: He's messing it up.

WALEI: Look, it's so small!

MALUNA: Get some ash salt for mixing with the stuff. Quick, get the betel ready. Quickly now!

WULTU: Split the betel. Oh! Look, the sprout is coming out from the side.

Kᴀɴᴛʏɪ (*a brother of Maluna*): I think you should get a big bowl to do a lot of ginger.

Mᴀʟᴜɴᴀ: Go on, get a bowl.

Wᴜʟᴛᴜ: Here's a big one. *Tultul* (*addressing Silmai by the title of his former office*), break one off, but don't tear the stalk.

Dᴀᴜᴡᴀʀᴀs: Here, try this cordyline. Don't pull the top off.

Wᴜʟᴛᴜ: Carefully, pull it carefully. The stalk—*ei*! It broke!

Wᴀʟᴇᴋᴀ: This man is doing it wrong and messing it up.

Wɪsᴜᴋ: Yaopei, the knife!

Wᴜʟᴛᴜ: We don't need it, we'll tear it off.

Mᴀʟᴜɴᴀ: You bring some salt to mix in with this, and hurry up with getting the betel nut ready.

Kᴀɴᴛʏɪ: I said I think you should get a big bowl and pour out plenty of water so it can take a lot of ginger.

Mᴀʟᴜɴᴀ: Aren't they asking for a bowl?

Wᴜʟᴛᴜ: Here's a big one. *Tultul*, tear one off. Tear it but don't break the stalk.

Dᴀᴜᴡᴀʀᴀs: Go and get a cordyline, but don't break off its shoot.

Wᴜʟᴛᴜ: Careful, careful now. Don't break the stalk.

Mᴀʟᴜɴᴀ: Come on, get the [white paint] marks painted on.

Wᴀʟᴇᴋᴀ: *Aiik*, no! I just splotched them on it, they're much too big!

Wᴜʟᴛᴜ: They're just marks, it doesn't matter if they're big.

Dᴀᴜᴡᴀʀᴀs: Why didn't they finish painting the face much earlier?

Mᴀʟᴜɴᴀ: Ah! Now take the bowl and put the stuff in it, they'll add the wood herb scrapings to it.

Sɪʟᴍᴀɪ: Hey! Give me some of the ash salt here to mix in with the paint here so it comes up bright—it won't without it.

Mᴀʟᴜɴᴀ: Haven't you got any yet? Haven't they brought you any?

Mᴀʀᴋɪ: Go get some, bring it here!

WULTU: Here's some coming now. Try it and see if it's enough.

WALEKA: We painted it too wet. Now it won't come up bright white. (*He means it will not dry in time, which is necessary for it to turn bright white.*)

MARKI: Fetch some water. Can't they hurry up with the water?

WALEKA: I did those marks . . .

WALEI: They are awful. And it [the spirit]? No! It will go barging into everyone! (*He implies that the spirit will be displeased by the bad painting and therefore hurt someone.*)

GALWUN: Bring us some water.

WALEI: Do the painting your way and bring me my nettles. (*The nettles will be fixed on the base and later rubbed on the patient as part of the treatment.*)

SILMAI: What's going on? They said they could do it and now look. . . . And that cordyline—what's that for? You lot, you keep laughing and mucking about. Go on like that and you'll mess it up.

DAUWARAS: You've brought an awful lot [of ash? Ginger?]. You should have brought just a little. Maybe it'll be all right. Why on earth did you think of bringing so much?

UNIDENTIFIED MAN: Because Father said to.

MALUNA (*sees a bold toddler, Takun, wandering up too close*): Who's this? Off you go!

SILMAI: Let's get on with it. Quick now, quickly. Daylight is leaving. And it [Panu'et] will go off, stand on the path, turn around, and come back. It will come strike some woman or child. It will overshadow [and do harm through] something belonging to you.

WALEI: Paint the marks on the face for us.

SILMAI: I thought you'd already done them a lot earlier to put them in the sun so they would come out well.

DAUWANIN (*calling to them*): Give me a bit of ash salt. You've got more than enough betel pepper catkins there.

PURKITEN (*replying to his daughter*): The betel pepper catkins are over there.

WALEI: Do you mean the head, we should do it like that? Look, should we do it like that for the head and then, for the face, like this? You must finish it.

MARKI: And the eyes, each side.

SILMAI: You people didn't learn how to do the mynah-bird–type painting on the face until just yesterday. Well, you didn't know my mynah-bird version. (*Silmai's version is named after the triangular markings on the head of the golden mynah bird, called* gapati gugalen *in Gnau, a noisy occupant of trees around their gardens.*)

WALEI: You put the little shells in (*to resemble to image's ears*) and then you do the mynah-bird–shaped face.

SILMAI: You lot don't know how to do it, so you've drawn it badly.

MAITATA: Those bits should be like this . . .

WISUK (*a small boy*): Like shit. (*He throws in his comment, speaking close to the microphone.*)

MARKI: Bring a little salt, some salt (*added for making the paint*).

PURKITEN: Dauwanin, bring some salt!

YAOPEI and MARKI (*both shouting*): Dauwanin! Bring a little salt!

WALEI: Bring a lot so it will "bite" and the color will come up bright. The ears, the curly spirals—come on, paint them on well.

WALEKA: The older brother—he's just taken the stuff I was using. Where's he gone to?

WULTU: There, they've painted the ears. That's done. Now put the dots along the lines of the jaws, along the cheeks on each side—just follow the line there. That's it. Hey! That's really good! Beautiful!

ANOTHER SMALL BOY (*speaking to Dauwaras to tattle on another boy*): He just stepped over you! Couldn't he bother to walk round you? He rushed past. He wanted to play. (*The boy violated a rule forbidding people from stepping over each other; they parallel some of the other rules of precedence.*)

DAUWANIN: Where has the ash salt gone?

GALWUN: Look out, there's mud there. . . . Get me the jaw so the marks can fit along the jaw.

SILMAI: Get a move on, hurry up, you lot there! Look, night is falling, it's coming soon.

WULTU: Night? Already? He's painting it as fast as he can so the spirit can go off back into the bush.

MAITATA (*commenting on the painting*): That squashed-up face— that's just right.

WALEI: Panu'et will spy out the lay of the bush, ready to go along a bad path. (*The reference is to the spirit leaving when it is sent off through wild bush, maybe going where they want to send it but by its own path. They call it "a bad path," meaning going cross-country through rough terrain.*)

WALEKA: Go on now. Paint the marks on already so it can leave by the bad path.

SILMAI: Are you lot ever going to do it? I could do it all by myself. Ha! The frogs have started piping (*this is the signal of evening falling*). Get on with it, quick!

WALEKA: Go carefully with the painting.

MARKI: When they've got it all ready, the others must come and stand and watch while we get Panu'et to treat her—someone to stand with the nettle ready to sting her, ready holding the leaf.

(*Marki, like many other men, keeps repeating bits of procedural instructions that everyone already knows, something that will become obvious from the rest of the transcript. It is a notable feature of any public gathering, a litany of prompting and reiterating what should come next. Silmai's comments about night falling are false alarms; they are meant to hurry them up; no one takes them seriously. They still had about two hours or more to go before nightfall.*)

Decorating the figure

(*The next part has mainly to do with putting on the decorations, shells of different sorts, and a pig tusk nose ornament.*)

WALEKA: Bring the pig tusks.

MAISU: Now, stick them through ready. . . . Hey! What are they pointing down for? Put them in pointing up.

WALEI: There? But that's the neck. He's crazy!

SILMAI: Ahh, just like that, that's it.

MARKI (*teasing Waleka, who is fixing them on the Panu'et image*): Don't you know anything? Is this the first time you've come? I even know your version and how to do it. Doesn't he even know the way his own ancestors did it?

MALUNA (*catches sight of little Takun again*): Hey, Takun, off you go!

WALEKA: I don't know the way he does it.

MARKI (*to Walei about Waleka*): Why don't you—you're his cross-cousin—tell him how to do it?

MALUNA: Takun, off you go!

MARKI: If things go on like this, when these men die, who will be around to tell you how to do them? You won't know how. Well, maybe it doesn't matter. Maybe just leave it.

WALEKA: His way? No!
(*Someone whistles, meaning "Shut up, keep quiet!" Someone else brings bamboo tubes containing shell and feather ornaments. They were stored in the thatch of a roof, so the ornaments got dirty.*)

MARKI: These are dirty. Go and wash them so they are ready.

PURKITEN: Even if you wash them, is that going to make them good? When you put them away, the rats will get back to work and make their nests there.

MAISU: You, young men there, eating things you shouldn't be! You'll be lying asleep in the house there, with dirt and rat shit falling on you. You'll get sick!

MALUNA: Go and fetch a *tekanik* shell string (*referring to a woven string loop with small shells sewn on it*). Bring it quickly!

WALEI: *Wut*! He's gone and pulled too hard! It's cut through.

MALUNA: Go fetch a *tekanik*, there's one left.

DAUWARAS: If some are left, bring them here.... Not like that! Fasten them on the chest in front.

SILMAI (*spitting to clear his mouth*): There. And put them on the neck. Bring me our *tekanik* to hang them on the ears, both sides.

MAISU: No! *Aaaa*, these should be on the neck!

SILMAI: They should go close up to the chin.

MAISU: That's it! That's it. Some for the chin.

SILMAI: There, now! You lot didn't know my way of doing it. This should be tied here and hang down.

DAUWARAS: Where were they put?

MAISU: Go fetch a bone awl for us. Where did they put them?

WALEI: We didn't use it for fastening the things on.

DAUWARAS: Get some *saorangel* shell strings to go right up to the face there. At the neck is down too low.

WALEI: This one is only fit for throwing away—it's broken.

DAUWARAS: You two hold on to it or else the nettle will come off. (*He means the nettle leaves that have to be tied to cover the rounded base of the image; they are the part that touches and stings the patient during the treatment.*)

GALWUN: Fasten it with something.

MAISU: Maybe you should go and eat in case you need to go and fetch more material to cover the other.

SILMAI: Bring something, bring me a *dalabi* mat to go on top of them. (*He is referring to an oval coconut-fiber mat covered on one side with small, flat Nassa shells—formerly the main valuables used as bridewealth.*) Haven't you got enough finery to show? (*This is said to tease or taunt the other man.*)

MALUNA: Just a little. That'll be enough.

WALEI (*addressing Silmai*): *Tultul*, where should we put it?

SILMAI: No. You bring it here and put it against this coconut trunk, over here.

WALEKA: Could you bring us a *gilt* shell to tie on here and then take the *dalabi* to fasten here? Or maybe it doesn't matter.

WALEI: Oh, bring it! Tie them on, go on! Hey, hey, pull on it, you lot! Tie it on strongly!

WALEKA: Then loosen the *dalabi* so it slides farther down.

GALWUN: He's painted it so it's very ugly!

WALEKA (*laughing*): No, no, I haven't! It's just their way, the White man's way of doing it!

GALWUN: You, pull them really tight.

DAUWARAS: Take it and hold on to that up there.

MALUNA (*calling to his youngest son*): Yaopei!

WALEI: You over there, tie the little rings on quickly!

MALUNA: Yaopei!

WALEI: There are the things, the little one there.

MALUNA: Go and tell Yaopei to get the little knife.

GALWUN: What are you holding it [the Panu'et image] for? Go and put it down on the ground!

WULTU: If you hold it, you'll get it dirty, the nettle will get torn off.

MAISU: Right. Tie the things and then we're ready to go.

SILMAI: You there, tie the things on quickly!

GALWUN: We'll tie them on now. Tell me, should that one go low down? I was going to put it on that side.

WALEI: I'll fasten it on the other side

SILMAI: Tie it first on that side.

GALWUN: These people put theirs high up. (*Presumably he was referring to the way of wearing some piece of shell decoration.*)

WALEI (*to Waleka*): Look first!

WALEKA: Pull them and cut.

WULTU: You said to tie the little one on, but it's broken.

(*Now they are almost ready for the senior men to spit betel juice and spells onto the image at its ears, headdress, vital center, and the nettle base. Maluna and Silmai courteously invite each other to do this. The* Iyi-mungai *banana leaf with two hibiscus flowers stuck in it will also have two big blotches of betel juice spat on it with spells. Maluna will do this.*)

MALUNA: You spit on it.

SILMAI (*demurring*): You spit on it.

MALUNA: You spit. For your daughter. (*This must be a way of referring to the patient, Milek, a "sister" of Silmai, but a collateral one in a junior line.*)

WULTU: But wait, it's not ready.

GALWUN: But what's got into you to make you rush everyone into the spitting?! You can still work on it a bit and lower it.

SILMAI: He's teasing; it's just a joke.

GALWUN: These here—elder brother . . .

MALUNA: And all you—"little sisters"!—telling off your elder brothers!? (*The way Galwun and the young men tell them to stop rushing makes Maluna laugh, so he is teasing them back. A lot of laughter ensues.*)

WULTU: You spit on it. It didn't turn out right (*that is, the betel juice is not red enough*). What's missing?

MALUNA (*jeering*): The sister, the sister!

SILMAI: The son-in-law [Galwun] should hold the bowl and his father-in-law [Purkiten, husband of Milek] should get the ginger *wa'agep* mixture and pour it into it.

GALWUN: Yes, I know.

SILMAI: Aaa, no! Turn them up, turn them, the tusks!

MAISU: Ours are all right now.

GALWUN: Go on, turn them up so it looks right.

MALUNA: You lot! Turn them around to point upward, toward the nose holes, up like that.

DAUWARAS: Gaita, we'll go to this side. Or shall we go to that? (*They are carrying the image at this point.*)

SILMAI: Turn it around the other way up. Like that. Like that. As he's holding it, he can turn it around so the decorations are on top.

MALUNA: Listen, hold it like that. That's right. They can throw it, turning it, so the tusks go down like that on this side. When I was little, you would put them in so they pointed upward, then I saw how my father's generation would stick the tusks in, pointing down for women but twisting them up for men.

GALWUN: Put them in. It doesn't matter if it's the wrong way.

MALUNA (*reminiscing*): When I was in Wimalu, I got some terrific tusks. They shot a pig and I got the head and the tusks. They really stretched my nose and it hurt dancing for Wunitap with them in. *Ehhh*, they hurt so much!

SILMAI: Well then, you should go shoot your own pig for yourself (*i.e., if you don't like the size of the tusks they gave you*).

Putting spells into the image to make the spirit enter it and spitting betel on the leaf

WALEKA: Now bring it, quickly, over here.

MATUPIN: Go and blow [the spells] on it, in here (*indicating where the headdress goes*), put them into it.

DAUWARAS: Watch out, you're putting dirt on the nettles.

MALUNA: All right, I'll go and blow my spells on it.

SILMAI: *Wuutt!* Blow in the ears first, each side. Then you can jiggle the croton headdress into place.

WALEI: Go and bring the ginger mixture. And get the banana leaf.

SILMAI: Get the ginger and hold it under it, under the leaf, so it's covered. Then you must get the tobacco for blowing smoke over them and fetch the hearth ashes.

Dauwaras: Get some of Milek's own hearth ashes that she slept beside. Then someone rolls the cigarette.

(*The idea of getting her own ashes is that Panu'et will see that the ashes come from her fire and accept her request to leave her. If she were to take ashes from someone else's fire, it would be like trying to trick the spirit.*)

Silmai: Walei, the ashes can wait for now, leave the ashes.

Maluna: It's time for this [the image] to go.

Silmai: Put the leaf over the ginger mixture to cover it. It's not time yet for the ashes, not yet. First, the "peeling," touching it on her.

Maluna: Right, not yet! First, do the peeling treatment, then you can get the ashes, and then blow over the leaf and tear it up.

Silmai: That's right. First, go and blow spells in at the ears (*so the spirit will hear and understand the appeals*).

Labawan (*a boy overheard speaking to another small boy*): My father shot us that *thingumme* . . . the cockatoo there.

Matupin: Take it out of her [Milek's] way. She's going to stand over there when she comes. Take the leaf so it's out of her way and lay it over the ginger mixture.

Maisu: You mustn't put it down on that side. Lay it down on this side. If you lay it down over there, the nettle will be on the wrong side.

Silmai: Who's going to get me a fire stick?

Galwun: Here's mine so I'll know where you are with it. Come and stand over here. I'll pick a nettle and keep it for you. We're coming.

Matupin: Don't pull the nettle leaves off the stalk.

Purkiten: Hold on, hold on to the croton [in the headdress].

Maluna: The younger brother can hold it at this end while they spit the betel on it. Hey, the spit is getting on me! What a mess! You people! Oh well, it doesn't matter. You can mess me up.

Dauwaras: They are our things. It's all right to spit on them. When it's over, we'll take it and throw it away in the bush.

(*Noise of spells being blown by blowing and spitting into the image: pfff . . . pfff . . . pfff . . . gilei . . . gilei . . . gilei. . . . Maluna spits on the leaf and on the nettles covering the base of the Panu'et image. Purkiten blows the spells into its headdress and ears.)*

DAUWANIN: I'm bringing plenty of ashes now.

SILMAI: Wait, we're not ready, put them down. Come and put them down. First, hold this nettle. Come and help your poor mother come down here. Put the ashes down for now.

MARKI (*loudly*): She should go and stand over there.
(*Milek, the patient, gets ready to come to confront Panu'et.*)

DAUWANIN: Milek, Milek, come on out now. Come and stand over by the coconut, by the trunk there.

WALEI (*loudly*): Her brother [Marki] should give her the betel so she can start chewing it. (*This is so she has the betel quid with the* geplagep *in her mouth ready when she faces Panu'et.*)

PURKITEN: I've got the smoke ready. Should I blow the smoke over the things?

MARKI: Not yet, not yet. Wait 'til she comes.

PURKITEN: I think you should give it her to chew. Give it her to chew while she's waiting over there before coming here.

MALUNA: She should chew it as she comes forward to spit in a spray. What she should say is: "Can't it see who I am, my paths, my bush? I only have one lot of bush that's mine, and others go there too. It doesn't recognize me. It must go off somewhere far away, to the empty bush, and leave me alone. It's not as though I had a lot of paths and bush plots to go to. They can use other bush plots. I've got only this one and others are using it too."

DAUWARAS: Bring them to us—over here. (*To Milek*) Eat it. Keep your mouth closed. Go and stand over there.

MEINI (*to Milek*): Eat it, keep your mouth shut as you come.

SILMAI: Bring them over. Blow the spells on them, the ginger and stuff there. When she comes, give her the betel with your spell to your ancestors in it. She should chew it . . . and then you can give her the ginger mixture after that. The ginger is for her; you must put Panu'et's own spells in it. It is not as though yours are different; yours are just the same as everyone else's.

MALUNA: That's it. You give her this ginger and put some aside. When you give her the first part, give only a little bit. Then take it [the Panu'et image] and throw it down on the ground while she looks at it.

MATUPIN: One of you standing at the head end, hold it [the image] with your senior [literally, "grandfather"].

MAISU: There! The spirit has gone down into it. You think this is nothing! The spirit has gone inside it. Come hold it and feel it [i.e., feel how heavy it is]! Now turn it so the face is upward. Come and stand here now. That's right.

The confrontation

MATUPIN (*to Milek, who looks so frail and has a long stick for support*): Hold your stick tight. Lean on it.

MAISU: The ashes don't matter. Leave them.

WALEI: Can the ashes be left out? Are you going to get some to blow over her or not?

MALUNA (*yelling*): So are you going to listen to me or not?! The hearth ashes, where are they?

DAUWARAS: Bring them and throw them down.

MALUNA: There's only one way to do it, one path, and that's the one I follow.

MAISU: You lot, listen to me!

SILMAI: Now get ready to tear the leaf. Aren't you going to tear it?
(*They are about to begin singing. If Milek announced herself to the spirit, it was inaudible. She stands in the presence of the spirit as the image touches her. Purkiten holds it while Marki holds the leaf over her. Matupin is flicking her with a sprig of nettles. The Panue'et image swings back and forth. Purkiten rubs its nettle base on her back and the back of her neck. Milek indicates with her hand that she wants him to rub higher up on her neck. He rubs her chest, her legs, abdomen, and face. The singing continues; it is part of the spirit presence. The subject of the verses is known; the individual words are said to be in a language*

278

of the ancestors, but they can only guess at some of the meanings. I have transcribed the sounds but the way I set them out as words and lines of verse is rather arbitrary [see G. Lewis 1980: 59–65].)

TAWO: Start with the "Woman" verse first.

MARKI (*shouting excitedly*): No, you've got to sing the "Sago" verse first, don't you? It was the sago that struck her!

MALUNA: Sing the Woman verse first. (*He starts it off, and the others follow his lead.*)

VARIOUS MEN (*singing*):

Anya mauru mawa au rimetau ei wisililu meitao

an selei ao seli wisililu meitao yelelei

iwa yelu rimawa wisililu

mei lao wa-o selei wisililu meitao

TAWO: *Sililu meitao mete selelelei*

mei anga lu sililu mawa malililu meitao

meitao sililu, wisililu meitao, selei sililu

MAISU: Go into the Sago verse now—you're singing the Woman verse; sing the Sago one.

MANY MEN (*singing a verse about the stone adze pounding sago; some of the words clearly sound like the names of varieties of sago palm*):

Wilakala wila walala wa kirp iwalala wil walala

warki wakemei yiulem walema

erki walemi ilei alemei yila lamei

erki walemi ilei alemei wawel keristu walemao,

keristu walema walem laota walema kekepag walema

ekapag walema kerisu walema kerisu.

MILEK (*in a voice that can only just be heard*): *Eii*, I'm dying here! (*The image is swinging back and forth, touching and stinging her.*)

MATUPIN: Sing each verse singly, once.

Maisu and other men:

> *Wiyem alalau siyao melelau siyao milalau siyao*
>
> *melelau siyao elkakao siyao ayu*
>
> *keitapao serakim kaitapao siyao ei siyao ei*
>
> *mauren gigru'ei maurin gigru'ei* [this is the "Pandanus" verse].

Maluna: Don't hide the face. Turn it upward.
(*The singing continues with a verse about* galip *nuts* [Tahitian chestnuts] *and the striped possum* [Dactylopsila sp.]):

> *Maurin gigruei wawunkakra yilawa kakra yilawa*
>
> *melyi'it ao yilawa wawum barya yilawa peryiai*
>
> *wipunk karara yiwak kawa simena kawa simena*
>
> *wawa laota wawa gegapa simenei—babi!* [Enough!]

Wultu: Go on, turn the face!

Maisu: Sing her one verse.

Marki: Sing the "Striped Possum" verse. You must sing the Striped Possum verse!
(*Singing*) *Yuli peikao yauli peikao, yauli peikao yuli peikao yauli peikao*

> *watukil kenau kerawit wita yuli peikao yauli peikao*
>
> *watukil sirpet kerawita yuli peikao yauli.*

Tawo and Maluna (*loudly*): That's enough. . . . Enough! Now you should blow spells on it, you throw it down into the ground, and you stand up over here. Throw it down so it goes over there!

Tawo: Hold it up and over her, wave it over her, wave it first, then throw it down! (*To Milek*) Open your legs. (*To others*) Wave it over her!
(*The nettle end of the image is passed between her legs, swung back, waved over her head, then dashed into the ground at Milek's feet.*)

Saimo and Tawo (*calling out to the spirit*): Don't you know her? You've struck our Sagrat [one of Milek's old nicknames] here. Use your eyes [to see who it is] and leave her alone!
(*The image of Panu'et is laid down on the ground.*)

Cutting the image open: Tearing the leaf

MAISU: Bring some ashes. He's got the cigarette there. Bring the ashes.

MALUNA: Bring the ashes here now.

TAWO: Her "son" must bring some here to the spells on the mixture for her. (*He is referring to Maluna, who, although senior, is classified as Milek's "son".*)

TAWO and MALUNA: Saimo, Saimo! Wait, they've got to cut the *thingumme* first! Wait! Leave the cigarette. Get a knife and cut it. I just saw her son-in-law carrying one over there.

MAISU: Quick, bring us the small knife!

TAWO: Cut the pouch open there so that cold can get into it.

MALUNA: Where's Dauwanin's husband gone? He's got the knife for cutting the pouch.

TAWO: Put it down for her over here. . . . Take the knife and cut, cut, cut, like this! Come on, cut its pouch now!

SILMAI: And pull out some of the cuscus fur, some of the white possum fur there. (*Shouting*) Pull some of it out there!

TAWO: The possum fur there, the white possum! What? Now who did I see wearing it?

MALUNA (*loudly*): What? The white possum there? Leave that out. Aren't you going to take some bird feathers? (*He is reminding them of the first example in the Delubaten myth with its origin for the leaf-tearing rite in an episode when some men sprang up, created from bird feathers, when such a leaf set with hibiscus flowers was torn over them.*) Leave that fur—the striped possum fur and the other rubbish. Where do you come from anyway?!

WULTU: Who was using it before?

MALUNA: That's enough!

SILMAI: Now stand at the head end, cut the pouch quickly, hold that end [of the leaf]. Blow over the ashes. Bring the cigarette, bring them so we can get on and finish up.

TAWO (*spits and then addresses the spirit in a loud voice*): Ssssa! So, do you know her?

SILMAI (*spitting and trilling the spell as he tears the leaf*): Sssssa! Rrrrr! Rrrr!

MATUPIN (*spitting*): Do the spells. Put the spells into her!

MAISU: Wait! You must put spells into the ginger mixture and give it to her!

TAWO (*spitting, addressing the spirit*): Go off now to Bi'ip! (*To others*) Put the spells in for her. Throw it off to go in this direction.

Treatment to expel the illness

MARKI: Bring some of Panu'et [its inside material] for doing her treatment, the patting and hitting. Put spells into it for getting it out of her and throwing it away.

SILMAI: The Panu'et stuff there for treating her.

MATUPIN: Do some light patting.

SILMAI: Chew some of the ginger for doing the patting, then eat some more of it when you blow the spells on it and give her some over your shoulder, standing with your back to her.

MAITATA: If you've shot something—a snake, lizard, mouse, whatever—for her Panu'et treatment, then put spells in it and strike her with it, then throw it away.

PURKITEN: Dauwaras, you see that *we'ati* flower? Well, you should've seen the one that was growing over there.

WALEI: But the two of us showed it to them, we asked them to look at the flower first and say if it was the right one for Panu'et. We went and showed it to Saimo. He said it was the right one for Panu'et.

(*Flowers are not named and classified. Knowledge of special ones, like the flower for the mixture used in the Panu'et ritual, is passed on by a senior man who shows another man which one it is; it has no common name by which to label it for common knowledge and make it openly identifiable.*)

SILMAI: They all went off over there.

WALEI: I became old enough only recently. I collected it and went to show them. It was growing low down near the shallow pool where the water collected. Well, look at it.

MEINI: Go and lean it against the coconut tree belonging to Gaita, over there.

(*Meini is a young woman married into Watalu Hamlet. She sees that after the Panu'et image had been cut open, it is leaned against one of the coconut palms belonging to her husband. She is frightened that this contact might somehow cause harm to enter her or her family or the coconuts. So she asks them to lean it against someone else's palm.*)

SAIMO: That one's a tall coconut, so what's the worry?

WULTU: She's thinking of Panu'et, the spirit, and the danger. But it's the Eagle Spirit, the wind, that's blowing through the fruits at the tops of the trees.

SABUTA: They say they're frightened that the spirit will strike them if they eat the coconut.

MAISU: Oh, yes! But what if Panu'et goes into it and the spirit eats out the insides [of the coconut]?

MALUNA: (*Laughs heartily.*)

PURKITEN: Bring some of the mixture to pat her [Milek] with.

MAISU: Maybe if it leans on the palm there, the spirit will gnaw out the insides of the coconuts.

PURKITEN: Maluna, when you treat her, throw it away in the direction of her uncles. To that side. *Psssah* [spitting]!! Go off to see Wani with his fine sons there. Go off and see the *Luluai* [village headman]. Take your eyes away from me. What have I got? I don't have plots of bush here and there to go to, just one bush plot that's mine. One bush plot there for me to go to.

MALUNA (*addressing the spirit*): Don't your ancestors know her? So you strike her? Where else can they go? I say that when they go off to their bush plot, you should be watching out over them.

MAISU: Use the "Birds" spell to hit her with so she'll feel light. Use the words of the "Birds" spell so her mind is clear and she'll feel light. (*The imagery of feeling better is lightness, which contrasts with feeling heavy, weak, befuddled, confined, tied up.*) I know all about this. I sent the young men off to fashion Panu'et for her. Because it struck her, so she got it. (*This is the assertive rhetoric that accompanies his gestures of hitting and extracting something as he treats her. It seems addressed to the audience, not the spirit.*)

MALUNA (*still calling to the spirit*): Go off and visit Malden, he's fine. Stop over to see him and stay in Bi'ip!

WALEI: And go off and see Wani, he's fine too!

MAISU: There now, her arm cracked! (*This is a prognostic sign of a good outcome. He has pulled on her arm or hand at the end of doing his treatment to see if he could get her joints to crack. Others do so, too.*)

MALUNA: Off you go! Go and see Dauwaras. Visit the Luluai! And Weimbari there!

MATUPIN: I've done its spell for her! There, that's it! She'll soon feel light now. (*To Milek*) Stamp your feet! Stamp your feet. Shake your head! Clear your head!

TAWO: *Prrrrr* [noise of trills in the spell]!

MALUNA: Get us a fire-lighting stick. A fire stick, quick! Saimo, light mine [a cigarette?].

TAWO: *Prrr! Mmmmm! Mmmmm! Mmmm* [choked noise of the "Birds" spell being done]!

WANI: Now go and bring some water!

MALUNA: Dauwanin, go and heat some water for your mother to wash with.

DAUWARAS: Help her back to her house.

MATUPIN: They should bring the water to wash her now.

TAWO: *Prrr!*

MAISU: One at a time now!

MATUPIN: Let her sit down by the fire there and rest a bit. Then you can bring the water to wash her. Tell them.

PURKITEN: Belei, Belei! Bring some water, bring water for washing!

GALWUN: Haven't they finished heating it up yet?

TAWO: *Prrrr...mmm...mmm! Prrr...mmm...mmm...mmm... prrr...mmm...* Get the fire going. Make a fire up for her.

SILMAI (*addressing the spirit*): They've had lots of people coming to sit. (*He is referring to Milek's illness and, before her, Dauwaras and his long drawn-out, tragic illness.*) For weeks and weeks, they've been kept here, waiting, waiting, sitting around. Now they're exhausted. Leave them alone now so they can get on with their gardens.

SILMAI and TAWO and MATUPIN (*talking at the same time*): For so long now.... The child of the lineage wrecked by illness.... Always having gatherings for sickness.... Sitting down all the time. ...Things in the garden going to waste.... Abandoned.... Take a proper look! ...Take your eyes off them! (*The idea is that illness can result from the spirit paying too much attention to someone.*) ...Leave them alone now to get on with their gardens and their garden work!

MALUNA: Let them get back to work now. The harm has ruined everyone. Go off and leave them alone. Let them stay healthy and fine.

MATUPIN: We have taro and bananas to plant. We need things to cook and feed people with. If we don't, then what about tomorrow? Tomorrow is going to come. What then?

MALUNA: Are you going to have to sit there, your head hanging down? (*He is implying that the spirit is hanging its head in shame because it has nothing to offer.*) That would be terrible!

MATUPIN: It [Panu'et] is pleased by the treatment we've done.

SILMAI: Yes, it approves [*wawilp*; the verb they both use means to approve or be pleased by something so that the agent appealed to gives the desired response].

The act of termination: The bathing

MARKI: Go and bring some water for warming up.

WEIRI: Husband of Milek! Bring some of the ginger mixture for these children. They've been eating lots of sago mushrooms.

(*The remains of the ginger mixture are soon distributed among the small children and women to protect them, more or less as a preventative measure just in case of risk, since the spirit has been concentrated among them. Weiri, the mother of four small children, adds the point that they have been eating sago mushrooms that sprout on discarded piles of sago pith and are therefore closely associated with Panu'et, adding to the risk.*)

DAUWANIN: Pour some water out and bring it over.

MALUNA: Wash her now.

MILEK (*in a quavering voice*): I don't want it.

DAUWANIN (*to her mother*): This is warm water.

SILMAI: Wash her! Wash her skin.

Wopi (*Waleka's little brother draws attention to two of Weiri's small daughters*): Look! Banu and Teraweia are running off! (*They are scared something will be done to them.*)

MATUPIN: Put your hand over the end of the water tube to sprinkle it on her.

GALWUN: So she has just a little water for rubbing on now. Then, tomorrow or the day after, she can wash properly.

(*This seems to make a distinction between the present washing and a real washing to mark the end of her illness, which he expects soon but without setting an exact time for it. The present washing done right after the treatment thus seems to be a prescriptive or make-believe gesture rather than the real act of termination.*)

DAUWANIN: Father, give Saoga [Dauwanin's little daughter] some of the mixture. She has been eating all sorts of things.

BILKI (*to Galwun, his own son*): Have they made a fire? If not, you're the son-in-law, get some wood and make one.

MATUWIL (*speaking to a small child*): Take some, eat it.

GALWUN: Dauwanin, take some and go and give it to your group of women [referring to the Watalu women from the hamlet where Dauwanin was born.]

WEIRI: Over there, you! Come and get some to eat!

MALUNA: I think that's enough. Go and get the taro mash to eat.

(*As at any gathering with visitors, they have made a mash of taro and yams mixed with scraped coconut in its milk. Those who remain in the village ate theirs in the middle of the day and put some aside in coconut shells and the wooden mashing bowls for the others who had gone to fetch the image.*)

TAWO: Now get the mash to eat, it's for her sake. (*He uses a special idiom that means to eat something all together at a ceremony to support or honor someone. But the person for whom the ceremony is held explicitly does* not *eat with them. He or she abstains, eating alone and apart; it is a special way of singling out the patient. The actual idiomatic phrase he uses literally means, "They break her/his backbone."*)

BAGI: Put some aside for Milek, a little bit. Put a little aside.

MALUNA: They've finished up all the coconut milk. There's no liquid left [to go with the mash]. With liquid, the mash is good, but without it, it's not. Take some to them, take some to the men.

SABUTA: Hey, Papa, Father!

DAUWANIN (*to Milek*): I've made a fire for you over there.

TAWO: Carefully now, go and sit beside it.

WANI (*seeing a child fooling around*): Put that fire-lighting liana down. He's got hold of that arrow. Watch out, the way it's pointing, he's going to stick it in my eye.

TAWO (*to the other men sitting on the bench*): Move over, move up toward the top end.

MARKI: Fetch the food, let's eat. Come on, it'll get cold!

PURKITEN: Take this, it's cockatoo. It's for you to eat.

DAUWANIN (*calling over to the men*): If you're eating, here's some water for washing [your hands].

GALWUN: If you go and sit down close to the fire like that, it'll dry out your blood and turn you into woodworm.

(*Dauwanin can be heard reassuring Saoga, who is three years old, not to be frightened by the ginger mixture, made with sago and breadfruit beetle grubs. The Gnau consider this dish to be a prime example of delicious food.)*

DAUWANIN: They're teasing, it's a grub, a grub, breadfruit tree grubs. Go on, eat it!

MATUPIN: *Tultul*, take this. They've turned it down.

(*He explains that the mash he offered was not eaten by some of the others because they could not eat it. The reason is strict rules of precedence and seniority apply to eating food that contains coconut grown or scraped into coconut milk, rules that depend on the status of the person who scraped or planted the coconut tree. The rules affect a number of the men attending on this day.*)

MATUPIN: Sit down first; you can leave later.

PURKITEN: Take this, they couldn't eat it.

DAUWANIN: Purkiten, they all had to refuse it.

WANI: Huh? Can't you eat it if Tawo scraped it?

(*People often have to think to work out how the complex rules apply, as illustrated in the chat that follows.*)

DAUWARAS: Yes. Well, Father is . . .

WANI (*Dauwaras is Wani's son*): Of course, he doesn't make it taboo. He's going to eat it.

TAWO: There! The two of us are going to sit down now and eat it together. "Father," indeed!

SAPUTEM (*an old, frail man*): Yes, he's in the junior line and his father was senior. The two of us were initiated together.

DAUWANIN (*to Milek, her mother*): Just rub your skin a little with it to wash, then go and sit beside the fire.

SILMAI: His mother came first, so I can eat it.

TAWO: As father's younger brother, I was initiated first.

DAUWANIN (*to Milek*): First, stand up so you can wash properly.

WALEI: The mash they made and left standing is now hardened . . .

SAPUTEM: If you put in some coconut to mix with the mash, the coconut water will help with the stuff that's too dry.

PAPIA (*a girl*): Baiwan, come and eat. (*Women's voices start to be heard more often.*)

BAIWAN (*one of Tawo's daughters*): I'm full!

DAUWANIN: Galwun, come and get the food for them.

BAGI (*another young woman*): He's still eating the mash.

WULTU: Oh, look! That selfish bunch ate up everything! Her poor son-in-law is sitting with nothing to eat (referring to Maitata, who is married to Milek's step-daughter, Belei, the daughter of a co-wife who died years ago.)

WALEI: Oh, well, maybe he'll just have to go without. He's like one of us anyway!
(*Their rules of hospitality are that guests should be fed before hosts, so if Maitata has nothing, he is being treated as if he were a member of the family or the hamlet.*)

DAUWANIN (*still trying to get Milek to finish washing*): Pour it over yourself so you'll get well. Go on . . . first wash there and there. . . . Father, can they take some fire over to her house for her?

WALEI: Those dogs! What's got into them? All they do is eat!

DAUWANIN: They threw it away [some of the ginger mixture?]. Saoga, Saoga, just look at her belly (*i.e., What on earth has she been eating?*)! She was heating it up and the bamboo cooling tube caught fire!

WALEI: Get some cold water to pour over her to cool it.

DAUWANIN (*to Milek*): Don't you want the cold?

MILEK: Pour some on me, pour some on me.

WALEI: See if there's some of theirs over there.

DAUWANIN: She's teasing, she doesn't mean it. She's frightened it will hurt.

WALEI: Hey, see if there's some cold water left to cool it!

KENKEN: There's some of ours up in the porch.
(*The rest of the recording is filled by the men's general chatting as they wait to eat and some betel nut is brought.*)

References

Abel-Smith, Brian. 1976. *Value for money in health services*. London: Heinemann.

Ackerknecht, Erwin H. 1971. *Medicine and ethnology: Selected essays*. Berlin: Hans Huber.

Adams, Francis, ed. 1846. *The seven books of Paul Aegineta*. Vol. 2. London: Sydenham Society.

Ahern, Emily M. 1979. "The problem of efficacy: Strong and weak illocutionary acts." *Man*, n.s., 14 (1): 1–17.

Allen, Bryant J. 1983. "Infection, innovation and residence: Illness and misfortune in the Torricelli foothills." In *A continuing trial of treatment: Medical pluralism in New Guinea*, edited by Stephen Frankel and Gilbert Lewis, 35–68. Dordrecht: Kluwer Academic.

Augé, Marc. 1975a. "Logique lignagère et logique de Bregbo." In *Prophétisme et thérapeutique: Albert Atcho et la communauté de Bregbo*, edited by Colette Piault, 219–36. Paris: Hermann.

———. 1975b. *Théorie des pouvoirs et idéologie: étude de cas en Côte d'Ivoire*. Vol. 11. Paris: Hermann.

Bambrough, Renford. 1979. *Moral scepticism and moral knowledge*. London: Routledge and Kegan Paul.

Barth, Fredrik, and Colin Turnbull. 1974. "On responsibility and humanity: Calling a colleague to account." *Current Anthropology* 15 (1): 99–103.

Bastide, Roger. 1972. *The sociology of mental disorder*. London: Routledge and Kegan Paul.

Beattie, John. 1966. "Ritual and social change." *Man*, n.s., 1 (1): 60–74.

Beecher, Henry K. 1959. *Measurement of subjective responses*. Oxford: Oxford University Press.

Bernard, Claude. (1865) 1949. *An introduction to the study of experimental medicine*. Oxford: Henry Shukman.

Boas, Franz, and Helen Codere. 1966. *Kwakiutl ethnography*. Chicago: University of Chicago Press.

Bouteiller, Marcelle. 1950. *Chamanisme et guérison magique*. Paris: Presses Universitaires de France.

Brock, A. J. 1929. *Greek medicine*. London: J. M. Dent.

Brody, Saul Nathaniel. 1974. *The disease of the soul*. Ithaca, NY: Cornell University Press.

Browne, Stanley G. 1975. "Some aspects of the history of leprosy: The leprosie of yesterday." *Proceedings of the Royal Society of Medicine* 68 (August): 485–93.

Browne, Thomas. 1977. *Sir Thomas Browne: The major works*. Edited by C. A. Patrides. Harmondsworth, UK: Penguin Books.

Bureau, René. 1975. "La religion du prophéte." In *Prophétisme et thérapeutique: Albert Atcho et la communauté de Bregbo*, edited by Colette Piault, 87–121. Paris: Hermann.

Butler, Samuel. (1872) 1945. *Erewhon; or, Over the range.* London: Jonathan Cape.

Cami, Pierre Henri. 1972. "Un radeau de la Méduse, ou naufrage et gastronomie." In *Dupanloup ou les prodiges de l'amour*, 93–99. Paris: Pauvert.

Campbell, E. J. M., J. G. Scadding, and R. S. Roberts. 1979. "The concept of disease." *British Medical Journal* 2 (6193): 757–62.

Cannon, Walter B. 1942. "'Voodoo' death." *American Anthropologist* 44 (2): 169–81.

Chapin, Norman MacPherson. 1981. "Medicine among the San Blas Kuna." PhD diss., University of Arizona.

Clements, Forrest E. 1932. *Primitive concepts of disease*. Berkeley: University of California Press.

Curtis, Helena. 1979. *Biology*. New York: Worth Publishers.

Danby, Herbert. 1933. *The Mishnah*. Oxford: Clarendon.

Douglas, Mary. 1966. *Purity and danger*. London: Routledge.

D'Souza, Frances. 1988. "Famine: Social security and an analysis of vulnerability." In *Famine*, edited by G. Ainsworth Harrison, 1–56. Oxford: Oxford University Press.

Durkheim, Émile. (1897) 1951. *Suicide: A study in sociology*. Translated by John A. Spaulding and George Simpson. Glencoe, IL: Free Press.

————. (1912) 1968. *The elementary forms of religious life*. Translated by Joseph Ward Swain. London: Allen & Unwin.

Durkheim, Émile, and Marcel Mauss. (1903) 2017. *De quelques formes primitives de classification*. Paris: Presses Universitaires de France.

Eddy, Mary Baker G. (1875) 1971. *Science and health, with key to the Scriptures*. Boston: First Church of Christ Scientist.

Ellenberger, Henri F. 1970. *The history of the unconscious: The history and evolution of dynamic psychiatry*. London: Allen Lane.

Evans-Pritchard, E. E. 1937. *Witchcraft, oracles and magic among the Azande*. Oxford: Clarendon.

Fabrega, Horacio. 1974. *Disease and social behavior: An interdisciplinary perspective*. Cambridge, MA: MIT Press.

Feinstein, Alvan R. 1964. "Scientific methodology in clinical medicine: Introduction, principles, and concepts." *Annals of Internal Medicine* 61 (3): 564–79.

————. 1967. *Clinical judgment*. Baltimore, MD: Williams and Wilkins.

Field, Margaret J. 1960. *Search for security: An ethnopsychiatric study of rural Ghana*. London: Faber and Faber.

————. 1969. "Spirit possession in Ghana." In *Spirit mediumship and society in Africa*, edited by John Beattie and John Middleton, 3–13. London: Routledge and Kegan Paul.

Finkler, Kaja. 1980. "Non-medical treatments and their outcomes." *Culture, Medicine and Psychiatry* 4 (3): 271–310.

Firth, Raymond. 1959. *Social change in Tikopia*. London: Allen and Unwin.

Fisher, H. A. L. 1935. *A history of Europe*. London: Edward Arnold.

Forster, Edward B. 1972. "Mental health and political change in Ghana 1951–1971." *Psychopathologie Africaine* 8 (3): 383–417.

Fortes, Meyer. 1950. "Family and marriage among the Ashanti." In *African Systems of kinship and marriage*, edited by A. R. Radcliffe-Brown and Daryll Forde, 252–84. Oxford: Oxford University Press.

————. 1959. *Oedipus and Job in West Africa*. Cambridge: Cambridge University Press.

————. 1977. "Custom and conscience in anthropological perspective." *International Review of Psycho-Analysis* 4 (2): 127–54.

Frank, Jerome D. 1961. *Persuasion and healing.* Baltimore, MD: Johns Hopkins University Press.

Freidson, Eliot. 1970. *Profession of medicine.* New York: Harper & Row.

Gellner, Ernest. 1970. "Concepts and society." In *Sociological theory and philosophical analysis,* edited by Dorothy Emmett and Alasdair MacIntyre, 115–49. London: Palgrave Macmillan.

———. 1979. *Legitimation of belief.* Cambridge: Cambridge University Press.

Ginsberg, Morris. 1932. *Studies in sociology.* London: Methuen.

Glover, Johnathan. 1977. *Causing death and saving lives.* Harmondsworth, UK: Penguin Books.

Gluckman, Max, ed. 1964. *Closed systems and open minds: The limits of naivety in social anthropology.* Edinburgh: Oliver & Boyd.

Good, Byron J., and Mary-Jo Delvecchio Good. 1981. "The meaning of symptoms: A cultural hermeneutic model for clinical practice." In *The relevance of social science for medicine,* edited by Leon Eisenberg and Arthur Kleinman, 165–96. New York: Springer.

Goody, Jack. 1957. "Anomie in Ashanti?" *Africa: Journal of the International African Institute* 27 (4): 356–63.

Gruenberg, E. 1963. "A review of mental health in the metropolis." *Millbank Memorial Fund Quarterly* 41:77.

Gussow, Zachary, and George S. Tracy. 1970. "Stigma and the leprosy phenomenon: The social history of a disease in the nineteenth and twentieth centuries." *Bulletin of the History of Medicine* 44 (5): 425–49.

Hacker, Peter M. S. 1972. *Insight and illusion: Wittgenstein on philosophy and the metaphysics of experience.* Oxford: Oxford University Press.

Haliburton, Gordon MacKay. 1973. *The Prophet Harris: A study of an African prophet and his mass movement in the Ivory Coast and the Gold Coast 1913–1915.* London: Longman.

Hallowell, A. Irving. (1955) 1967. *Culture and experience.* New York: Schocken.

Hašek, Jaroslav. 1974. *The good soldier Svejk.* Translated by Cecil Parrot. Harmondsworth, UK: Penguin.

Heine, Bernd. 1985. "The mountain people: Some notes on the Ik of northeastern Uganda." *Africa: Journal of the International African Institute* 55 (1): 3–16.

Higham, T., and C. Bowra. 1938. *The Oxford book of Greek verse in transla-tion.* Oxford: Clarendon.

Hobhouse, Leonard. 1906. *Morals in evolution: A study in comparative ethics.* London: Chapman and Hall.

Hollis, Martin. 1970. "The limits of rationality." In *Rationality,* edited by Bryan Wilson, 214–20. Oxford: Blackwell.

———. 1977. *Models of man: Philosophical thoughts on social action.* Cambridge: Cambridge University Press.

Hollis, Martin, and Steven Lukes, eds. 1982. *Rationality and relativism.* Cambridge, MA: MIT Press.

Horton, Robin. 1967. "African traditional thought and Western science." *Africa: Journal of the International African Institute* 37 (1): 50–71.

———. 1982. "Tradition and modernity revisited." In *Rationality and rela-tivism,* edited by Martin Hollis and Steven Lukes, 201–60. Cambridge, MA: MIT Press.

Iliffe, John. 1987. *The African poor.* Cambridge: Cambridge University Press.

Jahoda, Gustav. 1970. *The psychology of superstition.* Harmondsworth, UK: Penguin Books.

Janet, Pierre. 1919. *Les médications psychologiques: études historiques, psy-chologiques et cliniques sur les methodes de la psychothérapie.* Paris: Alcan.

Janzen, John M. 1978. *The quest for therapy in lower Zaire.* Berkeley: University of California Press.

Jaspers, Karl. (1913) 1963. *General psychopathology.* Translated by J. Hoenig and Marian W. Hamilton. Manchester: Manchester University Press.

Kafka, Franz. 1915. *The metamorphosis.* Leipzip: Kurt Wolff Verlag.

Kapferer, Bruce. 1983. *A celebration of demons.* Bloomington: University of Indiana Press.

Kennedy, John G. 1973. "Cultural psychiatry." In *Handbook of social and cul-tural anthropology,* edited by John Joseph Honigmann and Alexander Al-land, 1119–98. Chicago: Rand McNally.

Kingsley, Mary H. 1899. *West African studies.* London: Macmillan.

Kleinman, Arthur. 1980. *Patients and healers in the context of culture: An ex-ploration of the borderland between anthropology, medicine, and psychiatry.* Vol. 3. Berkeley: University of California Press.

———. 1986. *The social origins of distress and disease: Depression, neurasthenia and pain in modern China.* New Haven, CT: Yale University Press.

Kleinman, Arthur, Peter Kunstadler, E. Russell Alexander, and James L. Gale. 1978. *Culture and healing in Asian societies.* Berkeley, CA: Shenkman.

Kropotkin, Peter. (1902) 1939. *Mutual aid: A factor in evolution.* Harmondsworth, UK: Penguin.

Kraupl Taylor, F. 1966. *Pschopathology: Its causes and symptoms.* London: Butterworths.

———. 1979. *The concepts of illness, disease and morbus.* Cambridge: Cambridge University Press.

Kuhn, Thomas S. 1970. *The structure of scientific revolutions.* Chicago: University of Chicago Press.

Kunitz, Stephen J. 1970. "Equilibrium theory in social psychiatry: The work of the Leightons." *Psychiatry* 33 (3): 312–28.

———. 1983a. *Disease change and the role of medicine: The Navajo experience.* Berkeley: University of California Press.

———. 1983b. "The historical roots and ideological functions of disease concepts in three primary care specialties." *Bulletin of the History of Medicine* 57 (3): 412–32.

———. 1987. "Explanations and ideologies of mortality patterns." *Population and Development Review* 13 (3): 379–408.

La Fontaine, J. S. 1985. "Person and individual: Some anthropological reflections." In *The category of the person*, edited by Michael Carrithers, Steven Collins, and Steven Lukes, 123–40. Cambridge: Cambridge University Press.

Lasker, Judith N. 1977. "The role of health services in colonial rule: The case of the Ivory Coast." *Culture, Medicine and Psychiatry* 1 (3): 233–53.

Laughlin. C. D. 1978. "Adaptation and exchange in So: A diachronic study of deprivation." In *Extinction and survival in human populations*, edited by C. D. Laughlin and Ivan Brady, 76–94. New York: Columbia University Press.

Leach, Edmund R. 1968. "Ritual." *International Encyclopedia of the Social Sciences* 13:520–26.

Lehmann, J. 1972. "La fonction thérapeutique du discours prophétique." *Psychopathologie Africaine* 8 (3): 355–83.

Leighton, Alexander H. 1959. *My name is Legion: The Stirling County study of psychiatric foundations for a theory of disorder, sociocultural environment, man in relation to culture.* New York: Basic Books.

Leighton, Alexander H., T. Adeoye Lambo, Charles C. Hughes, Dorothea C. Leighton, Jane M. Murphy, David B. Macklin. 1963. *Psychiatric disorder among the Yoruba: A report.* Ithaca, NY: Cornell University Press.

Leslie, Charles, ed.1976. *Asian medical systems: A comparative study.* Berkeley: University of California Press.

Levi, Primo. (1960) 1987. *If this is a man.* London: Sphere Books.

Lévi-Strauss, Claude. (1950) 1966. "Introduction á l'oeuvre de Marcel Mauss." In *Sociologie et anthropologie,* by Marcel Mauss, ix–liii. Paris: Presses Universitaires de France.

———. 1963. *Structural anthropology.* Translated by Claire Jacobson and Brooke Grundfest Schoepf. New York: Doubleday.

Levy, Jerrold E., and Stephen J. Kunitz. 1971. "Indian reservations, anomie, and social pathologies." *Southwestern Journal of Anthropology* 27 (2): 97–128.

Lévy-Bruhl, Lucien. (1910) 1923. *How natives think.* London: Allen and Unwin.

———. (1927) 1928. *The "soul" of the primitve.* London: Allen and Unwin.

Lewis, Gilbert. 1975. *Knowledge of illness in a Sepik society: A study of the Gnau, New Guinea.* London: Athlone Press.

———. 1977. "Fear of sorcery and the problem of death by suggestion." In *The anthropology of the body,* edited by John Blacking, 111–43. London: Academic Press.

———. 1980. *Day of shining red: An essay on understanding ritual.* Cambridge: Cambridge University Press.

———. 1986. "The look of magic." *Man,* n.s., 21 (3): 414–37.

———. 2000. *A failure of treatment.* Oxford: Oxford University Press.

Lewis, I. M. 1971. *Ecstatic religion: A study of shamanism and spirit possession.* Harmondsworth, UK: Penguin Books.

Lindenbaum, Shirley. 1979. *Kuru sorcery: Disease and danger in the New Guinea highlands.* Palo Alto, CA: Mayfield.

Littlewood, Roland, and Maurice Lipsedge. 1982. *Aliens and alienists: Ethnic minorities and psychiatry.* Harmondsworth, UK: Penguin Books.

Lloyd, G. E. R. 1979. *Magic, reason and experience.* Cambridge: Cambridge University Press.

Locke, John. (1690) 1824. *An essay concerning human understanding.* New York: Valentine Seaman.

Lukes, Steven. 1970. "Some problems about rationality." In *Rationality*, edited by Bryan Wilson, 194–213. Oxford: Basil Blackwell.

———. 1973. *Emile Durkheim: His life and work*. London: Allen Lane.

———. 1982. "Relativism in its place." In *Rationality and relativism*, edited by Martin Hollis and Steven Lukes, 261–305. Cambridge, MA: MIT Press.

Macalister, A. 1902. "Leprosy." In *Dictionary of the Bible*, edited by James Hastings. Edinburgh: A. & T. Black.

Marsella, Anthony J. 1978. "Thoughts on cross-cultural studies on the epidemiology of depression." *Culture, Medicine and Psychiatry* 2 (4): 343–57.

Marshall, Lorna. 1961. "Sharing, talking and giving: Relief of social tensions among the !Kung Bushmen." *Africa* 31 (3): 231–44.

Mauss, Marcel, and Henri Beuchat. 1906. "Essai sur les variations saisonnières des societiés esquimaux: étude de morphologie sociale." *L'Année sociologique* 9 (1904–5): 39–132.

Maynard Smith, John. 1966. *The theory of evolution*. Harmondsworth, UK: Penguin Books.

McGregor, Donald. 1975. *The fish and the cross*. Hamilton, NZ: Privately printed.

McKeown, Thomas. 1976. *The modern rise of population*. New York: Academic Press.

McNeill, William H. 1976. *Plagues and peoples*. Harmondsworth, UK: Penguin Books.

Melrose, Dianna. 1982. *Bitter pills: Medicines and the third world poor*. Plymouth, UK: Oxfam GB.

Middleton, Margaret, and Sarah H. Francis. 1976. *Yuendumu and its children: Life and health on an Aboriginal settlement*. Canberra: Australian Government Publishing Service.

Mill, John S. 1910. *Utilitarianism, liberty, and representative government*. London: J. M. Dent.

Miller, Jonathan. (1978) 2011. *The body in question*. London: Jonathan Cape.

Mitchell, William E. 1978. *The bamboo fire: An anthropologist in New Guinea*. New York: W. W. Norton.

Montaigne, Michel de. (1588) 1927. *The essays of Montaigne*. Book 2. Translated by E. J. Trechmann. Oxford: Oxford University Press.

Morgan, Lewis Henry. 1851. *League of the Ho-dé-no-sau-nee, or Iroquois*. Rochester: Sage & Brother.

———. (1877). 1964. *Ancient society.* Edited by Leslie A. White. Cambridge, MA: Belknap Press.

Morley, D., J. E. Rohde, and G. Williams. 1983. *Practising health for all.* Oxford: Oxford University Press.

Murdock, G. P. 1980. *Theories of illness: A world survey.* Pittsburgh: University of Pittsburgh Press.

Obeyesekere, Gananath. 1968. "Theodicy, sin, and salvation in a sociology of Buddhism." In *Dialectic in practical religion*, edited by Edmund Leach, 7–40. Cambridge: Cambridge University Press.

———. 1976. "The impact of Ayurvedic ideas on the culture and the individual in Sri Lanka." In *Asian medical systems: A comparative study*, edited by Charles Leslie, 201–26. Berkeley: Unversity of California Press.

Papua New Guinea National Health Plan. 1974–78. Konedobu: Department of Public Health.

Papua New Guinea National Health Plan. 1986–90. Konedobu: Department of Public Health.

Parsons, Talcott. 1951. *The social system.* Glencoe, IL: Free Press.

Peel, J. D. Y. 1968. *Aladura: A religious movement among the Yoruba.* London: International African Institute.

Piault, Colette, ed.. 1975. *Prophétisme et thérapeutique: Albert Atcho et la communauté de Bregbo.* Paris: Hermann.

Pitt-Rivers, Julian. 1975. "Peter Brook and the Ik." *Times Literary Supplement*, January 31, 1975.

Popper, Karl R. 1972. *Objective knowledge: An evolutionary approach.* Oxford: Clarendon.

Prince, Raymond. 1961. "The Yoruba image of the witch." *Journal of Mental Science* 107 (449): 795–805.

Rasmussen, Knud. 1931. *The Netsilik Eskimos: Social life and spiritual culture.* Copenhagen: Gyldendal.

Rawls, John. 1973. *A theory of justice.* Oxford: Oxford University Press.

Read, K. E. 1955. Morality and the concept of the person among the Gahuku-Gama. *Oceania* 25 (4): 233–82.

Reiser, Stanley Joel. 1978. *Medicine and the reign of technology.* Cambridge: Cambridge University Press.

Richards, Peter. (1977) 2000. *The medieval leper and his northern heirs.* Cambridge: Boydell & Brewer.

Richter, Curt P. 1957. "On the phenomenon of sudden death in animals and man." *Psychosomatic Medicine 19* (3): 191–98.

Rivers, W. H. R. 1924. *Medicine, magic and religion.* London: Kegan Paul, Trench, Trubner.

Robertson Smith, William. 1889. *Lectures on the religion of the Semites.* London: A. & C. Black.

Robinson, Joan. 1964. *Economic philosophy.* Harmondsworth, UK: Penguin.

Rubel, Arthur J. 1964. "The epidemiology of a folk illness: Susto in Hispanic America." *Ethnology* 3 (3): 268–83.

Russell, Bertrand. 1945. *History of Western philosophy and its connection with political and social circumstances from the earliest times to the present day.* London: Allen and Unwin.

Sapir, Edward. 1929. "The status of linguistics as a science." *Language* 5 (4): 207–14.

Sen, Amartya. 1981. *Poverty and famines: An essay on entitlement and deprivation.* Oxford: Oxford University Press.

Shakespeare, William. (1595) 1992. *A midsummer night's dream.* Edited by Shane Weller. London: Dover Thrift Edition.

Shepherd, Michael, Brian Cooper, Alexander C. Brown, and Graham Kalton. 1966. *Psychiatric illness in general practice.* Oxford: Oxford University Press.

Shryock, Richard Harrison. 1948. *The development of modern medicine.* London: Gollancz.

Sigerist, Henry Ernest. (1951) 1967. *Primitive and archaic medicine.* Oxford: Oxford University Press.

Skorupski, John. 1976. *Symbol and theory.* Cambridge: Cambridge University Press.

Sorokin, Pitirim A. 1946. *Man and society in calamity.* New York: E. P. Dutton.

Spiro, Melford E. 1967. *Burmese supernaturalism: A study in the explanation and reduction of suffering.* Englewood Cliffs, NJ: Prentice-Hall.

Susser, Mervyn, and William Watson. 1962. *Sociology in medicine.* Oxford: Oxford University Press.

Sydenham, Thomas. 1742. *The entire works of Thomas Sydenham.* Edited by J. Swan. London: Edward Cave.

Szreter, Simon. 1988. "The importance of social intervention in Britain's mortality decline c. 1850–1914: A re-interpretation of the role of public health." *Social history of medicine* 1 (1): 1–38.

Tambiah, Stanley J. 1968. "The magical power of words." *Man*, n.s., 3 (2): 175–208.

Thomas, Keith. 1971. *Religion and the decline of magic: Studies in popular beliefs in sixteenth and seventeenth-century England*. Harmondsworth, UK: Penguin.

Thomson, William McClure. 1882. *The land and the book; or, Biblical illustrations drawn from the manners and customs, the scenes and scenery of the Holy Land*. London: T. Nelson and Sons.

Titmuss, Richard. 1962. "Medical ethics and social change in developing societies." *Lancet* 280 (7249): 209–12.

———. 1970. *The gift relationship: From human blood to social policy*. London: Allen and Unwin.

Topley, Marjorie. 1970. "Chinese traditional ideas and the treatment of disease: Two examples from Hong Kong." *Man*, n.s., 5 (3): 421–37.

Turnbull, Colin M. 1974. *The mountain people*. New York: Simon and Schuster.

Turner, Victor W. 1957. *Schism and continuity in an African society: A study of Ndembu village life*. Manchester, UK: Manchester University Press.

———. 1964. "An Ndembu doctor in practice." In *Magic, faith and healing*, edited by Ari Kiev, 230–63. Glencoe, IL: Free Press.

Twumasi, P. A. 1975. *Medical systems in Ghana: A study in medical sociology*. Tema: Ghana Publishing Corporation.

Waldstein, A. 1905. "Leprosy." In *The Jewish Encyclopedia*. New York: Funk and Wagnalls.

Wallace, Anthony F. 1972. *Culture and personality*. New York: Random House.

Warner, W. Lloyd. 1937. *A black civilization: A social study of an Australian tribe*. New York: Harper Bros.

Warren, Dennis M. 1974. *Disease, medicine and religion among the Techiman-Bono of Ghana: A study in culture change*. Bloomington: Indiana University Press.

Waxler, Nancy E. 1981. "Learning to be a leper: A case study in the social construction of illness." In *The social contexts of illness and patient care*, edited by Elliot Mischler, 169–94. Cambridge: Cambridge University Press.

Webster, James B., and A. Adu Boahen. 1967. *History of West Africa: The revolutionary years, 1815 to independence.* New York: Praeger.

Wellhausen, Julius. (1883) 2013. *Prologomena to the history of Israel.* Cambridge: Cambridge Library of Biblical Studies.

Wells, H. G. (1904) 2004. "The country of the blind." In *The country of the blind, and other stories.* http://www.gutenberg.org/ebooks/11870.

Westermarck, Edvard. 1906–8. *The origin and development of the moral ideas.* London: Macmillan.

Williams, Bernard. 1976. *Descartes: The project of pure enquiry.* Harmondsworth, UK: Penguin.

Wilson, Bryan R. 1973. *Magic and the millennium: A sociological study of religious movements of protest among tribal and third-world peoples.* London: Heinemann.

Wilson, E. O. 1975. *Sociobiology: The new synthesis.* Cambridge, MA: Belknap Press.

Winch, Peter. 1970. "Understanding a primitive society." In *Rationality*, edited by Bryan Wilson, 78–111. Oxford: Blackwell.

Wootton, Barbara. 1959. *Social science and social pathology.* London: Allen and Unwin.

Wynn, Allan. 1983. "The Soviet Union and the World Psychiatric Association." *Lancet* 321 (8321): 406–8.

Young, Allan. 1976. "Internalizing and externalizing medical belief systems." *Social Science and Medicine* 10 (3–4): 147–56.

———. 1981. "When rational men fall sick: An inquiry into some assumptions made by medical anthropologists." *Culture, Medicine and Psychiatry* 5 (4): 317–35.

———. 1982. "The anthropologies of illness and sickness." *Annual Review of Anthropology* 11 (1): 257–85.

Zborowski, Mark. 1952. "Cultural components in responses to pain." *Journal of Social Issues* 8 (4): 16–30.

Zempléni, Andras. 1966. "La dimension thérapeutique du culte des rab: Ndöp, Tuuru, et Samp, rites de possession chez les Lebou et les Wolof." *Psychopathologie Africaine* 2 (3): 295–439.

————. 1975. "De la persecution a la culpabilité." In *Prophétisme et thé-rapeutique: Albert Atcho et la communauté de Bregbo*, edited by Colette Piault, 153–218. Paris: Hermann.

Zilboorg, Gregory. 1935. *The medical man and the witch during the Renaissance*. Baltimore, MD: Johns Hopkins University Press.

Zilboorg, G., and George W. Henry. 1941. *A history of medical psychology*. New York: W. W. Norton.

Ziman, John M. 1976. *The force of knowledge*. Cambridge: Cambridge University Press.